Desk Book
of
New Techniques
for
Managing People

Les Donaldson

Prentice-Hall, Inc.
Englewood Cliffs, New Jersey

Prentice-Hall International, Inc., *London*
Prentice-Hall of Australia, Pty. Ltd., *Sydney*
Prentice-Hall of Canada, Ltd., *Toronto*
Prentice-Hall of India Private Ltd., *New Delhi*
Prentice-Hall of Japan, Inc., *Tokyo*

© 1979, by

PRENTICE-HALL, INC.

Englewood Cliffs, N.J.

Library of Congress Cataloging in Publication Data

Donaldson, Les
   Desk book of new techniques for managing people.

   Bibliography: p.
   Includes index.
   1. Personnel management--Handbooks, manuals, etc.
2. Interpersonal communication--Handbooks, manuals,
etc. 3. Persuasion (Psychology)--Handbooks, manuals,
etc. I. Title.
HF5549.D546   658.3'002'02   79-11396
ISBN 0-13-202085-8

Printed in the United States of America

For

My Mother

Also by the Author;

How to Use Psychological Leverage to Double the Power of What You Say, 1978, Parker.

Human Resource Development: The New Trainer's Guide, Les Donaldson and Edward E. Scannell, 1978, Addison-Wesley.

What This Book
Can Do For You

◆During the past twenty years, managers have been bombarded with new theories about managing people. Many of these new theories have not held up in all circumstances, even though many have worked well in certain situations. But, during this same period, results-minded managers developed their own approach to managing people. Drawing on the theories and research of management thinkers, they utilize only those concepts that held up when applied in actual supervisory positions on the job. Ideas that proved to be impractical, that didn't work in the field, have been weeded out. Only those ideas and techniques that *did* work, that *did* get results, have been retained.

The key feature of this new approach is that results-minded managers have found practical ways to use the unique psychological drives of each individual employee to get things done. Managers can direct those drives, even though they are different for each person, toward the achievement of the goals of the organization.

This new system was developed *by managers* and is usable by managers at all levels. It recognizes a "new breed" of employee but at the same time retains management authority. This new system is the only way managers today and in the future will be able to manage both the old and the "new breed" of employee. I have seen a number of successful managers

3

using this new system, which is a synthesis of the main ideas developed for business from the fields of psychology, sociology and anthropology.

You can use the knowledge from this new management system to solve the problems you encounter with people in your everyday business relationships. In this book, you'll see how to motivate your subordinates to commit their energies to doing the job you want done, even when the job is one they ordinarily resist. You'll read actual case examples in this book that clearly show how to use the new "directive psychology" approach. The subordinate, for example, is treated with courtesy, dignity and human understanding, but he is at the same time psychologically "commanded" to perform.

Throughout this book, you'll find practical examples of how to solve the problems you face with people. You'll find examples of how directive psychology is used to deal with reluctant, dissatisfied, uncooperative, egotistical, negative thinking, hostile and poorly performing subordinates.

This book also includes ideas on how to use the new approach to generate higher rates of productivity, better quality products and higher profits. You'll gain the advantage of the synthesis of new theories and practical experience that has been developed by results-minded managers who demanded a practical approach to managing their business.

You'll learn new techniques that gain cooperation from subordinates on your staff or on the production line. The book is devoted to practical solutions to business problems. Each chapter begins with a "Problem-Solution Index" that identifies the specific problems that are dealt with in the chapter. You can use the index to find solutions to specific problems that occur in your own organization.

You'll see how to apply the key features of this new approach in practical ways to motivate your subordinates. You'll be able to follow the guidelines in this book to tie into the unique psychological drives of each individual employee. You'll learn one simple technique that directs all human drives, even though they are different for each person, toward the goals of the organization.

In the first chapter of this book, you'll learn the psychological basis for this new management system. You'll see how managers reacted to a basic fallacy in the ideas proposed by behavioral scientists. While accepting some of the new behavioral concepts for dealing with people, they quietly rebelled when told to change their own behavior each time they talk with a different subordinate. From this refusal to play at being something they were not, grew the approach to managing people.

In Chapter 2, you'll see how to develop subconscious directives, a new motivation technique that helps you channel your subordinates' subconscious drives toward the completion of business goals. In Chapter 3, you'll learn two ways to use directive psychology to evoke subordinate commitment, and you'll see examples of managers who actually gained subordinate commitment to substantially higher levels of performance.

Chapters 4, 5 and 6 deal with employee performance problems. In Chapter 4, you'll see how to deal with negative attitudes and absenteeism. Chapter 5 covers high turnover rates and how to deal with people who are in self-imposed ruts. Chapter 6 explains how to use participation techniques without losing direction and control.

Chapters 7, 8 and 9 cover subtle psychological techniques for dealing with problem personalities, career dissatisfaction problems and ways to optimize results.

In Chapter 10, you'll see how to use the new psychological techniques in negotiation. You'll read case examples that show how to deal with emotional outbursts or sarcasm and how to win a favorable contract.

In Chapters 11 and 12, you'll see how to use the new psychological techniques in training, counseling and appraisal sessions. Chapter 14 gives examples of developing a winning team.

In Chapter 15, the final chapter, you'll gain new insight into eliminating and solving employee grievance problems. This chapter provides insights that will help you reduce the employee grievances in your organization to a manageable few.

Les Donaldson

ACKNOWLEDGMENTS

I am indebted to hundreds of managers and salespeople who participated in the training workshops I conducted over a five-year period. I am
further indebted to hundreds of trainers who participated in the training
skills workshops that I conducted. Both of these groups placed the practical
problems they faced at work up against the theories they were learning.
Their practical approach resulted in a synthesis of theory and experience
that evolved into the practical management principles related in this book.

I am grateful for the background knowledge gleaned from the writers
listed in the bibliography of this book and especially to Harold Leavitt,
Abraham Maslow, Elton Mayo, David McClelland, Wayne Minnick,
Jesse Nirenberg and Carl Rogers whose writings impacted heavily on my
thinking in developing *Desk Book of New Techniques for Managing People*.

Les Donaldson

Table of Contents

7

◆ 1 ◆
The Secret Power of
Directive Psychology

19

◆Directive psychology" is a new motivational technique that directs subordinate activity toward a management goal by giving an order to the subordinate in such a way that it becomes a subconscious directive, motivating the subordinate's behavior. This new approach to managing people was developed by managers who have lost patience with the more traditional "human relations" approaches to management. The new approach, while still concerned with good human relations, places the responsibility on the subordinate for achieving the assigned goal. The psychological response, if there is one, is the subordinate's problem, not the manager's.

The new approach to managing people evolved from the power of directive psychology. Business managers attending a management productivity seminar discovered that the power of psychological drives could be utilized to reach company goals. They developed a system of application and then tried it successfully in their own organizations.

The power of directive psychology comes from using your subordinate's motivational drives to reach the goals that you set. By learning to utilize the drives, you develop the power to direct your subordinate's energies and guide his activities toward the accomplishment of your objectives.

In this chapter, you'll learn how to recognize differences in people's behavior that tell you what their motivational drives are. You'll see how to use directive psychology to channel each individual's psychological drives toward the goals you set. You'll see how to evoke the psychological trust that protects your power and leadership position. You'll learn three techniques from directive psychology in Chapter 1 that you can put to use immediately. You'll see how to get action on the job and learn to deal with and correct subordinate incompetence and inefficiency. You'll learn techniques that have been tried and proven successful in increasing productivity. If you use them, you'll see results in a few weeks that you may previously have thought impossible.

Job actions that seem disproportionate to the actions required are clues to your subordinate's psychological drives. You need only recognize that any unusual activity is such a clue and you will be able to determine the employee's underlying need that is impairing productivity. You can use the techniques revealed in this chapter to analyze the employee's behavior, determine the cause of impairment and take corrective measures.

HOW TO DETERMINE PSYCHOLOGICAL DRIVES THAT CAUSE EMPLOYEE RESISTANCE TO MANAGEMENT DIRECTIVES

Activities During Social Events That Reveal Psychological Drives

The underlying needs that are strongest or most deprived will develop the most psychological thrust. This thrust will direct the person toward activities that satisfy these needs. A person who is strongly motivated by purely social needs, good companionship, conversation or friendship will seek out situations where those needs can be fulfilled. You can analyze the social or recreational activities of your subordinates as another way of determining their psychological drives.

A person who seeks out racing and gambling as his primary sources of entertainment is likely to be motivated by a desire for a big win or a quick move to the top. He is likely to take more risks and bigger chances on the job than most other employees.

An individual motivated by the desire for prestige and status is likely to fulfill this need through membership in outside organizations when the need is not fulfilled on the job. A friend of mine faced this situation and solved it by becoming involved in city government.

An Employee Who Turned to Outside Interests

Joe, a department head, was qualified for more responsibility but could not get promoted unless he agreed to a transfer. He was settled in the city he worked in, owned property and had a family and many friends there. He chose not to accept a transfer, which kept him from getting promoted.

As time went by, he became more and more frustrated. His job became routine, and he finally decided to enter local politics. Joe was successful in obtaining a seat on the city council. He initiated many innovative programs, which won him acclaim and recognition. Joe was obviously driven by his need for prestige and recogniiton.

The need for belonging to a group, often called a "social need," motivates people to seek out social activities. Social needs are motivators on the job, as well as at home, and are quite normal. But when you see a subordinate spend an unusually large amount of time in social activities that are work oriented, you will know that his social needs are the predominant drives directing his activity.

Daily Conversation That Reveals Psychological Drives

The third way that people reveal their psychological drives is through conversation. Conversation provides a safety valve that permits people to short-circuit the tension that builds up as a result of the frustration caused when they are unable to achieve their goals.

A person who believes he is due for a salary increase, for example, will feel frustrated until he receives the increase. As the frustration builds, a tension develops in the nervous system that motivates this person to take an action that will relieve the tension. If he is unable to secure the raise, he must find some other way to relieve the tension.

The most common way to relieve tension is through conversation. This can be done by verbally criticizing those who are causing the tension, by developing some rationalization to explain not solving the problem or by angrily denouncing the unjust company policy or the unfairness of the situation.

Conversation, then, does two things: it permits the release of negative emotions that result from frustration, and it permits the thinking through of the problem and alternative courses of action. One alternative that is sometimes chosen is to resign, another is to reduce output on the job. But, in either case, you are clued in to the psychological drive of this person by his conversation.

A Rash Employee Resignation

Recently, a friend of mine complained of difficulty in meeting his financial obligations. He talked about inflation and how his total financial obligations had gone up even more than the published cost of living increases.

Since my friend usually did not complain about such things, I suspected that he was having trouble getting a salary increase and was really venting the anger he held toward his boss. I asked hom how things were going on the job, and he let loose.

He criticized the unfair administration of salary policy, complained bitterly about his boss's method of rating him and talked of leaving the company. By venting his anger to me, he relieved some of his tension and was much calmer for the next few weeks.

Unfortunately, the motor in my friend's car blew up shortly thereafter, before he had resolved the salary problem, and he resigned. No one could understand his rash action. He quit his job at a time when he needed it most. He told me that when the motor went out it was the last straw. He had to do something to rebel against the unjust situation.

A boss who had watched and listened could have seen the signs of frustration and done something before the resignation. Psychologically the frustration became too great. Facing what he perceived as an impossible situation, my friend gave up and quit in protest.

His resignation could have been avoided. By carefully listening to the daily remarks made during social conversations, individual psychological drives can be determined. You can then tie into these drives to help your subordinate and, at the same time, utilize his drives to reach your objectives.

HOW TO DEVELOP "PSYCHOLOGICAL CHANNEL GUIDES," A FOUR-STEP SYSTEM TO ACCOMPLISH ORGANIZATIONAL GOALS

Psychological channel guides may be used to keep your subordinates on the right track. With an employee who has a tendency to stray away from an objective, you can utilize his own internal control system to bring him back on the track.

Using an Overriding Objective as a Channel Guide

All people are motivated to seek balance and harmony in their environment. When an element in that environment is disruptive to the structure or harmony of the system, each person within that environment becomes uncomfortable and is motivated to bring the system back into balance in order to feel comfortable again.

When you establish a goal or objective that is different from the ones people are accustomed to, they feel uncomfortable. If the goal is too small it creates just as much discomfort as one that is too large.

Psychologists say that people can successfully achieve new goals if they have, or can learn, the necessary job skills and if they perceive the goal as being obtainable. The secret, then, of expanding production or increasing efficiency is to establish an overriding objective that creates a mild discomfort—a discomfort that the employee believes he can alleviate by using his own skills more productively or efficiently. If the new objective is too high, if the employee sees it as being unobtainable, he will rebel either consciously or unconsciously against achieving it.

The overriding objective then must be one that permits small steps to be taken, each step being a small improvement on the previous one. For example, you might set the overriding objective as, "To reduce our operating expenses 10 percent by the end of the year." This provides the channel guide (a 10 percent reduction) but permits time for the necessary changes and improvements. In addition to the overriding objective, there must be specific directives that the employee can follow, that he clearly sees will achieve the goal.

Establishing Specific Directives That Prevent Side-Effect Losses

Too often supervisors are told to do something about costs or production without clearly stated specific directions. One foreman, who was given loose directions, reduced his production cost by lowering the quality specifications. Before the change was discovered, substantial damage was done to the quality image of the product. Specific directives such as, "Reduce costs by lowering the waste factor, reducing overtime and increasing the line speed," along with a reminder to maintain quality standards will provide the psychological guidance and direction that will convince your subordinates that the job can be done.

Requiring Absolute Conformity to Critical Policy Issues

Everyone needs structure and guidance in areas that are critical to the success and morale of the company. There must be some rules, procedures and policies that require absolute conformity.

It should be clearly established, for example, that any employee who violates the law in the exercise of company business will be discharged. A saleman who refuses to follow established pricing policy, a person who uses company materials or supplies for his private gain, or a person who drinks on the job should know that they will be immediately discharged. This knowledge will provide the guidance that keeps them on the track.

Verifying Procedures on a Random Basis to Insure Conformity

Since you can't be everywhere at once, the only way to insure conformity is to use a modified "management by exception" approach. Instead of directing your attention only to problems that stand out because they are different from the norm, randomly inspect operations that are running smoothly.

As long as your subordinates know that you may "turn-up" to inspect their procedures at any time, this knowledge will help keep them on the track.

One plant manager used to unexpectedly check shipping orders. He would require the entire truckload to be rechecked in his presence. Although he did this infrequently, the message was clear. He could, and would, spend the time and money to insure conformity to checking and billing procedures.

He used the same random sampling technique to check credit terms, sales discounts, return credits and pricing procedures. No one knew when they would be checked, but they knew it could be anytime, which helped guide them and keep them on the track.

HOW TO USE THE NEW APPROACH
TO DEVELOP EMPLOYEE TRUST

Research has shown that specific actions and discussion techniques are responsible for people gaining trust. These techniques appeal psychologically to people and evoke their trust, even though they may not consciously be aware that it is happening. There are four basic techniques that you can use to evoke psychological trust from your subordinates. They are:

1. Express your ideas as opinions.
2. Speak in a relaxed and quiet way.
3. Show respect for the other person.
4. Encourage open discussion.

Express Your Ideas As Opinions. One way to avoid autocratic or demanding statements, which psychologists have shown people rebel against, is to express your ideas and concerns as opinions. People resent being told something as though it was an irrefutable fact. They tend to distrust people who make these autocratic statements and, conversely, trust people who preface ideas with "In my opinion." If the idea really is irrefutable, you don't have to be too concerned about them not accepting it, eventually they will come around.

If there are some weaknesses in the idea, or if it is not one hundred per cent applicable in all situations, the use of words like "I believe," "I think," "I feel," "As I see it" and "In my opinion" actually enhances your trustworthiness. By leaving open the possibility that other opinions may also exist, you evoke psychological trust and leave no reason for what you say not to be accepted. This is far more persuasive than flatly asserting your idea as the one way to go.

Speak in a Relaxed and Quiet Way. People who are inwardly calm and are concerned for other people generally speak in a soft relaxed manner. If you adjust your inner feelings and attitudes, you will automatically begin to speak more softly and quietly.

This is somewhat like the old "chicken or the egg" question, however. Which comes first, the attitude or the action? Fortunately, it doesn't matter in developing trust. If you can learn to speak in a relaxed and quiet way, you will evoke trust, and you can learn to speak softly and quietly if you practice every day.

Show Respect for the Other Person. People lose respect and distrust those who they believe are showing them a lack of respect, by speaking over their heads, being abrupt or arrogant or speaking down to them. Trust evolves when people see that you are sincere and honest, speak in pleasant tones, are respectful to your audience and keep level eye contact.

Encourage Open Discussion. Another way to show respect is through open discussion. Above all else, open discussion convinces people that you have nothing to hide, that, in fact, you are seeking better solutions and that your ideas may be the starting point. So ask for your subordinates' opinions on the ideas you propose. Listen carefully to what they say and evaluate it. The fact that you listen and respond to their ideas also shows that you have enough respect for their ideas to give them serious consideration.

How John Wendt's Rebellion Was Directed Into Constructive Channels

John Wendt, a production coordinator for a midwestern manufacturing plant, rebelled against new quality standards that were imposed by the engineering department. John, who had a reputation for meeting all production schedules, saw that the new standards would slow production to a point where he would not be able to meet his schedules.

John began a crusade to block the introduction of the new standards. He convinced the line foreman to hold off until current orders were filled.

He requested a revision of standards from engineering and complained bitterly to the general manager.

Tom, the general manager, called John in to resolve the problem. He knew John was a conscientious and dedicated employee and felt he would stop his disruptive tactics if his energies were channeled in a constructive direction.

Tom gave John a few minutes to explain the problems the new standards were causing and then assured John that he wanted to find a way to meet production schedules in the future as well as he had done in the past. Tom explained that the overriding objective was to eliminate the large number of rejects that had been coming back from their customers. The repairs and shipping charges often made the entire order unprofitable.

John agreed about the necessity of reaching this objective and was willing to find a way to do it. He asked if the new standards could be set aside if the rejects were eliminated. Tom agreed to set aside the standards for the individual components but insisted upon absolute conformity to the overall quality standard of the completed unit's operation.

Tom asked John to work in conjunction with engineering when he got an idea formulated and to keep him informed of his progress. John stopped trying to block the new standards and began searching for a way to solve the problem. He investigated a number of rejects that had stacked up in the warehouse and found that most of the malfunctions were due to a specific part.

He used the new standards for this particular part, got agreement to test the final product with only that part changed and found that the single change solved the problem.

Tom's method of channeling John's energies into constructive rather than destructive activities resulted in a considerable savings over the initial plans that called for new standards on all component parts, and John was able to meet all production schedules.

THREE DIRECTIVE TECHNIQUES THAT IMPROVE MANAGERIAL EFFECTIVENESS

You can improve your effectivness as a manger by using directive techniques that are psychologically based and have been tested and found effective in actual work situations. Directives based on management expectations, reversal techniques and psychological power are three techniques that you can use in your daily management activities.

How Directive Psychology, Based on Management Expectations, Can Get Action on the Job

Directive psychology is the establishment of an expected action by management that stimulates the subordinates to achieve the desired result. Research has shown that managers usually hold higher performance expectations than do their subordinates. These same studies found, however, that subordinates work towards the goals established by management. They either feel unsure of their own analysis of the situation or they think management has more information or experience to draw upon.

In study after study, researchers found that performance related more to management expectations than to the subordinate's own expectations. The higher the expectations of the manager, the higher the performance of his subordinates.

The implications are clear. You can issue a written or verbal directive stating the performance goals you wish accomplished. The higher the goals, within limits, the higher the performance. One caution is to keep the goals within realistic bounds. If the goals are set so high that your subordinates see them as ridiculous, they will not try at all.

The best goal, then, is one that requires a great deal of stretch on the part of everyone. A goal that is possible, but may require some changes, is appropriate if the required changes are included in the directive. Once you have issued the directive, you must clearly show that you expect it to be followed in order for the goal to be accomplished. In all conversations and written memoranda, constantly proclaim your high expectations of success and you will get action on the job that will reach your expectations.

How Reversal Techniques Can Solve Problems of Subordinate Inefficiency

Inefficiency, obviously, occurs for two different reasons. One is incompetence due to lack of skills, training, knowledge or ability. One writer discussed various competency levels in stages of conscious or unconscious competency. A beginner might be called an "unconscious incompetent." He is incompetent, but unaware of the skills required for the task, is unconscious of his incompetency. As soon as he becomes aware of the task requirements, he is a "conscious incompetent." Next, he learns the skills and becomes a "conscious competent." When the task activities become automatic and habitual, he becomes an "unconscious competent."

One of the problems with human development is that, along with the necessary habits that are acquired to become competent, we inadvertently pick up unproductive habits. These unproductive habits and poor job attitudes result in inefficiency on the job. Since inefficiency of this type is generally unconscious, it can be corrected by bringing it into consciousness, by making the subordinate aware that he is inefficient.

The reversal technique brings an employee's efficiency into consciousness without criticizing him. By leading the subordinate through a process of self-discovery, he becomes conscious of his inefficiency and is internally motivated to improve. This awareness can be brought about by asking the subordinate to "reverse roles" and evaluate himself.

For example, a supervisor who has a high turnover rate can be given figures for other departments and asked to compare his own with the others. If he has excuses, reasons or problems, let him talk to the other supervisors and see if they have similar problems. Remember, the role is reversed, it is up to the subordinate to evaluate his own performance after a thorough investigation.

In the final analysis, he still may not see the reasons for his inefficiency. In this case, you ask him, point by point, how each of certain actions (that you know are causing problems) is affecting the turnover rate. Eventually, he will get the point. Let him then suggest methods of improvement.

How to Use Psychological Power to Increase Productivity

Most subordinates want to do well on the job. They want to be highly productive and want their company to be successful. Productivity often lags, however, because of group pressures, poor attitudes or a simple lack of understanding of the importance of the individual's productivity on the total operation.

Sometimes the employee needs an excuse, sometimes a reason and sometimes a motive. You can use your psychological power to increase productivity by providing the excuse, establishing a reason or providing the motive.

One highly effective power tactic is to let a subordinate know that you are aware of exactly what he is doing. You can show him his records, his progress and how he stacks up against others. This provides him with a motive to improve. He knows he's not fooling you and respects the fact that you're letting him improve without criticism. He also knows that you'll be aware of the improvement when he makes it, because you are watching his results.

Another power tactic is to unexpectedly intervene in the middle of the job. Stop the subordinate and have him demonstrate, with explanations, exactly what he is doing. Check every item, assure yourself that the job is being done exactly right. Ask the subordinate for ideas on how to improve the operation. Once your reputation is established and you are expected to show up and recheck an activity unannounced, productivity will go up.

Of course, the tried and true methods of special attention, a slap on the back, departmental progress reports and an overriding goal for all to shoot for are powerful ways to increase productivity. The one most powerful tool of all, however, found to be effective in study after study, is to show genuine concern for the well-being and satisfaction of each and every employee.

How Directive Psychology Encouraged a Reluctant Employee to Become More Productive

Mike Tanner, a newly hired college graduate, was working on the assembly line in a bottling plant. The plant manager saw that Mike had management potential and planned to start giving him experience on each supervisory position, as soon as he was performing well on his current job.

Ed, the plant manager, was surprised when he read a three month review of Mike's performance. The report stated that Mike was performing below expectations, had a poor attitude and did not take advantage of opportunities to improve. It was recommended that Mike not be placed on the management training program.

Ed called Mike in for a formal review. During the review, Ed found Mike to be very confused. He wanted to advance into management but had been told by his father, who was a union official, that management exploited workers, promoted on the basis of politics and, generally, could not be trusted. When Ed asked if Mike felt that way, he said he doubted that it was true but was not sure.

Ed then asked Mike to evaluate his own performance. Mike recognized and admitted his low performance level. He explained that he felt the other workers expected him to hold back. Ed then showed Mike the records of some of the people he worked with. Mike saw firsthand that the people he thought expected low performance were themselves high performers.

Ed asked Mike to evaluate his own performance in relation to the other workers. Mike said his performance was obviously lower than any of the other workers. "How do you feel about performing at a low level," Ed asked. Mike said he was not happy about his record. Ed then asked Mike to suggest what improvement he would expect from someone else performing at his level, if he were the foreman.

Ed said he would expect that person to match the performance of his co-workers within a week or two. He volunteered to set a two-week improvement goal for himself. He concluded by saying that he could see that he must do much better if he expected to get ahead in the company.

Next, Ed asked Mike what position he would like to have next. Mike replied, "A line foreman's job." Ed then told Mike of the performance standards, cooperative attitude and general requirements that must be met to be considered for the job. Mike felt he could meet them.

Ed gave Mike specific performance goals that must be met within the next three months and advised him that his attitudes would also be evaluated. Mike experienced some problems in adjusting his attitude, but his performance increased rapidly. At the end of the second three-month period, his supervisor recommended him for the formal management training program. Mike was accepted and eventually became an effective supervisor.

USING SUBORDINATE DRIVES TO REACH
YOUR OBJECTIVES

Using a subordinate's own motivational drives to reach organizational objectives had its early beginnings in human relations studies. In the fifties, scientists proposed an array of human relations techniques aimed at increasing human productivity by creating socially rewarding work conditions, treating employees with courtesy and respect and asking for their participation rather than telling them what to do.

But, problems developed because people don't consistently react to these humanistic approaches in the same way. To take the "people difference" into account, new systems were developed. In the sixties, for example, personality profiles were drawn, managerial styles were described and charts and graphs were used in an attempt to plot behavior and learn to control it.

The new theories, after all was considered, boiled down to one simple statement: A *high concern shown for people would paradoxically result in higher production than would a high concern for production*. Numerous studies in selected industries verified the theory. An insurance company study showed that supervisors who were concerned with their subordinates had significantly higher productivity than did those who showed more concern for production. A railroad study, an office workers study and twelve plant studies corroborated the findings at the insurance company.

As the new philosophy spread, many failures were reported and management began to revert back to the old method of concentrating on production. In a trucking company study, for example, it was found that some workers do better under tight control and close supervision. In a California electronics firm, production actually fell when management instituted a human relations program.

The behavioral scientists continued their studies and reported that the "concern for people concept" was sound but needed modification, because people are different and like to be treated differently.

The human relations concept of "Do unto others as you would have them do unto you," gave way to the new concept of "Do unto others as they would like to be done to." Management consultants were advising that different management style should be adopted for each different subordinate personality type.

Managers didn't totally buy the new concept. They resented changing their natural behavior to some other behavior that was actually determined by their subordinates. They felt they were being manipulated, and they quietly rebelled. They accepted only the behavioral scientists' concepts and techniques that were practiced and tested and developed from them their own techniques for using their subordinates' drives to reach their objectives.

How to Determine Individual Psychological Drives
That Block Management Directives

Everyone gives clues to their psychological drives in their actions at work, during social events and in their daily conversations. People continually express and satisfy their underlying needs through conversation. Since psychological drives evolve from these underlying needs, you can analyze each subordinate's conversation and determine what his psychological drives are.

Actions on the Job That Reveal Psychological Drives

As people confront the problems and challenges that they face on the job, their underlying needs come into play. These needs form the framework within which the employee sees the problem. His visualization of the organizational goal as a way to fill his own needs adds psychological thrust, or impetus, to his actions. If he has an underlying need for security, for example, he visualizes high productivity as a means of job security, and his attention will be drawn to those elements of the job that would interfere with productivity and impair his security. He will be motivated to take actions that reveal this need for security and thus reveal his psychological needs.

A Foreman Who Was Psychologically Driven
to Resist a Management Objective

In one situation in a manufacturing plant, there was an old stamping machine which was being used to fill small orders for customers who were under no time constraints for delivery. The machine broke down often but was kept in reasonable repair by using surplus parts left over in the storeroom after a change to new machinery the previous year.

The stamping machine was to be removed when it could no longer be repaired from the surplus parts. At that time, the machine would be junked and not be replaced. The foreman in charge came to the realization that once the machine was eliminated, his work crew would be reduced below the minimum number of ten employees that were required in a gang if it was to be supervised by a foreman. If there were fewer than ten members in a work gang, they were supervised by a gang leader.

The foreman realized that he would be reduced to gang leader status and lose his foreman's pay should this occur. From that day on, the foreman's actions were guided by his desire to retain the security he felt in being a foreman. On several occasions, he bought new parts to keep the old machine running. He also allocated a disproportional share of his time to the old machine, to keep his position secure.

◆ 2 ◆

How Managers Use
Subconscious Directives
to Get Results

◆Managers in the sixties and seventies, who tried and were not satisfied with the old behavioral approaches to managing people, decided there had to be a better way. They saw the value in the human relations approach but recognized a need for a stronger method to direct subordinate activities.

One manager attending a "productivity" seminar succinctly expressed the feelings of the group. He said, "I don't mind taking the time to explain the reasons for a job to a subordinate and I'm glad to listen to his ideas and opinions. I'll do all I can to help keep him happy and make the job enjoyable for him, but I'll be darned if I'm going to worry about whether or not he feels good about his job. That's his problem." This remark opened a discussion that eventually led to the new approach to managing people.

These managers sought the psychological factors that affect people who work toward the accomplishment of an objective with such power and enthusiasm that they seem to be possessed by an irrepressible force. These individuals face insurmountable odds and conquer, overwhelm those who oppose them and move directly and expeditiously to their goal.

The managers' research revealed that such behavior generally occurs without the person being aware of it. He is driven by an "unconscious directive," a directive that blinds him to environmental constraints and compels him to proceed toward his goal. These managers then delved into unconscious motivation and, from their research, developed the concepts that became the basis for the new approach to managing people.

In this chapter, you'll see how man's survival instinct, which subconsciously generates high energy levels, can be utilized to direct people unwaveringly to their objectives. You'll see how one portion of this energy can be harnessed and utilized for the accomplishment of your objectives.

By establishing subconscious directives to guide these high-energy actions, you'll be able to get better results from your subordinates.

A THREE-STEP METHOD FOR IMPLANTING SUBCONSCIOUS DIRECTIVES

Subconscious directives develop from our instinct for survival. Emotional energy that builds up for man's protection when he feels a threat to his survival directs behavior toward objectives that remove the threat. This emotional reaction to threat generates a very high level of energy to match our sense of urgency. If we sense the situation as one of immediate fatal danger, our emotional reaction will generate the highest possible energy level in order to preserve our life.

A lower level of energy is generated to restore comfort when we are mildly intimidated or socially embarrassed. Any challenge, social rejection or any activity that is inconsistent with our best interests, as we perceive them, will evoke this emotional reaction. Since we have learned to control our behavior in social situations, however, this energy motivates us subconsciously. Within socially accepted guidelines, we are directed by these subconscious forces to restore our "comfort balance."

Some people have learned to be sly, some manipulative, some brash and some humorous in restoring this balance. In one way or another, everyone learns to restore their own comfortable feeling by relieving the emotional tension that occurs when we find ourselves in a situation that is outside our "comfort boundaries."

Each person's comfort boundaries are different. One person may feel comfortable engaging in barbed verbal exchanges, while another will only feel comfortable in discussing areas of mutual agreement.

In either case, when the situation develops beyond one person's comfort boundaries, he feels threatened and his emotional tension triggers a subconscious response.

The particular behavioral activity that is motivated by a subconscious directive will be a behavior that successfully restored the feeling of comfort in the past. In other words, behavior is used that alters the situation so that it again falls within the "comfort boundaries."

When conditions are favorable, boundaries may be widened, new behaviors may be learned and ego-enhancing directives may be implanted in the subconscious mind. You can draw upon your subordinates' motivational thrust that keeps them within their "comfort boundaries," to get the results you want on the job. By penetrating resistance barriers, overcoming avoidance reactions and then stating the directive in an ego-enhancing way, you can implant a subconscious directive that will utilize your subordinates' system of self-preservation to get the results you want on the job.

How to Penetrate Subordinate "Resistance Barriers"

Before a subconscious directive can be implanted, the subordinate must be in a state of readiness. He must be mentally receptive to the idea that a certain action will remove a threat or enhance his esteem. There are two barriers that must be penetrated to establish this state of readiness. They are the subordinate's desire to do something else and his "comfort boundary."

Subordinate Resistance to Doing the Current Job

Research has shown that job resistance occurs when a person holds a desire to do something other than the job he is currently assigned to do. The attempt by the military to place new recruits in jobs and locations of their choice is based on this premise. If a person likes what he is doing or is doing what he wants to do, his results will be better. The absence of conflicting feelings will reduce resistance to your ideas.

In order to eliminate the barrier, you must bring it out in the open, discuss it and help the subordinate see how to resolve the conflict. Psychologists have found that the tension associated with emotional disturbances can be relieved through conversation. By questioning your subordinates about their personal goals and what they want to do most, you help them relieve their tension. At the same time, you are gaining information that will be helpful in resolving the conflict.

To resolve the conflict and eliminate the barrier, the subordinate must either see that his current job will lead to his personal goals or see that he can get the job he wants by doing well on his current assignment. Often, people simply don't see that they can achieve their personal goals on the job. A careful discussion of how job performance will fulfill personal goals will help eliminate this barrier.

The other way is to point out specific requirements that have to be met in order to make the change to the more desirable job. If there are no requirements, the subordinate should be given a realistic appraisal as to how long it will be before he can change to the new job. Once he has this question answered or has a plan in mind to achieve it, it ceases to be a barrier and the subordinate will be open to ideas pertaining to the job at hand.

How the Desire to Stay Within Comfort Boundaries Creates Subordinate Resistance to Newly Assigned Tasks

Each of us has an area both geographically and psychologically within which we feel comfortable. In talking to other people, for example, we feel comfortable standing no closer than about eighteen inches and no farther away than two or three feet. The outer boundary is extended in group meetings or in the work situation where the physical requirements of the job require more distance.

If someone tries to converse with us from too great a distance, we have problems hearing and being heard and feel uncomfortable. Anytime we face a situation that falls outside our comfort boundary, we become tense and uncomfortable and our functioning is impaired.

These comfort boundaries can become "resistance barriers" when something you want done requires your subordinate to operate outside their individual comfort zone. This barrier can be overcome by helping the subordinate stretch the boundaries and expand the area that he feels comfortable in.

Incidentally, the reason many new management programs fail is that people don't feel comfortable with them. I have seen a number of excellent programs wasted because of this problem. In one program, salesmen were put through an expensive training program, in which they learned new ways to solve customer problems and increase their sales. Test results at the end of the program showed that over 95 percent of the salesmen had learned the new techniques and believed they would be effective.

In a routine check on sales performance six months later, the salesmen were still found to be using the old techniques. None of the salesmen were using the new techniques that they had been trained to use. When questioned, the salesmen said they believed the new techniques would work but they didn't feel sure of themselves.

Even though each of the salesmen used different words in describing his reluctance to use the new techniques, all the answers were basically the same. The salesmen did not feel comfortable with the new techniques. This problem was resolved by developing "role plays" in which each salesman practiced the new techniques until he became comfortable with them.

You can break through your subordinates' resistances that are due to comfort barriers by getting them to participate in an activity until they become comfortable with it. Psychologists have found that if a person performs a new behavior three times, he will feel comfortable with the new behavior. You will need to stay near a subordinate to make sure he exercises the new behavior correctly three times.

For example, if you have a foreman who does not feel comfortable complimenting people, then walk around with him and have him compliment three different people in your presence. If he has problems in how to pay compliments or what to say next, help him with suggestions. Make sure he handles the situation correctly three times. If you are ready to institute a new employee relations program at this point, the foreman's resistance due to comfort boundaries will have been neutralized.

A Shoe Company Employee Who Resisted a Work Change

An eastern shoe company had been experiencing a sales decline for over three years. Profits had decreased year after year until the company was operating on a break-even basis. At that point, the president of the company called in a management consulting firm to analyze the sales problem.

The consulting firm found that the sales decline had occurred due to a fashion change in shoes. Competing shoe companies had introduced new styles which had gained consumer acceptance. The company was losing sales due to the relatively old-fashioned lines of both men's and women's shoes. The consulting firm recommended that the company purchase new advanced equipment to manufacture the more acceptable modern shoes.

Joe Biggs, an older employee, was recognized as a leading operator of the shoe machine used prior to the change to new machinery. Everyone expected Joe to establish himself quickly as the leading operator of the new machinery. From the first day of operation, however, Joe's production was the lowest in the plant. Everyone, especially Joe's foreman, Bill, was surprised. They assumed Joe was having a problem learning how to handle the new machinery and would soon be back up to his old speed. All the workers waited and watched to see when Joe would start breaking records again. Instead of breaking records, Joe became less productive. Each day he produced fewer and fewer shoes. Some of the men asked Joe what was wrong, but he gave no answer. The men were concerned about Joe's performance but did not know what do do. Since Joe's operation was the final shoe assembly, he was holding up the entire production line.

Bill, the foreman, watched Joe for two days and decided that the problem was not that Joe couldn't operate the machines but rather that Joe just didn't seem to have the old interest that kept him producing more than anyone else. In the past, Joe's line had always produced more shoes than any other line. Bill decided it was time to have a talk with Joe and try to overcome Joe's obvious resistance to the job change he had gone through.

Bill called Joe into his office, chatted a little about the new machines and then worked the discussion around so that the problem was brought out in the open. After a few questions, Joe said he resented making the new shoes. He felt the new styles were silly and couldn't understand why anyone would buy them. "Why should I produce a lot of dumb shoes that won't sell once they are in the stores?" Joe asked. "How can a man face his family at night," he asked, "after making those silly looking new styles all day?"

Bill listened to Joe talk until he expressed all his frustrations. Joe felt he was wasting his talent. He was a skilled craftsman being wasted on the new styles, a job anyone could do. He would never gain the respect from the men that he had when he ran the old machines.

Bill suggested that maybe Joe would be of more service to the company if he worked on boots instead of shoes. Boots were made on the new machines but the style changes were minor for boots. Joe liked the idea and felt he could see some results for the effort he put in on the boot line. Bill assigned Joe to the boot line the next day and the results were immediately better than before. Joe was producing at an acceptable level in a few days and in two weeks was once again the highest producing operator in the plant.

After a month on the boot machine, Bill saw that Joe was completely comfortable with the new machine. Now, Bill felt, he only needed to find a way to tie into one of Joe's personal goals to get him to work the machine on the new shoe line. Thinking about Joe's past behavior, Bill realized that one of Joe's goals was to be recognized as the best operator in the plant.

Bill asked Joe to come in for another chat when he was on break. When Joe came in, Bill explained that he didn't think he was getting a high enough rate of productivity on the shoe machine lines and wondered what Joe thought about it now that he had worked the new machines on the boot line. Joe agreed that the new lines should be producing more than the operators were getting.

Bill asked Joe if he would mind working one of the machines on the shoe line for a week or two to set the pace for the other operators. That way everyone would see what could really be done and Joe would get the credit. Joe agreed to work just long enough to set the pace, and then go back to the boot line.

Once Joe began to establish new records on the shoe machine line, he soon forgot the boot machine. Bill's use of the new management technique of getting Joe to feel comfortable with the new machine and then tying into one of Joe's personal goals overcame Joe's resistance to the job change. Joe continued to perform at a highly productive level and set the example for the other operators. He never asked to go back on the boot line again.

A FOUR-POINT SYSTEM THAT NEUTRALIZES EMPLOYEE "AVOIDANCE REACTIONS" TO DIFFICULT JOBS

Often, the problem of subordinates trying to avoid difficult jobs is not due to the job difficulty, but rather to the subordinates fixed "avoidance reaction." Most managers try to simplify the job or convince the subordinate that he can easily learn the job. These approaches usually fail because they are directed at the wrong problem.

One reason that people avoid a certain job is because of an assumption made about the job from an attitude or belief held about something else. If a foreman believes that a manager or a foreman should avoid performing any task himself and should only be required to direct others, he may assume that any actual performance of labor will be demeaning. He will, therefore, avoid any job that he sees as demeaning to a man of his position.

The new way to handle these problems is to learn the basis of the avoidance reaction and neutralize it. There are four primary points to cover in neutralizing "avoidance reactions."

1. Create an opposing drive. If you place primary emphasis on getting the job done, and order the subordinate foreman or manager to personally do the job, the subordinate is faced with an "approach-avoidance" drive. He is driven to please you by getting the job done, and, at the same time, he is driven to avoid the uncomfortable feeling he has when doing a job he felt was demeaning. The avoidance reaction can thereby be suppressed and the subordinate is able to perform the task you have given him. He sees value in doing the job that outweighs the discomfort of feeling demeaned, so he complies with your directive.

2. Add value to the approach drive. Industrial managers developed a system to neutralize the avoidance reaction and let the "approach drive" direct the subordinate's behavior. Managers add extra value to the performance of the actual job by giving the subordinate praise or compliments immediately after accomplishing the work task. By letting the subordinate know that the manager considered his willingness to step in and do the actual work himself a highly desirable management trait, the uncomfortable avoidance feelings were neutralized.

3. Evoke the avoidance drive. Psychologists tell us that avoidance-approach conflicts can also be resolved by challenging the psychological base for either the avoidance or the approach reaction. In the example of the foreman who feels demeaned when required to perform some of the workers' tasks, you might challenge the avoidance base. You would say, for example, "you must enjoy an opportunity to do some real work with your hands."

The foreman is reminded of his uncomfortable feeling when doing "hands-on" work. He will either complain or express his feelings about a foreman's responsibilities. If you argue, he will dig in and support his position with logic and reason. If you encourage him to talk, on the other hand, he will express his views as personal feelings and reduce the strength of his resistance.

4. Extinguish the avoidance drive. Ventilation can be encouraged by empathetic questions and comments. You might say, "I can see this bothers you. Tell me why you feel this way. I can see your concerns. What happened to make you feel this way?" After the foreman has thoroughly ventilated and expressed his feelings and emotions, his avoidance feeling will have been extinguished.

After the avoidance reaction has been neutralized, you can then express the positive aspects of the job. Psychologists have found that, immediately after ventilation, a person will generally listen to the sympathetic person who permitted him to express his feelings.

HOW TO ESTABLISH "SUBCONSCIOUS DIRECTIVES" TO DEVELOP SUBORDINATE RESPONSIBILITY

To establish a subconscious directive you must get the other person to accept responsibility, to become accountable for the action you want him to take. The accountability creates a value to the responsible person.

A subconscious directive can be established by getting a subordinate to restate his commitment to getting the results you want at least twice on subsequent days. If not, his commitment may wane.

There is a more important reason for the repetition, however, which is to establish cognitive consonance. If the employee makes a statement with which he is in disagreement, he experiences cognitive dissonance, which creates discomfort for him. He must either change his previously held conflicting feelings, or he must reject the statement to alleviate the discomfort.

If he rejects the statement, then the repetition the following day creates the discomfort again. This time, he is less likely to reject the statment, because he has now learned that rejecting the statement only relieves the discomfort until you face him again. By continually insisting that the employee verbally state that he will take the action or follow the procedures you establish, he will eventually build up supporting attitudes for your directive, and the subconscious directive will be established.

The directive can be further reinforced by waiting and watching the subordinate perform the required activity. Again, three is the magic number. If you can watch the subordinate perform the new activity three times, he will in most cases, begin to feel comfortable with the new behavior and the directive is supported again.

How Bob Wilson Used Subconscious Directives
to Build Sales During an Economic Slump

During an economic slump, Bob Wilson decided that he must do something to develop new sales to offset the loss of regular business. Bob soon discovered that his salesmen were resisting his instructions by avoiding government agencies. Bob questioned his salesmen and found that they felt uncomfortable calling on government accounts and consequently continued to call on their traditional accounts, even though they knew there was very little business available from these accounts.

Bob took his two top salesmen with him and personally made a government agency sales call. On the first call, he made the presentation, while on the second and third calls, he had the two salesmen alternately make the presentation. By making the calls himself, demonstrating the presentation procedure and letting the salesmen make a presentation, Bob helped the salesmen become familiar and comfortable with government accounts.

Bob called the two salesmen into his office the next morning and told them what he expected. He wanted each of them to get one new government account each week, until sales were back up to the level existing prior to the slump. Each of them would be held personally responsible for achieving these results. These instructions created an opposing drive to neutralize the salemen's desire to avoid government accounts.

Next, Bob added value to the approach drive by offering a special cash prize to be awarded at a recognition dinner, which would be held as soon as the results were back up to their normal level.

Bob offered his help and asked if they saw any problems in getting the job done. This gave the salesmen an opportunity to discuss their reluctance to call on government accounts. During this brief discussion, they expressed their feelings and worked out ways to handle any problems that might come up during the sale.

Bob then clearly established the sales directive. He stated the volume and dollar objectives that had to be achieved. Both salesmen expressed a belief that they could get the job done. The subconscious directive was established and would thereafter subconsciously guide the salesmen toward their goal. Five months later, both salesmen received their cash awards. One eventually sold more, on a yearly basis, to government accounts than to his regular customers.

TWO WAYS TO USE SUBCONSCIOUS DIRECTIVES TO OVERCOME PERFORMANCE SLUMPS

Performance slumps require extra effort on a sustained basis until performance is brought back up to par. There are two ways to use subconscious directives to evoke this extra effort. One is to create a "completion pattern" and the other is to direct subconscious drives toward higher goals.

Creating Subconscious "Completion Patterns" to Improve
Subordinate Commitment

Research has shown that when a person begins working toward the completion of a task or a project, he subconsciously develops a plan to accomplish the task. The details and strategy of this plan taken together form a "completion pattern." Once this pattern is set, the person is subconsciously directed to complete the pattern or complete the task.

This subconscious drive directs the person's attention to any object or incident that contains information that might be helpful in completing the project he is working on. In other words, the person becomes aware of all the implications of each thing he encounters that relates to the task he is concerned with. Without this subconscious directive his attention would be diverted to other things and he would miss the opportunity to utilize all the available data.

You can promote the development of a subconscious completion pattern simply by stating a specific objective that your subordinate is to be held responsible for. He must understand the specific goal and realize that he will be responsible for reaching that goal.

Once the goal has been clearly defined, you must get your subordinate started on the project. Get him to take some action, even if it is nothing more than a note to you outlining his planned approach. Once he takes the first step, he has created an incomplete pattern of action directed toward the goal you gave him. He will then be subconsciously motivated to complete the pattern.

Directing Employee Subconscious Drives Toward Higher Goals

Most people have the ability to perform at a much higher level than they normally do. Research has also shown that people generally use only a small fraction of their total intelligence. This means that if people become motivated to achieve higher goals, they are most likely equipped to accomplish them. The problem is one of stimulating the desire or evoking the drive within the employee that will subconsciously drive the employee toward the higher goal. The following five-step procedure will generate the subconscious drives to achieve higher goals.

(a) Determine a Need. In order to get an employee interested in working more productively, you must find out some of the things that he needs or desires. If he needs recognition, for example, he will work harder if he knows that a higher performance level will bring an award or some form of a pat on the back. If he needs or desires security, then he will work harder if he sees that his efforts will make his job more secure.

You can determine what a person's needs are by listening to him carefully in conversation and by asking questions to determine his goals and problems. He, of course, needs solutions to his problems, as well as methods of reaching his goals. A simple question, such as "How are things going?," followed by "No problems at all?," will usually bring out many needs. Most people will gladly tell you their problems and goals if you ask them. Employees also reveal their needs and desires during their work routine, as discussed earlier. Once you know what a subordinate's needs are, you can relate job activities to those specific needs.

(b) Build Awareness. Research has shown that people generally do not see the relationship between their jobs and their personal needs. If these relationships are brought into people's awareness they become more cooperative and productive on the job. If you find out for example that a certain employee wants to be important, respected or recognized for his abilities, you must bring into his awareness that improving his job performance is a way to obtain that respect. You do that by making occasional remarks that remind him of the respect people get who do "top" work.

A reminder, such as "Everyone respects a top performer," will bring into his awareness the fact that he can gain the respect he desires by doing better work. Once he is consciously aware that he wants respect, he will be more responsive to suggestions that relate to gaining respect.

(c) State a Specific Benefit. Once an employee sees the relationship between his work and his personal needs, you can evoke his subconscious drives by mentioning a specific benefit that he will receive when he accomplishes the assigned task.

For example, if you know a subordinate is saving for a down payment on a car, you can relate the benefit specifically to the car. You might say, "Joe, if you work at 110 percent proficiency all month, you will earn a $500 incentive bonus which will help make the down payment on your car." This reminder will trigger the subconscious drive to earn the down payment on the car.

(d) Provide Comfort. As mentioned earlier, it is vitally important that the employee feel comfortable in the task. If he doesn't, he will soon revert to his old ways. To avoid this, help the employee get into the new production without unreasonable effort. He should have to stretch, but it should be a comfortable stretch. Make sure the tools and materials he needs are close by, so that he doesn't lose time getting them. Make sure the environment is comfortable, cool enough, warm enough and has enough space for free movement. Finally, watch the employee get through three complete cycles of the activity. Usually, people feel comfortable with something they've done three times.

(e) Reinforce the Benefit. Behavioral research has shown that once an action has been performed, it will be strengthened and repeated if it is rewarded. The reward is generally called a reinforcement. It has further been found that behavior may be shaped by reinforcing behavior that tends toward the desired behavior. This is referred to as "reinforcing close approximations."

The implications drawn by management were that an employee

could be encouraged to be more productive if management could find a way to reward the small improvements with small rewards and reward the completion of the task with greater rewards.

The answer, of course, was to make periodic inspections of the employee's work after he had enough time to make some improvement. He was then verbally reinforced by praise and recognition for the specific progress he had made.

You can encourage the continuation of improved performance by reinforcing each closer and closer approximation with verbal rewards. The final reinforcement is the persuasive remarks made after the task is completed. These remarks are made to assure the employee that what he did was the correct thing to do. For example, you might say, "You did a fine job and deserve the bonus you're going to get. You'll have that new car faster than you thought possible."

These reinforcing remarks help convince the employee that what he did was the correct and proper thing to do. No sorrows, no remorse. He'll feel good about his accomplishment and want to continue at that level. The employee will be subconsciously directed to continue working toward these rewards in the future.

How the Manager of One Division Provides 70 Percent of the People Promoted to Managerial Positions in Six Company Divisions

Pete C., the manager of a west coast paper mill, provides more people for managerial promotion than any other division of the company. Over a recent five year period, 70 percent of all managerial promotions in six major divisions of the company went to people from Pete's division.

Pete personally interviews every new employee that comes to work in his division. He discusses the new employee's goals and ambitions, he digs out the resistances the employee feels and determines what the employee is likely to avoid in his daily work. Pete then candidly discusses the problems, as he sees them, and points out specific tasks that must be accomplished and goals that must be met.

Pete places the responsibility on the new employee. In effect, he places the new employee on a management training program by requiring the employee to manage his own progress. The new employee must report back on his progress and any problems that he encounters.

Pete discusses the progress and helps the employee feel comfortable in dealing with the problems. He stresses that problems are growth building. They provide opportunities for decision making which develops managerial skill. Pete is understanding and expects mistakes. He makes his employees feel comfortable with making mistakes, and they make very few as they learn responsibility for their own actions.

Finally, Pete makes no promises he can't keep. He never tells an employee that he will earn a promotion by perfecting his skills. Pete tells them about the personal satisfaction they will gain and, of course, that they will be prepared should an opening occur. His employees admire and respect Pete and take pride in their personal accomplishments. They also now know that their chances of being promoted are very high because of the reputation Pete has developed.

◆ 3 ◆
A New Approach to Gaining Commitment to Organizational Goals

◆We have all seen people who expend barely enough energy to complete a given task. They work slower, take longer and get less done than fellow workers who seem more committed to the task. People who feel committed to their work produce more of a higher quality product in less time. The commitment they feel directs their activity and evokes their high efforts.

The new approach to managing people resolves this problem by using techniques that build strong subordinate commitment to organizational goals. Once the subordinate becomes committed, his own psychological drives overcome his apathy and evoke his best efforts.

In this chapter, you'll learn the techniques developed by top managers to deal with employees who lack commitment to their work. You'll see how directive psychology was adapted to the work situation to evoke verbal commitment, how problem employees were brought under control and how quality standards were raised and better results achieved.

You'll learn how to use the principle of directive psychology to gain more commitment from your own subordinates by applying the techniques unveiled in this chapter. You'll learn how to deal with problem employees who lack commitment to the job and how to deal with absenteeism. You'll see examples of how to overcome faulty product problems and how to eliminate quality improvement barriers.

BUILDING SUBORDINATE COMMITMENT TO THE JOB

Building commitment is simply getting your subordinate to *want* to do a job or task rather than *having* to do it. When a person wants to do something he will take the responsibility for getting it done and assume accountability for getting it done properly. Psychologists have found a number of methods to develop commitment, most of which fall in the category of linking job needs to personal goals. These motivational techniques are effective but require time.

Businessmen, however, needed and developed a shortcut method for dealing with problems where lack of commitment was concerned. They developed the method of placing the responsibility on the subordinate and requiring him to verbally state his commitment to getting the job done. The subordinate's own psychological drives then come into play and create real commitment or a personal crisis for the subordinate. Most often, real commitment occurs. In those cases where it does not, a subordinate can be helped through his crisis, and productivity can be maintained. In either event, the problem belongs to the subordinate. Either he becomes committed to his job or he must deal with his own psychological frustration.

How to Use Direct Psychology to Evoke Verbal Commitment to the Job You Want Done

When a person verbally states that he will achieve a specific goal, he is committing himself. He then becomes accountable and is responsible for accomplishing that goal. Most people are willing and many are eager to accept responsibility. By accepting responsibility, they are able to demonstrate their competence.

One problem in gaining commitment is the lack of clear directions and the failure to establish clear goals. Often, a supervisor will assign an employee to a job without specifying what the employee is to do and what final outcome is expected. Employees who do not have specific goals to work toward and/or do not have clear directions explaining what is to be done have nothing to be committed to.

People are goal oriented. They commit themselves to specific work goals, not to work alone. To develop commitment, the goal must be specific and clearly defined, so that the employee understands precisely what he is working toward. Once you have clearly explained the goal, checked to insure understanding and cleared up any questions the employee may have, you are ready to ask for the employee's verbal commitment to get the job done.

Getting Commitment: A Step-by-Step Guide

For example, let's assume you want a production employee to get 46 units produced today, when only 40 are normally produced. To get the extra production, the employee is going to have to commit himself to 46 units, and the only way you can be sure of getting that commitment, is to ask the employee to state it verbally. The following procedure will generate commitment and result in verbal commitment:

1. State the goal clearly and precisely.
2. Ask the employee for his opinions on how the goal can be achieved.
3. Have the employee develop, or help develop, the procedures and work methods necessary to achieve the goal.
4. Summarize the procedures and methods, and restate the goal using the employee's words.
5. Ask the employee to accept the goal—to state that he will achieve the required production.

State the Goal Clearly and Precisely. One of the most troublesome problems for management is how to make sure that employees perform the specific job that management wants done. If there were no misunderstandings and no mistakes, productivity would be greatly increased. Unfortunately many jobs have to be repeated because an error was made. These errors may result because of unclear instructions or misinterpretation of the instructions by the employee.

There's a story, often told for illustrative purposes, about the foreman in a body shop who was behind schedule. He handed a curved section that had been cut from the front fender of a car to an apprentice and said, "Go straighten this out." The apprentice returned, shortly thereafter, with the fender section completely flattened. The foreman of course, had meant for the apprentice to smooth out the dent, not destroy the fender by flattening it's natural curvature.

One way to avoid these problems is to think about the words you use, and ask yourself if they can possibly be misinterpreted. If they can, think of words that are less confusing. The foreman in the dented fender example, might have said, "Smooth this dent out so that the fender is returned to its original shape."

Even though your instructions may be very clear, there is always the possibility of misinterpretation. You can overcome this problem by having the employee summarize what he is going to do. If he misunderstood your instructions, it will show up in the summary and you'll be able to correct it.

Ask the Employee for His Opinion on How the Goal Can Be Achieved. When you ask subordinates to express their opinion, you are showing your respect for what they have to say. This act of respect incites a feeling of pleasure within the subordinate. We all feel good when someone asks our opinion. This pleasure or good feeling always accompanies the satisfaction of our psychological needs and reinforces the action that excites the pleasure.

When employees express their opinions under these pleasurable conditions, they establish their own motivational connection between the task to be done and the pleasure associated with applying their own opinions to the task. Like all our other pleasure-seeking psychological motivations, the desire for the pleasure associated with the task remains in the subconscious and provides the basis for the *subconscious directive* that motivates the subordinate to complete the task.

Have the Employee Develop or Help Develop the Procedures and Work Methods Necessary to Achieve the Goal. Involving the subordinate in the development of the procedures and work methods required to do the task, does two things. It gives you the opportunity to correct or clear up any errors or weaknesses in the subordinate's opinions, and it provides further involvement for the subordinate which leads to commitment.

During the second step, in which the subordinate expressed his opinions, if you had challenged or rejected his opinions, you would have nullified the feeling of respect you were trying to show. In this step, however, you can help the subordinate discover the errors, if there are any, as you convert his ideas into practical application.

Dave, who manages a grocery store, used this procedure with one of his department heads. Dave first asked the department head for her opinion on where to place a new merchandising rack containing fragile glass figurines. The department manager expressed the opinion that the rack should be placed at the end of the first aisle in order to catch people's attention as they first started their shopping.

During the following discussion of the procedures and methods of installing the rack, it became evident that people would be likely to bump into the rack as they pulled their shopping carts out. It was agreed to move the rack to a safer location to avoid breakage. The subordinate still felt good about her ideas being used because she participated in developing the procedures that led to the change.

Summarize the Procedures and Methods and Restate the Goal Using the Employee's Words. It is important to summarize what is to be done to ensure a clear understanding of the procedures and methods to be followed and to excite again the subordinate's good feelings about being involved. A restatement of the goal or final objective directs the attention and energies toward that specific objective.

Unless the specific objective is clearly pictured, the subconscious directive has no target to shoot at. This picture can best be developed in the subordinate's mind by using the words and phrases used by him in his original opinion.

Ask the Employee to Accept the Goal—to State That He or She Will Get the Required Production. The final step in getting commitment is to have the subordinate verbally state that he or she will achieve the goal. This statement is the subordinate's acceptance of the responsibility for achieving the goal. Watch the facial and body movements that accompany the statement of acceptance. If the subordinate seems open and cheerful about accepting the goal, your job is done, and you have commitment. If, on the other hand, the subordinate seems hesitant, looks down or away or uses qualifying phrases such as "I'll try," "I guess" or "If we can," then you don't have commitment.

When you recognize a lack of commitment, explore the reasons the subordinate has for not feeling committed to the goal. Usually there will be one or two minor problems that the subordinate expects trouble from. You can neutralize these fears by discussing the problem areas and finding a solution for them.

Begin by asking the subordinate questions to spotlight his reservations. Ask the subordinate "What problems do you see?" or "Do you see anything that might go wrong?" When these questions are answered, you have the problems that need to be resolved. After resolving these problems, ask the subordinate again to accept the goal as a personal objective.

How Chuck Marki, a Southern Furniture Manufacturing Plant Foreman, Got Commitment from an Immature Employee

A southern furniture manufacturing company was experiencing an extended sales decline. The medium-priced and slightly higher-priced quality lines were both in decline and the company had decided to add a low-cost line to generate additional sales in the low-priced couch and chair market.

Couches and chairs were relatively easy to build by unskilled labor if the laborers were closely supervised. Chuck Marki, the plant foreman, was assigned three young men with limited work experience and was responsible for guiding them in the manufacture of the couches and chairs.

Two of the young men were conscientious and applied themselves to the job in a mature way. The third young man, however, acted in a very immature way. He often forgot what he had been told to do, made numerous mistakes and started new jobs while leaving unfinished work for someone else to finish.

Chuck talked with the immature employee to explore his lack of commitment. Chuck found that the young man had not previously been required to take responsibility for even small personal tasks. Chuck pointed out to the young man that his careless approach to work was not a very mature method of keeping a job or working with other people. To help him develop a more mature approach, Chuck offered to give the young man special guidance.

Each time a new job was started, Chuck carefully explained the job, the time constraints and how he expected the job to be done. He then had the young man summarize what was to be done. As he summarized, he was also asked to describe his actions in getting the job done. Chuck "grilled" him for details, what steps he would go through and how he would handle any problems that came up.

Slowly, the new employee formed good work habits. He corrected his earlier immature attitude and became a dependable employee. He soon began to take pride in his work, and Chuck no longer had to work with him on a daily basis. The new immature employee had matured on the job.

How to Get Commitment from Problem Employees

Every organization has at least a few employees who do just enough to get by. They are not committed to the goals of the organization and see their job merely as a means of existence or a place to put in time. If there was no hope for getting improvement from these employees then they would have to be ferreted out of the organization. Fortunately, however, most people can be guided and made more productive.

The following five steps will increase the commitment and productivity of problem employees:

1. Explore the problem employee's lack of commitment.
2. Ensure understanding.
3. Ask for acceptance of a specific goal.
4. Ask how the goal will be accomplished.
5. Demand a written summary of the steps to be taken in accomplishing the objective.

Exploring the Problem Employee's Lack of Commitment. Managers working with problem employees have found that there are a variety of reasons for an employee's lack of commitment. Researchers, too, have found and classified four basic types of problem employees. The first type is the hostile personality who has been wronged or who imagines he has been wronged by the company in the past. This person is always looking for an argument in which he can lambaste the company. Many of his actions on the job are intended to provoke a superior into an argument.

The second type has been identified as being an insecure group who feel unable to cope with the world and the problems of their daily activities. The third group is one that sees the world through "rose-colored glasses." They feel everything is great and don't see the necessity for specific actions to get the job done. The fourth group is one that simply has not learned responsibility. These are generally new people who are younger and haven't seen the relationship between the work they do and the success of the company.

A general discussion with your subordinates will help you determine which of the four problem types you are dealing with. A few questions, such as "How re things going?" or "Do you have any problems," will elicit the answers needed to determine the problem type you are dealing with. You can then avoid arguments with those who are hostile, avoid increasing the fear of those who can't cope, prevent the ramblings of those who see everything as rosy and explain responsibility to those who feel none.

Ensure Understanding. The second step in dealing with problem employees is to make sure they understand exactly what is to be done. Your understanding of each type will help you determine when you have understanding. The hostile employee will try to argue about it, the one who finds it difficult to cope will express fears about it, the one who sees everything as "rosy" will gloss over it and the one who lacks responsibility will probably have it all mixed up. In every case, you must ask each of them to tell you or summarize to you what the goal is.

It is necessary that problem employees summarize what you've told them the job goal is, or they will use the excuse later that they didn't understand what was to be done. Once they have repeated what you have said, they can no longer use this excuse.

Ask for Acceptance of a Specific Goal. Once you are sure that the problem employee understands what is to be done, ask him to agree to complete a specific goal. This could be one partial step in the process for the person who has difficulty coping, or the complete goal for the others. Use the power of your position, if necessary, to get agreement. When it's time to follow up, you don't want any doubt about the specific job the subordinate was supposed to do.

Ask How the Goal Will Be Accomplished. When dealing with problem employees, it is not enough to get them to say they will do a job, you must ask them for details. Ask them to tell you the steps they will take in getting the job done. If anyone complains about all the discussion and repetition of details, merely remind them that because of problems of understanding in the past, you are making certain that everything is clear. As a manager, you are required to correct problem causes as they occur.

Demand a Written Summary of the Steps to Be Taken In Accomplishing the Objective. Where verbal summaries have not been effective in the past, you must require written summaries. The hostile employee is going to try to argue over this requirement. Don't argue, let him have his say, and then tell him very forcefully that because of the problems of the past, the steps must be written out. Require them to be written out, on the spot, in your presence. Do not let him return to work or use any excuse to avoid writing them out. Once they are written out, follow up on each step to make sure he is following the written plan. If not, take him into your office and ask for an explanation. If the explanation is not satisfactory, let him know his job is on the line. Either he follows the plan he developed, or you let him go.

How a Manager Used Directive Psychology to Get Commitment from an Employee Who Was Habitually Absent

Dan Beldon, the manager of a midwestern manufacturing plant, decided to get directly involved with the individual employees who were causing his plant's absenteeism record to be so high. Dan began by calling in George Restin, who had the worst absentee record in the plant. It was early February, and George had already been absent three times that year.

Dan began by explaining to George that his unusually large number of absences was causing problems for both production and shipping. Dan explained to George that he wanted to discuss the reasons for the absences, in order to help George eliminate them.

George said he didn't think he had been absent very often, whereupon Dan pointed out the specific dates of the absences. Confronted with specific dates, George agreed that the absences were excessive but said he could not help it.

When Dan asked George what he could do to eliminate his absences, George replied "Nothing." All the absences were either caused by traffic tie-ups, washed out roads or windstorms. According to Geroge, all his absences were acts of God, things he couldn't affect.

Dan then pointed out that other employees had managed to overcome these problems and get to work. George said that if someone had told him how they did it, he would have been glad to come to work.

Dan, at that point, asked George how they could work out a way for him to solve these problems in the future. George said he'd call in, and the foreman could send someone to get him. Dan suggested that, perhaps, there was someone he could arrange to ride with. George agreed there was and that he would call someone else before taking the day off in the future.

Dan asked George to summarize exactly what procedure he would go through the next time something happened that looked like it might create a problem for him in getting to work. George said he would call either of two friends, Jim or Bill, and see if they would pick him up. If not, he would call the foreman and ask the foreman if there was a route open that he could use to get to work.

Dan then asked George to give him his assurance that he would not be absent in the future. Dan explained that George's absence caused an increase in expense for two departments and the company had to have someone on that job that they could depend upon to be there every day. George agreed to follow the procedures and said he would not be absent in the future.

Dan then pointed out that if George really worked toward this goal, he could win an attendance award. There were awards for each six months without absences, and there was no reason that George couldn't earn these awards, just as many of his friends were doing.

SOLVING FAULTY PRODUCT PRODUCTION PROBLEMS WITH DIRECTIVE PSYCHOLOGY

Problems with faulty products can be improved or eliminated when the problem lies with your employees. Even in these cases, where machinery is at fault, your employees can minimize the problem and make necessary corrections very rapidly if they are motivated to do so. To develop an employee attitude consistent with your desire to eliminate faulty products, you must set high quality standards and stimulate employee pride in high quality finished products.

How to Get Subordinates to Set Higher Quality Standards

To eliminate faulty products, higher quality standards must be set. The quickest way to get higher quality standards is to have them set by the people involved with the production. This might be one or more foremen or a combination of foremen and key workers. Once you decide who is to be in the group, call them together to discuss the problem and set the new standards.

There are two important elements that must be considered in getting subordinates to set higher goals. One is the establishment of a *mental climate* that will encourage the subordinates to commit themselves to higher standards, and the second is a *plan to overcome barriers* that may block the achievement of the new quality standards.

Establishing a Positive Mental Climate

Seven specific actions have been identified that establish a postive mental climate. Each of them, individually, will create a favorable response from a subordinate. When all are used together, a feeling of complete freedom evolves within the group, and ideas are freely exchanged. Suggestions are made, and creativity comes into play. A climate of cooperation and problem solving evolves, in which the group members develop the desire and the motivation to solve the problem. The following seven steps will help you achieve this climate.

1. State the Purpose or Objective of the Meeting. When people are called together they often assume an incorrect purpose for the meeting. Even when previously informed of the nature of the meeting, they forget or come to the meeting with many other things on their mind. To clear away these other thoughts and get everyone thinking about your objective, you must state very clearly what the purpose of the meeting is. This draws the group's attention to the problem at hand and away from other interfering thoughts.

2. Avoid Criticism. Once the meeting has begun, avoid criticism. You may wish to review past results, to point out the extent of the problem. When doing this, avoid any reference to salary, incentive or job security. Relating to work rewards, in connection with past errors, may be interpreted as criticism or threat. Criticism or threat will cause people to become resistant and refuse to cooperate. Very little can be accomplished under these conditions.

3. Develop Trust. One way to develop trust is to protect group members from criticism. If one member criticizes another, quickly intervene and say, "We don't want to criticize each other, let's concentrate on solving the problem." Another way to develop trust is to ask for experiences from the group that relate to the problem, then you use those experiences as starting points to solve the problem. The group members will see that their contributions are going to be used and will trust you and continue to work on the problem.

4. Treat Subordinates as Peers. No one likes to be talked down to. By simply saying "we" instead of "you," and "our" instead of "your," you will develop an air of equality. The subordinate feels he is being treated with respect and dignity and consequently opens up and shares his ideas and thoughts. He will continue to participate in order to retain the good feeling he gets from being treated as an equal by his boss.

5. Express Your High Expectations for the Group. Expressing high expectations shows the group you have confidence in them. It has also been found that subordinates are motivated to perform in relation to their boss' expectations. Within reasonable limits, the more the boss expects, the more they accomplish; the less the boss expects, the less they accomplish.

6. Mention the Benefits to Be Derived from Success. People are motivated to reach goals, and the benefits you mention become the goals for them to work toward. If your subordinates clearly see that solving the problem will be a step toward achieving their work or personal goals, they will be motivated to solve the problem.

At this point, it is quite logical to mention profits and their relationship to job security, salary and bonuses. Benefits, such as recognition for high quality performance, would also be appropriate. The self-satisfaction that comes from doing professional work, or any similar benefit you might think of, would also be appropriate to mention.

7. Place Responsibility for Success on the Group. Finally, place responsibility on the group. Make sure they understand that it is up to them to find the solution. This will not be just a discussion group to talk over what is wrong. The group is required to find an answer. Once the group understands that they must find the answer, that they have that job to do, they will work toward that solution.

Eliminate Barriers That Block Improvements

Once new methods and procedures have been worked out to make the quality improvements you need, the employees must be carefully trained to use the new techniques. The greatest stumbling block in making changes on the job is the habits the workers have developed in performing their duties. The worker feels comfortable with these old habits, since they make his work easy. Yet, as he tries to do things differently to reach the new quality standards, these old habits get in the way.

There are three training steps that will eliminate the barriers formed by old habits. You can follow this three-step plan to institute any change in methods or procedures on the job.

1. Identify the Habit That Results in Faulty Products. The previous group discussion, if successful, highlighted the areas where improvements were needed. By examining this area carefully, as it is being performed on the job, you will be able to identify certain repetitious habits. These habits should be described in writing so that they can be examined against the new procedures.

2. Determine the "Key" Change in Habit Required to Perform the New Procedures. Usually, you will find one key habit that interferes with the new procedure. Point out the habit to the employee, and determine exactly what movements or actions will need to be changed to break the old habit and form the new one.

3. Guide the Employee in Developing the New Habits Required for the New Procedures. After all the details have been worked out, the employee must be guided step by step through the new procedures. A foreman or training specialist should work closely with each employee learning the new procedure until the old habits no longer interfere with the new procedures. Usually, a new activity will become comfortable for an employee after he has performed it successfully three consecutive times. Follow-up checks should be made daily and then weekly until the new habits are strongly formed.

How to Develop Employee Pride in High Quality Production

In order to develop employee pride in high quality production, you must provide a picture that the employee can be proud of. You can do this by describing what the situation will be like. For example, you can point out what it will be like to be known for producing the highest quality products on the market.

You can relate to the prestige and respect that other people will show the employees once their reputation is known. Also, their peers and superiors will recognize them as professionals. You can continually relate to them as professionals and make statements to the effect that they can be proud of their professional results.

As progress becomes evident, reward the employees. Show them that their results are appreciated. Put up a wall chart so they can check their own progress. These posted results will encourage them to do better, because it gives them a goal. They want to see better results posted. When the improvements are made and the results are posted, they will feel proud of their results.

As time goes by and the goals are achieved, you will have to provide feedback to the workers to let them know that their output is contributing to the overall results of the organization. If each person sees how his work, or his department's work, affects the company's pricing, sales volume, profits, wages and salaries, he will feel more responsibility for and pride in his work.

This feedback, to reinforce the employee's efforts, tied in with some freedom to use his own skills to improve production techniques will result in personal pride and higher quality products.

How a West Coast Sales Manager Used Directive Psychology to Double His Weekly Sales Record

Fred Odin, the sales manager for a west coast plywood distributor, was being forced into a loss position as rising costs and a depressed market squeezed his profits down to nothing. Fred planned an all out drive to double his sales volume in order to return to a profitable position. In order to find the best and fastest route to success, Fred analyzed his area and found that a drive for new accounts offered the best possibility for new business.

Fred followed the procedures explained in this chapter. He stated clearly that his objective was to double the current sales volume. He explained that the group would have the responsibility and get credit for the accomplishment of the goal. A bonus of five percent would be paid on all sales to new accounts during the period.

The group discussed the problem and decided that time was their biggest barrier. Their current customers required extensive merchandising help, which took most of their day's time. It was suggested that two salesmen be relieved of their regular duties to concentrate completely on soliciting new accounts. Fred offered to hire two merchandisers to fill in while the two salesmen concentrated on the new accounts. This was later ruled out because of the great distances between accounts. A salesman then suggested that if the two merchandisers were hired to help on all territories, then each salesman could call on new accounts within his own territory. This plan was adopted, and two merchandisers were hired and started work the following Monday morning.

One problem that occurred was the salemen's reluctance to leave the merchandising work to the newly-hired merchandisers. The identification of the problem resulted in a required change in habits that scheduled the salesmen for new account calls prior to making their regular calls each day.

This guidance in lining up new calls first helped the salemen break the merchandising habit. Soon, new sales habits were formed and new business was being acquired. Fred came very close to doubling his sales volume in a six-month period, and by the end of the year, he did double it. His profits were better than ever and his salemen were proud to be on his winning team.

◆ 4 ◆

How to Use the New Directive Psychology Approach to Deal with Negative Attitudes

◆ Negative attitudes not only lower productivity, reduce quality and produce inordinate amounts of waste, they also breed dissention and frustration, which blocks subordinate objectivity, increases friction between employees and encourages absenteeism. In the past, these problems were ignored, or occasional attempts were made to soothe ruffled feathers, and sometimes people resigned or were fired.

The new approach to managing people resolves these problems by using concepts from directive psychology that neutralize negative attitudes. The subordinate is directed to a specific task that utilizes his pent-up tension. The application of additional psychological techniques is used to build positive attitudes that block the development of negative attitudes.

In this chapter, we'll look at the development of negative attitudes and how those attitudes affect performance. Then, you'll learn two ways to deal with negative attitudes that develop on the job. You'll see how to use the new directive psychology approach to defuse negative attitudes and build positive ones. Finally, in this chapter, I'll discuss the techniques of making an immediate challenge and command decision in order to redirect negative energy to achieve positive goals.

DEALING WITH PERFORMANCE PROBLEMS
CAUSED BY NEGATIVE ATTITUDES

Most of us are not qualified to deal with the psychological aspects of negative attitudes. In most cases, however, a psychologist is not required to deal with the problem. We simply deal with the employee's performance. An understanding of the effect negative attitudes have on performance, however, will help us deal with the performance aspects of the problem.

The Development of Negative Attitudes on the Job

People are not born with negative attitudes, they develop attitudes, some positive and some negative, throughout their lives. The reaction a person gets to an action he takes impacts heavily on the formation of that person's expectations for the future. These expectations become the base for attitude formation.

If a subordinate comes in with a suggestion on how to improve working conditions and his boss ignores it, or worse, remarks that working conditions are OK as they stand, the subordinate will build expectations that the boss will ignore his suggestions in the future. The subordinate may then extend the expectations to an attitude that, "It doesn't pay to make suggestions, because no one listens anyway." You can avoid contributing to the development of negative attitudes in similar circumstances by listening carefully and at least telling the subordinate that you will think about his suggestion.

Problems That Develop from Negative Attitudes

Negative attitudes impact heavily on productivity. If a person believes he can only produce at 70 percent of standard, he will support his belief by only producing at that level. Humans are guided in their activities by the image they hold of themselves. A person who believes it is possible for him to jump a four-foot fence will attempt to jump it. A person who believes the feat impossible for himself will not try and will not learn.

Negative attitudes can also keep people from working at a level that they feel comfortable with. If John feels he is capable of producing 100 percent of standard but feels that no one cares whether or not he makes standard, he will not. With a "who cares" attitude, there is no motivation to do his best.

Negative attitudes about company policy or supervisors may also interfere with productivity. If an employee feels the company is taking advantage of him, he may try to offset the unfairness by lowering his output. If a supervisor is harsh or unreasonably critical, the subordinate may try for revenge by lowering productivity or by sabotage in extreme cases. Regardless of their cause, negative attitudes reduce productivity. Anything you can do to create positive attitudes will improve productivity.

A Home Appliance Company That Reorganized to Overcome Negative Attitudes

An eastern home appliance manufacturing and marketing company was recently forced to reorganize, because employee attitudes had become so negative about the company's products that the company was literally splitting apart. The sales organization was complaining bitterly about production. The operations division was complaining about marketing, and marketing was complaining that neither sales nor production used the information they supplied.

Marketing had completed a research project that revealed a growing demand for microwave ovens. Plans and promotional strategies were developed to introduce a line of microwave ovens in the next quarter. The operations manager decided not to produce the new ovens. He argued that the investment was too great and the employees would have to be retrained to produce the new ovens. Overall, he argued that the cost would be prohibitive.

The sales force was now in the process of presenting the promotions on the new microwave ovens and when the production order was re-scinded, they had nothing prepared with which to promote the old line. The accusations and arguments deteriorated into widespread negative attitudes. Sales declined drastically, inventory piled up and profits evaporated.

At this point, a consulting company was brought in to find a solution to the problem. The consultants found that low morale had developed from the negative attitudes. No one really believed that the various divisions would ever cooperate. The consultants recommended, and the company instituted, a complete reorganization.

Under the new organizational structure, marketing decided and actually placed orders with the operating division. Marketing plans and promotional strategies were then provided to the sales department. Sales worked with marketing to establish reorder quantities. Marketing was given profit responsibility and was answerable for capital investment. The new structure was successful. Operations became cooperative and the negative attitudes disappeared.

TWO WAYS TO DEAL WITH NEGATIVE ATTITUDES

A negative attitude kills a person's objectivity. People are generally attentive to ideas and occurrences that support their own attitudes and filter out those things that challenge their attitudes. This blocks their objectivity and interferes with their judgment. In order to neutralize the negative attitude and restore objectivity, you must find a way to provide an immediate challenge for the subordinate that will require objectivity in its accomplishment.

The second way to neutralize negative attitudes is to use "command decision" techniques. You require the subordinate to make a decision that places him in opposition to the negative attitude. He is forced to utilize the negative energy to come to grips with the situation. Once he makes the decision, he uses the energy of the previously negative motivation to carry out your directive.

These two techniques, the "immediate challenge" and "command decision" were developed and used successfully by management in a number of situations. They work with all levels of subordinates in all types of situations.

How an Immediate Challenge Can Neutralize a Negative Attitude

One reason that negative attitudes persist is that they go unchallenged. People tend to be polite and avoid confrontation by letting negative comments pass without challenge. The person with the negative attitude takes silence to be acceptance and feels supported in his negative opinion.

As a manager, you can neutralize negative attitudes by challenging them immediately when they appear.

Begin by asking the subordinate for specific details of the incident that cause him to feel the way he does. If a subordinate says the company has a "lousy" promotion policy you might say, "What happened to make you feel that way, George?" When you get the details that his negative attitude is based upon, you can then challenge the attitude. You might show why you disagree or ask the subordinate to prove that the incident is reflective of the company's promotion policy.

Often, the subordinate who holds a negative attitude about a particular policy does not have enough information to make an objective judgment. By discussing the details openly with the subordinate and then challenging him to accept or disprove your opinion, you may neutralize his negative attitude.

Psychologists tell us that both emotion and logic are important in changing attitudes. It is not enough to provide overwhelming logic; you must also explore the subordinate's emotional involvement. It is important to let the subordinate express his feelings, thoughts and opinions and let him freely criticize or express anger.

During the expressions of anger or other feelings he will ventilate or "vaporize" the emotional feelings associated with the incident that caused the negative attitude.

I know a manager who was actually involved in a similar situation. He managed an assembly factory where production workers were frequently given trials as line foremen. If they were successful during their trial periods, they were put on a "promotable" list and were then eligible for promotion throughout the plant.

Recently, a worker was promoted from this list and another worker, George, remarked that this was another example of favoritism. Bill, the manager, immediately challenged George. "Why do you think it's favoritism," he asked. "That's usually the way people get promoted," George replied. "What happened to make you feel this way," asked Bill. George talked around the subject for awhile, but finally broke down and told how he had worked on a previous job for four years, conscientiously and diligently, and just when he should have been promoted, the owner's son was brought in and put in charge. That's why he left that company and came to work in his present company.

Bill listened patiently until George had poured out the negative feelings he had pent-up inside himself. Once the emotions were out of the way, Bill was able to explain the company's policy of giving everyone a chance for advancement through the trial foreman system. As George saw the system in operation, his negative attitude changed to a more positive one.

How to Use "Command Decision" Techniques to Redirect Negative Motivation

Negative motivation is the desire to work against the goals of the organization and evolves from negative attitudes. An employee with a negative attitude may try to talk other employees into working slowly, goofing off, taking unauthorized breaks and, in extreme cases, actually sabotaging the operation. The tension that is built up within the individual as a result of negative attitudes provides the motivation for these negative actions.

Psychologists have suggested, and line managers have developed, techniques to implement the suggestion that negative energy can be utilized in a positive direction. Managers have found ways to get the subordinate to apply the pent-up energy to positive organizational goals.

The basic application of this system is to assign the subordinate a task that forces him to make a decision in opposition to his negative feelings. I call this "command decision" techniques, because the decision results from your command. There is more required than just giving the command, however. You must get a verbal commitment from the subordinate that he will perform the required task. This places the decision and responsibility on the subordinate.

How an Office Manager Dealt With White Collar Negative Attitudes

One manager actually converted an employee who was "bad-mouthing" the company into a spokesman for his division by using these techniques. Hart, the office manager, called Johnny into his office. Johnny, a veteran saleman, had recently been transferred from another state. Johnny was bitterly complaining about the company from his first day in the office. When Hart heard what was going on, he called Johnny in to discuss the problem.

"Johnny, I hear you were treated poorly by management in your previous location. Is that true?" Hart asked.

"You bet it is," replied Johnny, "I'm still in a bind now because of some of the things that happened there."

"Why did you ask to come here?" inquired Hart.

"I heard at the last national sales meeting that this was a good office, that you had a top team and a salesman could make money and get ahead here," answered Johnny.

"One of the reasons for our success, Johnny, is that we take a positive attitude about everything. We have a rule here that no one is to be negative about anything. We always look for a positive way to say what we have to say," Hart informed Johnny.

"I see what you're getting at," replied Johnny. "My comments about the company are negative and that creates a negative atmosphere."

"That's right," continued Hart. "Now that you see the problem, you have a decision to make. I want you to start being positive. I want you to tell the other salemen how great this organization is. Will you start doing that?"

"How can I? I've been telling everyone what a 'bum' break I got before I came here," answered Johnny.

"Perhaps you could compare this office to the last one you were at. I'm not telling you what to say, I'm sure you can see that the company is basically a good one, or you wouldn't have been able to transfer here. You said you came here because you heard we were a great team. Perhaps you could start with that. It's your decision," Hart continued, "but it must be done in a positive way. Will you do it?"

"I see what you mean," replied Johnny. "I can say this place is great to work at, and that I like this a lot better than the old location. That way I'm being positive. I can still get it off my chest, but in a positive way."

"It sounds as though you've made the decision. I'll check in a few days to see how you're doing. Let me know if you have any problems here," Hart concluded.

Hart got his message across. He gave Johnny a command and then helped him work out a way to "save face." Johnny was still able to work off his negative energy in a positive way.

PREVENTING THE DEVELOPMENT
OF NEGATIVE ATTITUDES

Although managers have learned to deal with negative attitudes by placing responsibility on the subordinate and demanding that corrective action be taken, they have also been willing to utilize the techniques developed by psychologists to defuse and prevent the development of negative attitudes. You can use these techniques to prevent the development of negative attitudes in your organization.

Techniques That Defuse Negative Feelings

Negative attitudes develop from a series of negative incidents that are built up in a person's mind. Sometimes, even one incident is built up over time until it becomes the basis for a long term negative attitude. Anytime a negative feeling is held back or forbidden expression, it builds a negative attitude.

These negative feelings can be defused, however, and the development of negative attitudes can be prevented. One way that feelings are defused is through conversation. By expressing the anger, discontent or dissatisfaction that is felt, the person knows, at least, that his feelings are understood. The action involved in expressing negative feelings helps eliminate the tension and clears away the negative motivation that interferes with productivity.

You can defuse negative feelings by following the steps outlined here:

1. Question the Subordinate to Permit the Negative Feelings to Be Expressed. Ask what the person thinks, how he feels and what action is needed to correct the situation. The person with negative feelings will expend those feelings while giving the answers to your questions.

2. Listen Attentively to Everything the Subordinate Says. It is important to show empathy, and careful listening does this. Make a few brief comments to express your understanding and show your concern, but let the subordinate do the talking. You don't have to agree with what is said, but you must understand why it is said in order to be empathetic.

3. Ask the Subordinate's Opinion About Any Concerns You May Have. Don't argue with the opinion that the subordinate expresses, you are providing food for thought and learning the subordinate's reaction. Your goal is to defuse his negative emotions.

4. Summarize and Express Understanding. Summarize what the subordinate has said in order to let him know that you listened carefully, then express your understanding of why he feels the way he does. Say to him, "I see why you think that" or "I understand why you feel this way." Again, you are not expressing agreement. You are expressing understanding, which helps defuse negative feelings.

Techniques That Build Positive Attitudes

An experience that is pleasing or satisfying to a person leaves a good feeling about the experience, the people and the activities involved in the experience. A work crew that is friendly and supportive to a new worker will generate good feelings in the new worker toward both the job and the workers. If the work is also satisfying, then the employee's attitude is doubly reinforced. The following four techniques will insure the development of positive employee attitudes.

1. Provide a satisfying or pleasurable consequence for actions that achieve business goals.
2. Provide rewards for specific behavior that is cooperative in business relationships.
3. Provide positive feedback on the employee's job performance.
4. Provide the employee with a feeling of acceptance.

Provide a Satisfying or Pleasurable Consequence for Actions That Achieve Business Goals. Positive attitudes are formed about work activities when the work activities are pleasurable or are followed by pleasurable consequences. Work will not always be pleasurable, but you can always provide a pleasurable consequence for the work. You can verbally comment on the work or on the result of the work.

When a particular activity is complete, show the employee you appreciate the job he did. Tell him you are pleased, and thank him for doing a good job. An employee who feels his work is appreciated feels good, even if he doesn't like particular aspects of his work. The knowledge that someone, especially a superior, thinks well of him as a result of his job performance leads to the development of positive attitudes about the job.

Provide Rewards for Specific Behavior That Is Cooperative In Business Relationships. Research has shown that cooperative behavior is more productive than competitive behavior in most business situations. Cooperative behavior fosters positive attitudes about fellow employees, the job and the company. You can encourage these conditions through your reward system. Base your bonus or incentive plan on group results rather than on individual results. Provide other rewards such as parties, picnics or special rest facilities as rewards for specific group performance. All of these things will build positive employee attitudes.

Since you can't always provide monetary rewards, be prepared with psychological rewards. Use praise, give recognition and afford the employee an opportunity to talk about his own record. Although most managers know the value of praising and giving recognition, many are unaware of the psychological need people have to talk about their own results. After all, who is better informed about his work than the employee himself.

Today's enlightened managers discovered that sales meetings were much more productive when the salesmen were allowed to relate their experience to the group. The salesmen learned from each other and developed positive attitudes about the organization and their jobs. "Buzz" sessions have been added to operations meetings and most training sessions with the same favorable results.

Provide Positive Feedback on the Employee's Job Performance. If an employee doesn't know how his performance measures in relation to management expectations, he is in a state of quandry and cannot possibly hold positive attitudes about the job. Feed back information to your subordinates on how they are progressing to overcome this problem. Place special emphasis on the progress they are making, so they realize that you are aware of their efforts and accomplishments.

Employees who know exactly what is expected of them, are aware of where they stand in relation to those expectations and possess knowledge that they have time to reach those objectives, develop positive attitudes. The employee feels good about his ability, his progress and the knowledge that his superiors are aware of his efforts.

Provide the Employee with a Feeling of Acceptance. One of the easiest of the many social forms of acceptance is the consideration of an employee's ideas. Managers have found that an employee feels accepted and develops positive attitudes about the company, even when his ideas are not used, if they are given serious consideration by management. You can solicit ideas from your employees on a continual basis, continually showing acceptance by seriously considering their ideas and feeding back reasons for rejection when they are not used.

How a Manufacturing Plant Manager Stopped a Strike by Defusing Negative Emotions

The plant manager of an eastern manufacturing company was called into a meeting between the plant Labor Relations Manager and Local Union Representative. The two negotiators had reached agreement, but both felt the plant workers would not vote to accept the contract because of their highly negative emotional state.

The workers felt the company had, in the past, exploited them by requiring them to clean their tools and machine on their own time. They also felt other rules and regulations were designed to exploit the employees and were grossly unfair. These problem areas were corrected in the new contract.

The following morning, the plant manager called a meeting of all the plant union employees. He told them that an agreement was nearing completion and would soon be presented to them by the local union officials. He said that it had been pointed out that there were a number of complaints that he should hear. "I wanted," he said, "to talk with the employees to get their views first hand."

The employees voiced their complaints and grievances for over two hours. The manager had recorded their comments and at the end of the session, he read them back to the group. "I believe I understand your complaints and understand the reasons you feel the way you do. I cannot change the past and neither can you. We are now faced with a decision about the future. For my part, I have agreed to a new contract which I believe corrects the things you are concerned about. You will soon have the same decision to make. You must decide whether or not to ratify that contract."

The plant manager let the employees get their resentment off their chests. He questioned them and listened to their complaints. He summarized and expressed understanding of their complaints, and ordered them to make a decision. This use of command decision techniques cleared the air between management and the workers. They voted to accept the new contract, and the strike was avoided.

◆ 5 ◆

How to Use the New Directive Psychology Approach to Move People Out of Self-Imposed Ruts

◆ In recent years, managers found that the previously touted self-motivation approaches were not effective for all subordinates. In many cases, where the employee was given freedom and left to his own devices, as recommended by some authorities, he simply did not make the necessary effort to improve. To overcome these problems, managers developed the new directive psychology approach to move people out of self-imposed ruts. Managers found that direct statements of improvement expectations tied into the subordinate's psychological drives moves people out of these self-imposed ruts and triggers a desire for self-improvement and higher productivity. This approach was based on the new psychological theories that people perform at higher levels if they see the relationship between the job goal and their personal needs. The new approach utilizes this psychological base but adds an element of managerial power, the command to perform.

In this chapter, you'll learn proven techniques that cause subordinates to raise their aspiration level on the job. You'll see how to alter job structure to reinforce subordinate attempts to improve, how to overcome employee fear of taking risks and how to foster the subordinate's awareness of his need for new or improved skills. Finally, in this chapter, you'll see what to do when a subordinate loses confidence in himself and stops trying to achieve his goal.

THREE NEW APPROACHES TO GUIDE THE DEVELOPMENT OF SUBORDINATES WHOSE PERFORMANCE IS UNSATISFACTORY

Three techniques that managers found especially effective in developing employees who were not performing at a satisfactory level were "developmental risks," "raising expectations" and "persuasive demands."

These three techniques used together provided the subordinate an opportunity to develop, coupled with personal motivation and managerial direction. These techniques have been successfully used in manufacturing, service, technical and professional organizations.

How to Use the New "Small Risk" Approach
to Support Subordinates Who Fear Taking Developmental Risks

A management development study at General Electric revealed that the most significant change in subordinate behavior occurred when the subordinate was trained on the job by his manager. On the job, the subordinate could see the results of his boss's actions, and where they were successful, he copied them.

When the subordinate tried a new way of doing things, he was given immediate feedback from the environment and from his boss as well. This immediate awareness of the results of his actions led to constant improvement.

One of the reasons this approach worked so well was that the structure of the job supported the behavior that the boss was teaching. Often, a trainee attends a class or workshop away from his job and learns useful techniques that seem to fall apart when he tries them on the job. This is the result of a non-supporting job structure.

You can overcome these problems by using the new approach to managing your subordinates. One technique from the new approach is to change the structure of the job to suggest small risks, which the subordinate is encouraged to take. After a subordinate learns a new technique either off or on the job, he is encouraged to take a risk and try what he has learned in small steps. His job structure is redesigned so that he is rewarded for trying rather than for success alone.

By this process of taking small risks, the subordinate learns not to fear trying new procedures, and as he tries them, he develops into a more experienced and more valuable employee. The job structure change may involve giving him a new developmental assignment, or it may simply require that his supervisor comment on his risk-taking in a favorable manner.

Another way the new "small risk" approach can be used is to establish proficiency levels and encourage the subordinate to move into new proficiency levels before he is completely ready for them. The subordinate should be shown that some risk is involved but that you have confidence in his ability to catch up to the assignment.

One example of how this was used occurred in a Los Angeles sales division of a national manufacturer. The manufacturer decided to discontinue distribution sales and establish his own sales division. A sales manager was sent to the area to hire and develop a sales team.

The sales manager decided to use the "small risk" approach to develop his organization. He hired twenty salesmen, gave them two weeks of intensive training and started them calling on small retail accounts. One month later, while they were still "green," he asked for volunteers to call on larger accounts.

Six people volunteered for the new assignments. The sales manager worked with each of them and helped them learn the requirements of selling to large independents and independent chains. Two months later, he selected three of the six to begin calling on the large local and national chains.

Each time he encouraged one of his salespeople to take a risk and move into a more difficult selling situation, he worked closely with him and helped him become successful. He developed an outstanding sales force which produced sales managers to staff other areas of the country as the company expanded.

How Raising Your Level of Expectation Affects
Subordinate Development

Psychologists tell us that we behave in ways that create self-fulfilling prophecies. In other words, if we believe that something will happen, we subconsciously act in ways that lead to fulfillment of that belief. If we believe a subordinate is going to fail some task, we will unconsciously convey that feeling to the subordinate. We also say and do things that impede his efforts and cause him to lose his self-confidence.

Educational psychologists at Harvard tested the intelligence of a group of students and then selected and listed the names of a group from those tested. The list included students from the lowest and progressed up through the highest-scoring student. The teachers were duped by being told that the list contained only the highest-scoring students in the school.

A year later, the psychologists returned and gave the same test to the students. The students whose names had been given to the teachers as the highest-scoring the previous year, scored substantially higher on this year's test. They improved their scores by 20 to 25 points, which would not be expected of even the brightest students. The increases were substantially higher than those made by students not on the list.

The answer to the question, "How did these students improve to such high levels?" is found in the self-fulfilling prophecy. Psychologists say that people behave in ways that fulfill their expectations. In this case, the teachers, believing they were dealing with superior children, treated them with praise and encouragement. They gave the children special attention and treated them with affection and respect.

Even the dullest students in the class responded to this special handling. The children sensed the confidence the teachers placed in them, responded to their encouragement and lived up to the teachers' expectations.

The same experiment was recently repeated in another state with similar results. It is clear that high expectations coupled with encouragement, respect and support elicits outstanding effort.

Managers cannot usually hide their low expectations. If they feel a subordinate is going to perform poorly, they give their feelings away through their inactivity. They unintentionally reveal their lack of confidence by saying nothing, by withholding praise, by not speaking enthusiastically to the subordinate and by acting indifferent.

You can resolve this problem and provide motivational support to your subordinates. Accept the fact that your most ineffective subordinate can improve. Once you accept this fact, support that subordinate by showing him special attention. Help him improve his performance in one specific area, then praise and encourage him to continue in other areas.

One manager who runs a large processing plant, helps his product managers increase their prices on one item in the line. He could have them raise all their prices at once, but he doesn't. He demonstrates how to do it with one line and then lets them enjoy the satisfaction of using what they learned to raise the other prices themselves.

The secret of successful managers, those who hold and express high expectations for their subordinates, is that they expect to develop the needed talents and skills in their subordinates. In effect, they say, "I know this is a high goal, but I will help you reach it. I'll show you a couple of techniques that will get the job done."

The key, then, is what the manager thinks of himself. The successful manager holds high expectations because he *knows* that he can *select*, *train, guide* and *stimulate* his subordinates' performance to the level he expects.

How Jim Boven's Rising Expectations Paid Off in Higher Productivity

Jim Boven was recently promoted to foreman in a clothing factory. Jim had been an average worker who did his job and kept his clothes clean but was not considered a ball of fire. He was well liked by the other employees and enjoyed his new job.

As a foreman, Jim learned the importance of cost controls and productivity improvements. Jim became intrigued with the ideas of improving productivity and began to look for ways to help the employees increase their productivity. As he found small changes that resulted in higher productivity, Jim began to raise his expectations about how much productivity they could really get.

Jim began talking to his men and asking them for ways to get productivity up to the level which he thought them capable of attaining. Jim's attitude rubbed off. The way he treated the men showed that he had confidence in them and expected them to do a lot better as they found or developed new methods of production.

Jim started giving the employees goals to shoot for, and then he helped them find ways to reach the goals. He always encouraged them to find their own ways to increase productivity and convinced them that he expected them to do so. Jim's rising expectations had their effect. The workers looked for and found new ways to improve their performance. Their productivity rose, seeking the level of Jim's expectations.

How to Use "Persuasive Demands" to Generate Subordinate Development Actions

The third new approach to improving unsatisfactory subordinate performance is to use persuasive demands.

A "persuasive demand" is an order or a demand that is given with some persuasive appeal. The demand leaves no room for argument or rejection, but it is based on logic.

There are two occasions when a subordinate is extremely susceptible to persuasive demands; one is when he is under heavy stress, and the other is when he is facing an assignment or situation of such magnitude that he feels incapable of handling it. At those times, the subordinate opens his mind and seeks information to use in the solution of his problem.

While the subordinate's mind is open, any action by the manager that is spelled out as appropriate problem-solving behavior will leave an *imprinted pattern* on the subordinate's mind. This behavior will be unconsciously repeated as appropriate when similar situations arise.

Using "Persuasive Demands" to Imprint New Employees Against Negative Suggestions

One opportunity that management has generally missed is the opportunity to start the new employee with the proper attitude. The old approach to breaking in a new employee was to place him in the care of another employee for his initial training. Often, the new employee is subjected to the negative attitudes of the embittered employee who is supposed to train him. The new employee is imprinted with negative suggestion.

The old approach of placing a new employee in the care or under the direction of the peers he would be working with, denied the new employee the opportunity to learn management expectations, attitudes and beliefs. Everything the new employee learned was filtered through the prejudices, jealousies, secretiveness and lack of teaching knowledge of the other employees.

New employees begin their employment in a state of stress. They don't know what to do, how much to do, when to do it or how to do it. They are very impressionable, in fact imprintable, at this time. The new approach places the new employee under the direction of a manager who explains management expectations and demands that the employee strive to learn the job and accomplish the goals of the job and the organization. He is imprinted to resist negative suggestions.

The Four Stages of "Persuasive Demands"

A persuasive demand will be most effective if used in a four-step sequence in which the subordinate is made aware of the situation and given an opportunity to make a decision. The following four stages comprise a "persuasive demand."

1. Explain the Situation or Problem. Before any decision or commitment can be made, the situation must be thoroughly understood. If an employee is being asked to do something new or different, he must be given an explanation of what, why and how. If, for example, new machinery is being utilized that makes higher production possible, the explanation should be given. If employees are being asked to work harder due to low profits, this should be explained. The employee should be told how his work fits into the organization's overall goals and how he will benefit from the program. If he sees how he personally benefits, he is more likely to be committed to the job.

2. Explore the Employee's Feelings. Knowing how the employee feels about the job will help you determine how closely you must supervise. Obviously, the employee who is enthused and likes the work will require less supervision than one who dislikes the work.

You can determine the employee's feelings by simply asking questions. Ask your subordinates how they like their work, what part they like best and what part they dislike. The answers to these questions will often surprise you. You may find that someone you thought liked their work actually doesn't.

The same thing applies to conditions on the job. The subordinate may like his work but dislike his immediate supervisor or the conditions of work. He may not like the starting time or the work location. It's important to know these things in order to deal effectively with the employee.

3. Offer the Employee an Alternative. Once understanding has been established, once the employee understands the job situation or problem and the manager understands how the employee feels, alternatives must be established. There must be different courses of action presented to the subordinate so that he may choose one to which he can commit himself.

In many cases the subordinate will commit himself to the action the manager wants, in which case everyone is happy. At other times the subordinate may opt for a different assignment or a new job, knowing that he can't perform as expected on the current one.

For example, an employee might be offered a sales bonus based either on volume or profit. The employee must choose one or the other. Once the choice is made, he is expected to commit all his energies to accomplishing that goal and he is persuasively commanded to do so.

4. Demand a Decision and a Commitment to That Decision. In many cases, especially under the "old" approach to managing people, the employee was never ordered to make a decision. The alternatives may or may not have been developed, but the employee was left to decide when and if he felt like making the decision. The new directive approach corrects the old inefficiencies. The manager, using the new approach, orders the employee to make a decision. Once that decision is made, you demand commitment.

If you have a sales supervisor, for example, with slumping sales volume and you determine that either sales calls are to be made by the supervisor or extra training must be provided the salesmen, you offer those alternatives. Once the supervisor selects one of the alternative methods, he is then told bluntly and specifically that he is expected to commit all his energies and skills to that decision. He is expected to perform.

The good manager will follow up to make sure that he does perform. This is the basis for the new approach to managing people. Once the subordinate makes his decision, after fully expressing his views, he is directed to proceed in the fulfillment of the required actions. The time for discussion is past, and the time for action at hand. The manager orders it and follows up to see that it's done.

How a Bottling Company Executive Used the New Approach
to Bring a High Turnover Rate Under Control

A few years ago, Tom Landry, a bottling company executive used the new management approach to curb the high turnover rate in a bottling plant. Turnover was over 14 percent during the current year and the trend was upward. Tom called in all the foreman to give him information on the problem.

Tom found that the problem was primarily one of boredom. Most of the employees were on jobs that had been specialized with new machinery adding to the routinization of the job. One foreman said that "other than the adjustments made by the engineers when changing bottle size, there is no real skill required to operate the equipment."

Tom asked if the employees could be trained to make their own adjustments. "Most of them would be afraid to try," the foreman replied. Tom asked the foreman if they would be willing to train their men if they could be encouraged to take the risk associated with learning the adjustment procedures. The foremen agreed, and a plan was developed to win the workers' support.

Tom next spoke to the assembled workers and explained the new plan to have each of them trained to adjust their own machines. He explained a two-fold purpose. One, the men would have more interesting work to do and two, the new skills would result in an increase in productivity. He expressed his *high expectations* for the improvement of skills and the increase in productivity.

The men voted to accept the training, and Tom immediately told them that he would expect improved performance as they learned the new skills. The program worked. The men took pride in learning the new skills and in their higher rates of productivity.

Tom's original objective was accomplished. A few problems that occurred in the early stages of the program resulted in a continuance of the high turnover rate for the first few months. As the men began to gain proficiency in the new skills, they gained confidence and began to take pride in their work. When this happened, the turnover rate dropped drastically and eventually stabilized at about one percent.

TWO NEW MANAGEMENT APPROACHES
THAT ENCOURAGE SUBORDINATE SELF-DEVELOPMENT

Many people never attempt self-development beyond the specific skill, profession or trade they require for their livelihood. Only those who realize that career promotions are based on individual development and have a desire to succeed are motivated to do anything about their own self-development.

It is commonly known, however, that self-development not only helps the individual but the company as well. As the individual learns and grows, he performs more productively on the job. So efforts on the part of the organization that encourage self-development benefit the employee and the organization as well.

There are two new management approaches that encourage subordinate self-development. One is a technique that encourages the subordinate's interest in self-development and the other is the use of directive psychology to start the subordinate participating in tasks that provide development on the job.

How to Develop Subordinate Interest in Personal Advancement

There are two opportunities for a manager to encourage a subordinate to take an interest in advancement. The manager can demonstrate a managerial philosophy that appeals to subordinates, and he can direct the subordinate's interest to career goals in management. Both of these techniques develop subordinate interest in personal advancement.

State and Demonstrate an Explicit Management Philosophy. A manager who clearly states an explicit management philosophy provides his subordinates with a clear picture of what's expected. Furthermore, when he demonstrates support for the philosophy with his actions, he provides a clear-cut model of what a manager is supposed to do.

If you say that a manager should check production records before leaving each day, and then you actually do so, you provide the model to support the philosophy. Your subordinates learn by your example. After a period of continual demonstration, they feel comfortable with the action you take and sense it as something they can also do. Once they believe they can do it, they begin to develop an interest in advancement. When they develop an interest in advancement, they will develop an interest in the self-development required to win a promotion.

Provide Career Counseling. The second opportunity the manager has to encourage interest in advancement is during career counseling sessions. By directing the counseling discussion toward the subordinate's career goals, you can encourage the subordinate's interest in the personal development that is required to achieve those goals. Then, following your techniques will provide the foundation for good career counseling.

1. Offer a Candid Appraisal to Promote Awareness of Production Problems. Be very candid in appraising the subordinate's performance. You can select those tasks that the subordinate does well and point them out with praise, but do not gloss over the problem areas. Many managers feel that the mere mention of a problem area will cause the employee to do something to correct his shortcoming. This is not true. The employee may hear the praise, miss the problem areas and leave the counseling session thinking everything is all right.

The new approach to management attempts to use questions to get the subordinate to see his faults himself. Questions that ask the subordinate to evaluate his own performance by comparing it with others often lead to the subordinate's self-discovery. When self-discovery does not occur or the subordinate fails to accept his lack of acceptable performance, you must candidly spell out exactly what is lacking and what must be done to correct the situation.

2. Encourage Subordinates to Establish Career Goals. Psychologists tell us that all of our behavior is goal-directed. Everything we say and do is intended to help us achieve some goal. If you can elicit the goals of your subordinates during a counseling session, you can direct their interest in the self-development areas that will lead them to their goals.

Often, employees have some vague goal in mind but no specific job in mind. For example, they may want to be a manager, but have no idea of the specific managerial position they want. Consequently, they have no idea of what steps they must go through and what they have to learn to become a manager.

During the counseling session, you can point out the various positions available in the organization and have the subordinate select the specific one he wishes to work toward. Once a specific goal is established, you can then talk to the subordinate about the specific skills and experience required for that job. Most subordinates will start on a self-development program if they are given guidance and see the specific goal they are working toward.

3. Clarify the Methods of Seeking Promotion. Once your subordinate has indicated his preference for a specific position, tell him exactly how that position is filled. Point out the requirements for the job and the procedures an employee must go through to be considered for the position. If it is customary for an employee to make written application for a job, when one comes open, spell that out to your subordinate. Don't leave any surprises for later, let him know immediately what he will have to do to be considered for promotion. If he doesn't like the rules, he may not try, but at least it's his decision and he won't be misled.

4. Require a Personal Assessment of Personal Strengths and Weaknesses. After a subordinate becomes aware of the specific knowledge and skills required for a position he aspires to, he must assess his own strengths and weaknesses in relation to that position, his strengths to be further utilized and his weaknesses to be used as an improvement base. Again, if the subordinate fails to see his own weaknesses after reasonable discussion, the manager must point out the weaknesses clearly and candidly.

How to Use Directive Psychology to Encourage the Development of New Skills

Managers who developed the new approach to managing people discovered that many psychological concepts could be used in practical ways. A subordinate's unconscious motives can be tapped, his avoidance drives can be utilized and clearly defined goals can be used to get people out of ruts and make them productive. These managers also discovered practical ways to get their subordinates involved in activities that incite their motivational drives and encourage self-development. The following list of activities was designed to encourage subordinate development of new skills.

Assign Extra Developmental Tasks. The assignment of extra tasks gives the subordinate time to move slowly into new skill areas. He still performs his regular job but has some opportunity each day to learn the new skill. This might be a special one-man project or a committee assignment. In either case, the assignment should be one that requires the subordinate to learn a new skill.

Assign a Research Project. Another way to get your subordinate involved in self-development activities is to assign him a research project. You might ask him to research and propose a new investment project or the development of a new product. Although these projects often result in the development of profitable new ventures, their primary purpose, in this situation, is to provide a means of self-development for your subordinates.

Assign a Cost Reduction Problem. Every manager needs an approach or system to use in reducing costs when conditions require it. You can assign the problem of developing a cost reduction system to a subordinate as a self-development task and then assign him a project to use the system on.

This approach gives your subordinates an opportunity to develop and practice managerial skills in advance of need. The potential manager can learn and practice decision-making techniques so that he is ready when the opportunity comes.

A Sales Manager Who Resigned When His Subordinates Stopped Trying to Achieve Company Goals

Bud Jenkel was a hard-driving salesman who consistently made or exceeded his assigned budget. He was well liked, a good communicator and held high expectations for success. Bud was promoted to sales manager in January, and everyone thought he would continue his successful pattern.

For the first three months, Bud's division showed tremendous growth, then it peaked out and began to subside. Bud held sales contests and trade promotions, and he increased advertising and made personal calls with his salesmen. He did everything he could to build enthusiasm back up, but everything he tried failed. At the end of June, Bud resigned.

The new sales manager who replaced Bud brought in a consulting firm to find out what went wrong. Their studies revealed that the very trait that enabled Bud to make his initial progress undid his efforts when it became extreme. Bud held high expectations that his men initially accepted but later rejected when Bud raised them to unrealistic levels.

The expectations that became self-fulfilling prophecies were initially perceived as being realistic. But, when Bud tried to encourage additional effort by using flowery phrases and positive platitudes, he actually lost ground. His subordinates did not perceive the new expectations as achievable.

Bud tried to move too far, too fast. He should have given the men time to become comfortable with old levels before pushing for new goals. A number of studies in large manufacturing companies found that when production goals were set too high, the workers stopped trying to achieve them. As in the case of Bud's salesmen, no extra effort will be put forth when the goals are perceived by the subordinates as impossible to attain.

The new sales manager used these findings to establish a reasonable and achievable set of goals. The men were allowed to become comfortable with each level of sales volume before pushing on to new goals. The new sales manager took six months to surpass Bud's three month record, but he then went on to establish new records for five years in a row.

◆ 6 ◆

The New
Split-Participation
Approach That
Gets Things Done

◆Since the early sixties, managers have been experimenting with participative management. The theory behind the approach was that by letting the workers participate in decision-making, planning and scheduling, higher levels of productivity would be achieved. Many companies were successful with participative techniques and did, in fact, experience high gains in productivity.

Unfortunately, as the system spread, failures were encountered. In many cases, productivity actually *dropped*. The system did not work in all cases, in all situations.

In this chapter, you'll see how managers learned to overcome the problems of group participation. You'll learn the new management approach of "split-participation" management. The split-participation technique takes the employee's needs and motivations into account but reserves the direction of the operation to management.

You'll see why the old participative techniques failed and how to use the new techniques to improve productivity. You'll learn eight needs in this chapter that employees have that can be fulfilled on the job without the loss of management control. Finally, you'll learn how the new approach brings out the full range of subordinate skills that can be utilized to accomplish organizational goals.

PROBLEMS WITH PARTICIPATIVE MANAGEMENT

There are five major problems that mitigate the value of participative management. The quality of decisions and the level of productivity is reduced by these problems. The problems evolve from natural human traits that emerge in group associations. The five problems listed here are adapted from an analysis of group errors in international relations presented in *Victims of Group Think*, (Janis, 1972).

These five problems are the major reasons for the failure of group participation techniques. They are (1) Unreasonable trust in the group, (2) Failure to call in experts for specialized information needs, (3) Failure to plan for problems or interference, (4) Acceptance of the first suggestion presented (5) Placement of social support of the group above the goals of the organization.

Unreasonable Trust in the Group

One major reason for the failure of participative management, is the trust that groups develop. As the members work together, they begin to ascribe an undeserved trust to the group. As friendly feelings build up for group members, the members begin to accept what is said without challenge. When the group makes a decision, it is taken for granted that the group decision is correct.

Often, the decision is correct in the sense that the actions decided upon get results. The problem is that the results may be at a very low level. A better decision would have brought better results. But, since the group is not made aware of the possibility of better results, they reinforce the low-value group decision by thinking it is the best one.

Failure to Call in Experts for Specialized Information

As group members develop problem-solving skills, they tend to go through the problem in a superficial way. They develop information for each step, but the information may not be technically accurate. A few members of the group may have a general knowledge or a superficial knowledge of an area that requires specialized information. If the specialized information were available, a high quality solution would be possible.

In this situation, where superficial information is available, members tend to accept the superficial information and fail to call in experts who could provide the specialized information that would solve the problem. This failure to utilize expert information results in lower quality group performance.

Failure to Plan for Problems or Interference

Group participation in decision-making often results in well-laid plans with no anticipation of problems or interfering actions that might block the accomplishment of the plans. "The best laid plans of mice and men . . ." If consideration of the possible interferences were listed and discussed along with the possible consequences of each of the planned actions, this problem could be avoided.

Sales managers who plan large sales volume increases generally check the availability of raw materials, plant capacity, availability of labor and shipping schedules. Any one of these elements could pose a problem, if not considered and planned for in advance. The same considerations apply when a group is involved in the planning, but these things go unnoticed in the group setting. This lack of notice or discussion may lead to the failure of the program.

Acceptance of the First Suggestion Presented

If the first suggestion is presented by a prestigious group member, the group will generally accept it without rigorous discussion. The group ascribes an infallibility to prestigious members. Since their suggestions are not subjected to intellectual investigation, the opportunity to detect weaknesses in the suggestion are lost. If weaknesses are not recognized, they can't be prepared for.

Placement of Social Support of the Group Above the Goals of the Organization

A primary concern of an on-going group is the social support the group gives each member. Group members develop a dependency upon each other to maintain their individual and group status. Janis describes this process as "concurrence-seeking." He said,

> Concurrence-seeking and the various symptoms of group think to which it gives rise can be best understood as a mutual effort among the members of a group to maintain self-esteem, especially when they share responsibility for making vital decisions that pose threats of social disapproval and self-disapproval.

The group members can close their eyes to outside criticism as long as they gain support from each other. This support is continued by unspoken agreement and becomes a social goal of the group. Eventually, this social goal becomes more important and more strongly directs the group's activity than do the goals of the organization. Individual members withhold ideas or opinions that might conflict with the social support of the group. Often, these ideas that are withheld would contribute to organizational goals.

A Participative Management Failure That Could Have Been Avoided

Midtex Manufacturing, an industrial machinery company, decided to try participative management techniques to reduce costs and improve profits. The company manufactures standard drilling machinery as well as custom-designed drilling tools. Recent cost increases on subcontracted parts have cut deeply into the company's profits.

The cost increases affected the custom-designed tools more heavily than the standard drilling machinery. The president appointed a division vice-president to take over the custom tool division and suggested the division begin producing some of the parts that had previously been subcontracted. The new vice-president immediately set up a new production line and initiated full participative management with all workers meeting in groups to establish their work goals and plan their day's schedule.

The plan was doomed from the beginning and failed. The men had no idea what level of production to expect. They set the quotas low and often didn't make them. Undue trust in the group and the lack of expert advice resulted in very low levels of production. The specialized knowledge of an expert in the field could have gotten them on the right track. Without this initial help, waste was high and errors occurred frequently.

The lack of planning for possible snags or breakdowns resulted in many hours of lost time. The men were willing to work, but just did not have the managerial expertise to deal with the large number of problems associated with a "start-up" operation.

This fiasco could have been avoided if management had been aware of the problems of full participation when skills are lacking. The split-participation technique would have evoked worker motivation but would have reserved control to management. This failure resulted in losses exceeding a million dollars, which could have been avoided.

SUCCESSFUL EXPERIMENTS
WITH PARTICIPATIVE MANAGEMENT

A large number of participative management experiments have proven successful in spite of the tendency for groups to place their personal goals above the goals of the organization. An examination of these groups in various research studies revealed that the primary supervisory concern was for the well-being of the group. Management showed a sincere interest in the personal success of their subordinates. They made the group members feel important to the company and view themselves as a useful and vital link in the organization's major activities.

It seems that the supervisor's efforts to provide personal and social support for his subordinates eliminated the need to develop group support. As long as their esteem and social needs were being met by the supervisor, they were emotionally free to concentrate on job objectives.

Psychologists tell us that if a child is raised to feel socially approved and accepted, the child will not be motivated to perform acceptance-seeking or approval-seeking behavior. In the absence of the satiation of these needs, the child is motivated to seek the higher-level needs of self-actualization.

The same principle can be applied with adult workers. The supervisor can, by supporting the worker's needs for approval and acceptance, encourage the evolvement of the worker's needs for self-actualization. By letting the subordinate know that he is meeting required standards, that his performance is acceptable, even though some improvement may be required, and by telling him how his work fits into the major activity of the organization, the subordinate's motivation for self-actualization will be free to evoke actions that improve performance.

Experiments That Failed

Early experiments in participative management often failed as a result of four basic errors made by management. (1) Management did not make clear to the workers what the production problems were. (2) Management did not demonstrate an expectation of reasonable success. (3) Employees felt increased productivity would result in layoffs and (4) Employees were not allowed an opportunity to report their feelings and express their attitudes about work problems.

By permitting the four errors to continue, one electronics firm actually suffered a reduction in productivity after changing to a participative management system. In the electronics study, a vital factor was the loss of confidence of the workers. Management had led the workers to believe that there would be greatly increased productivity. In fact, they built worker expectations too high.

The workers were expecting 15 to 20 percent increases. When the increases did not occur the workers lost confidence on the system. Other studies of individual behavior on the job have shown that if a subordinate fails to meet goals that he had set for himself, he loses his self-confidence and lowers his personal standards. Evidently the same thing occurs with groups. They lose confidence in a system and develop negative attitudes when they fail to reach group goals.

How One Company's Failure Led to the
Split-Participation Technique

A California canning company tried participative management in a southern California plant in the early sixties. In an attempt to improve productivity, foremen were eliminated and the workers were formed into eight-to-ten-man work groups. The groups were responsible for all phases of production.

Each day, the groups gathered, discussed the day's work load and planned out their activities. If a problem occurred on the job, the senior or skilled members of the group were consulted. During the first two months, the system seemed to be working. These leaderless groups actually showed slight increases in productivity. By the end of the third month, however, productivity had dropped. Declining productivity continued for six months and the system was scrapped.

At this point, management consultants were called in to analyze the system and determine the cause for the failure. Their research revealed that the work groups, operating without leadership and direction, had become more social in nature than work-oriented. Their primary function became one of group support. Their fear of layoffs held production down and their meetings became social support sessions.

Later, under the direction of trained foremen, the meetings were reintroduced to gather opinions and ideas from the workers that could be utilized for productivity increases. This controlled utilization of subordinate participation led to the new approach to managing people with split-participation techniques.

THE BUSINESSMAN'S PRACTICAL BREAKTHROUGH

Businessmen who recognized both the problems and benefits of participation techniques began to experiment on their own to find a better method of managing people. These men recognized the possibility of generating high gains in productivity by using the ideas and opinions of the workers. They also recognized the danger of non-directed leaderless groups. Again, the answer evolved as a combination of directive psychology and practical experience. The split-participation technique came into use.

Management learned that people were satisfied to make their contribution by giving their ideas and opinions and then letting their supervisors make the decisions. The important thing to the subordinate was to be listened to and kept informed.

How to Get Full Value from the New Split-Participation Management Techniques

You can use split-participation techniques to improve productivity and still keep managerial control. By making it clear in the beginning that you are establishing a method for your subordinates to communicate their ideas and opinions as opposed to a method where they take over management functions, you are free to use the best ideas and reject those that seem ineffective.

The following principles evolved from fifteen years of research, and study and experience provide a sound basis to encourage the highest levels of employee participation in a productivity improvement program.

1. Explain the General Goals and Objectives of the Organization. Managers have confirmed the research findings that show that employees are more productive when they know what the major organizational goals are and how their own work fits into those goals. By clearly explaining the organizational goals and objectives, you give your subordinates something to shoot for. Once they have a target they will offer their ideas and suggestions to help achieve those goals. Psychologists tell us that once people clearly perceive and accept a goal, they will be subconsciously motivated to act in ways that will lead to its accomplishment.

2. Define the Major Problems That Interfere with Reaching the Goals. People cannot prepare for problems if they don't know what to expect. You can gain employee support and prepare them for temporary setbacks by having them participate in a discussion dealing with these problems. This is an example of split-participation techniques. You utilize your subordinates in discussion, analysis and recommendation stages but retain for management the right to make the final decisions.

3. Rank and Isolate the Major Causes of the Problem. Managers have found that employees become committed to management goals if they are listened to and if their ideas are considered. They realize that all ideas cannot be accepted and used. If they are shown the respect of being listened to and know their ideas are evaluated, they feel they are a part of the organization and become committed to organizational goals.

One excellent way to develop this commitment is to have the employees participate in isolating the major causes of the problems that relate to their departments. If there is a large production waste problem for example, the employees who work in production can be asked to participate in isolating and ranking the probable causes of the problem. Once this ranking is completed, the list is turned over to management for action.

4. Spell Out Specific Performance Standards That Will Resolve the Problem. Once the problem causes have been considered you must spell out specific standards that must be attained. Unless the employees know precisely what they must do, there is very little likelihood that their performance will improve.

You may also improve their desire to attain the new goals if you can point out the results of some other group that is doing well. This may be an in-house or outside group. The important point is that the goals can be achieved, because some group is doing it.

5. Get Acceptance That the Goals Are Achievable Under Stated Conditions. Managers have found that people don't reject new goals because they don't want to do more, they only reject them because they don't believe they can be done. One of the reasons they believe they can't be done results from previous problems they have encountered. Most of these causes have been discussed, so you have a base of understanding to work from.

The way to gain acceptance for the new goals is to state the goal as being conditional upon correcting the previously determined problems. If one of the problems causing rejects was inferior processing material, then solving this problem is a condition for accepting the goal. You might ask, "Will you accept the standards when we start using the new processing material?"

6. Get Public Commitment to Reach the Goals. It is very important to have group members commit to the new goals in public. They should be asked to accept the goals in meetings or other public situations so they commit to the goals in front of their peers. Once they verbally commit to the goals, they feel a psychological drive to live up to the commitment, to enhance their esteem in the eyes of their friends and peers.

7. Challenge the Group to Find Creative Ways to Improve. A challenge also calls upon the individual to support his self-esteem. Many people are motivated by achievement needs and readily respond to specific challenges. This motivation can be enhanced by spelling out a specific benefit that will be earned by achieving the goal. Achievement-oriented people are accustomed to receiving rewards for their success in attaining goals.

8. Provide for Easy Communications. Creativity and improved production methods grow in an area of freedom. Provide free and easy access to all levels of management. Make sure that ideas generated at the bottom have a way to get to the top.

Employees also need freedom for experimentation and a means to communicate the results of their experimentation to management. Monthly meetings, written suggestions or a weekly visit by the manager are a few ways this communication channel can be established.

9. Support Subordinate Efforts. Management must support subordinate efforts if they are to succeed. First, an atmosphere of friendliness must be established. The subordinate then feels a part of the organization and feels free to experiment and make mistakes. Second, he needs feedback on how he is doing. He wants to know if the boss thinks he is doing OK or not. This may simply be a remark to the effect that you see that progress is being made.

10. Select an Overriding Theme. Managers who have been the most successful with split-participation techniques have generally set an overriding theme that directed the group's activity. One manager used the theme "The Charge of the Bulls." The group began to look at themselves as a group with the strength and determination of a herd of bulls. They were successful in overcoming their production problems and retained the name "The Bulls" long after the big "charge" was over.

11. Provide Social and Esteem Need Fulfillment for the Group. Social needs can be provided for through group discussion and planning sessions. Also, provision should be made for socializing during breaks from work and through club and team activities. Many organizations sponsor bowling or other in-house sports teams. The more socializing that takes place off duty the less is necessary on the job.

Just as we want to minimize social fulfillment on the job, we want to maximize the fulfillment of needs for esteem on the job. This can be done through recognition for successfully completing an assignment or for reaching certain levels of productivity. The important thing is that the group begins to feel like an elite group and knows that it is recognized as an elite group.

One way to do this, in addition to pats on the back and achievement certificates, is to recognize the group symbol. For example, you might place large signs in plain view proclaiming "The Bulls Do It Again." An awards dinner or evening out for the "Bulls" or anything that publicizes the group symbol will support the prestige of the group and evoke group cooperation and the desire to keep the group in the "limelight."

12. Maintaining a Fair and Equitable System of Promotion to Maintain Group Cooperation. Even though everyone knows they can't all be promoted, they want to make sure that they all have an equal chance. They want to be sure that promotions are available to all on the same basis. Knowing that promotions go to the best qualified on the basis of qualifications that everyone can easily evaluate will keep most employees cooperative and productive.

One way to satisfy your subordinates of the fairness of your promotional system is to establish minimum requirements for each position and publicize those requirements. The requirements can easily be publicized by word of mouth. During discussions or counseling sessions, when the topic is brought up, you can spell out the requirements for the position under consideration.

Once a promotion has been made, a letter can be issued announcing the promotion and congratulating the promoted person. You can use this letter to establish the validity of your promotion by listing the qualifications of the person promoted. You might also emphasize the importance of one of the promoted person's strong points as related to one of the more important requirements of the job. By showing your subordinates that you promote on a fair and equitable basis, you will win their cooperation on the job and keep their productivity high.

*How to Use the New Split-Participation Technique
to Get Results Without Losing Management Control*

The new split-participation concept is based on the pscyhological need for people to live in a rational environment, to understand their relationship to that environment and be able to participate in the planning that affects their lives in that environment.

The old system of management interpreted this to mean that employees, in addition to understanding the organizational goals and policies, had to be involved in the actual determination of their own working conditions, plans, schedules and productivity levels. For some employees this system worked well, but in many organizations it failed. As discussed earlier, employees did not share the same aspirations, or thought they did not, as management. In other cases, they simply became more interested in social support than in organizational goals.

The new approach to managing people uses the participation system by providing a clear definition of the organizational environment and goals. An opportunity for employee participation in those areas that affect their working conditions and productivity is provided by discussion periods, productivity meetings, suggestion forms and gripe sessions. At this point, however, there is a split between proposals and decisions.

Management, under the split-participation concept reserves the right to make all decisions. No man has the right in pluralistic society, especially a democratic one, to expect more than to have his ideas, opinions and suggestions evaluated. Management's job is merely to insure all employees that all suggestions are being given serious consideration.

The rejection of ideas should not be publicized but any individual should be able to ask and find out why his idea was not used. Management should be prepared to answer these requests truthfully and candidly. If they do, the split-participation technique will generate employee loyalty, participation, high morale and high productivity.

How an Operations Manager Used Split-Participation Techniques to Improve Results

Rod Grantly, the operations manager of a midwestern plumbing supply manufacturer, faced a decline in productivity throughout the plant as a result of 30 percent of his employees being replaced by workers from a recently closed plant. The union contract permitted employees from a closed plant to bump employees with less service in other locations. A large number had chosen Rod's plant, as it was geographically closer to the closed plant than any other.

Many problems developed as a result of different machines, operating procedures, policies and some dissatisfaction as a result of the old plant's closing, which required the relocations. Productivity had dropped over 10 percent and was still dropping. Rod realized that the men had the skills to do a better job. He also knew that the new men might have some new ideas that would help resolve the problem. Rod decided to use a split-participation technique to draw the men together and regain the lost productivity.

Rod called all the employees together and explained the problem. He expressed the attitude that the men wanted to meet the old objectives and would work toward that end. He formed the men into productivity improvement groups and asked them to elect a representative to pass their ideas and problems along to him. He would meet with their representatives once a day until their basic problems were overcome and then twice a week until the company objectives were resolved.

When Rod met with the group representatives he created a friendly climate and asked for creative solutions. He developed a list of problem causes and had the representatives rank them in importance. He demonstrated clearly that he appreciated and expected advice and opinions on the most important planning and decision-making activities. He also pointed out that he would not always be able to use the recommendations, but would give them careful consideration and serious evaluation.

Rod spelled out his short-range performance standards in specific terms and expressed his expectations for the long run. Rod told the group representatives that he wanted a 10 percent increase (high expectations) over the old standards within a year after the old production level was achieved.

Rod expressed the belief that if the committees of representatives could tap their full potential and utilize their experience to develop new ideas, they would easily achieve the goals. He asked for and got verbal commitment from the committee to achieve the goals.

The committee agreed to meet every Tuesday and Thursday and to write out any ideas and problems in advance. At the meetings, Rod asked each group representative to present the problems and ideas of his group to the full committee. They were then discussed and Rod dismissed the meeting prior to making a decision. In this way, he separated the decision-making process from the recommendation process.

Rod introduced the decided changes at the next meeting and explained why he had accepted certain recommendations. He said that he was taking the group to lunch for the next meeting, and if there were any questions about why some recommendations were not instituted, he would be glad to answer them prior to that meeting. He explained that any committee member could come to his office to discuss the reasons at any time.

At the next meeting, Rod was able to point to improvements that had resulted from the committee's recommendations. He made it clear that every committee member had played a part in the improvements. Each group representative was given a chart to post in his department to plot his progress.

As the productivity inched upward, the employees, seeing their progress on the charts, began to experience a sense of self-satisfaction with their work. They soon reached the old levels of production and surpassed the old records in two months.

Once the old production records were surpassed, the employees began to feel real pride in their work. They began to work eagerly toward the 10 percent improvement goal established by Rod. They offered ideas for improvements and the committee gained status throughout the plant. Three months after they had achieved the old production level, they reached the new goal. They made the 10 percent improvement in just one-fourth the time Rod had established as reasonable for the goal.

◆ 7 ◆
Subtle Confrontation:
The "One Style"
Management Breakthrough

◆The new "one style" approach to managing people permits the manager to be true to himself. He can retain his own personality by using one style—his own, and by adding "subtle confrontation" techniques to his management style. Subtle confrontation places the burden of change or correction on the subordinate.

In this chapter, you'll see how to use this new management approach to deal with employee personality problems and problems of job dissatisfaction. You'll learn the techniques that managers, like yourself, developed and improved in actual job situations to deal with problem personalities, power plays and intimidation as well as job assignment, promotion, demotion and job dissatisfaction problems.

HOW "SUBTLE CONFRONTATION" PROVIDES
A NEW APPROACH TO MANAGING PEOPLE

Currently, many consultants are recommending that managers change their personality to mesh with the personality of the problem subordinate. If the subordinate has a personality problem and the manager tries to match the problem personality, we simply wind up with a bigger problem. The new approach only requires the manager to *confront the problem* not become a part of it.

"Subtle confrontation" is a new persuasive method of evoking commitment from people by requiring them to face the problem and make a decision. Once they make the decision, they are required to commit themselves to perform to the best of their ability.

This new approach is participative in the sense that the subordinate is permitted to question, discuss and offer his opinions on the problem. Once this process is complete, however, he must make a decision. Once the decision is made, discussion ends and implementation *must* begin. The problem belongs to, and must be accepted by, the subordinate.

THREE SUBTLE CONFRONTATION APPROACHES FOR DEALING WITH PROBLEM SUBORDINATES

Many people avoid confrontation because they see confrontation as an aggressive action, and they fear consequences of aggression. Confrontation does not have to be aggressive, it can be friendly and quite *subtle*. Subtle confrontation does not result in aggressive reactions, loss of friendship, embarrassment or being put down. Subtle confrontation is simply a new approach to finding a compromise solution, acceptable to both parties. It is also a new management approach that gets a subordinate to examine his options and make a decision. The following three behavioral problems can best be dealt with by applying the new subtle confrontation approach to managing people:

(1)   Problem personalities
(2)   Subordinate power plays
(3)   Intimidation by other employees

How to Use Subtle Confrontation Techniques to Deal with Five Problem Personalities

There have been a number of "labels" placed on differing personality types by psychologists, student researchers and management consultants going back at least to the early fifties and probably earlier. One or more of the following five labels may have been previously used by other writers or may have been used to describe a different personality type. My purpose in using the labels is to identify behavior that interferes with production or the

cooperative relationships that are most productive. The destructive, disruptive, defiant, dictatorial and disorganized personality types that generally interfere with productivity can be controlled by using the new subtle
confrontation approach to managing people.

Confronting the Destructive Personality. The destructive personality type interferes with productivity by belittling and putting down others
or by taking unreasonable positions in group meetings or activities. The
destructive personality will block productivity by disagreeing, by criticizing, becoming sarcastic, using offensive language and belittling others.
Each of these destructive behaviors can be neutralized by subtle confrontation.

To deal with destructive disagreement, confront the disagreement by
demanding facts, figures and explanations. If the facts and figures support
the argument, then give the argumentative person credit for bringing the
information to your attention. If the argumentative person cannot supply
the facts and figures, then treat his remarks as an expression of his feelings.
You might say, "I see you *feel* strongly about this and I will *consider your
feelings* where possible."

In all cases, *do consider* the feelings of the argumentative person as
well as all other people involved. Then, when the decision is made, subtly
confront the argumentative person by asking how he feels about supporting
a decision that he previously opposed. The question gives him the opportunity to get any anger or resentment off his chest. Next, ask if in spite of
these feelings, he will do his best to carry out the decision. If he says yes,
then he has verbally committed himself to the decision. If he later works
against the decision, you can remind him of his verbal promise to support
the decision. Should his reply be that he cannot support the decision, you
offer him the opportunity to resign or transfer to another position. He
should clearly understand that to retain his position, he must support the
decision.

To deal with destructive criticism, sarcasm or an attempt to belittle
someone, again confront the situation. Point out that the criticism or
sarcasm is interfering with productivity, then ask the offending person if he
has specific recommendations. Speak directly to the offending person and
state that you want all remarks and criticisms aimed at problems or systems,
not at people. When decisions are reached, always confront the critics by
asking them to commit themselves to the decision.

To deal with offensive language, simply confront the user. Just ask the offender to discontinue using offensive language. If the offensive language continues, ask the offender why he continues to use offensive language after you requested that it be stopped. If the offender expresses an honest desire to stop but simply finds it impossible to break habit, help him find professional help. If he simply ignores the request or treats it as a joke, give him a decision to make. Either he stops the profanity or finds other employment.

Confronting the Disruptive Personality. Dealing with the disruptive personality type simply requires that you confront his disruptive behavior. If, for example, the disrupting person acts stubborn, you ask him to explain his position, listen carefully to his remarks, repeat his position as you understand it and then express your own opinion in a way that does not conflict with his.

If the disruptive personality type continues with his stubborn stance, point out to him that he seems to be resisting for some reason other than those he has stated. Ask him to reveal the reason if there is one. If he says there is no other reason, then state that you have listened to his arguments and that you don't see how they apply to the current situation. Clearly state your decision and ask him if he will cooperate. If he says no, remind him that to continue on the job, he will be required to do so. It's his decision to cooperate or leave.

The same techniques apply when the evidence presented is not valid, when no reasons at all are given for his rejection or when he continually reverts to previously settled arguments. In all cases, listen carefully to insure understanding and summarize what he has said to show that you do understand. Always give the disruptive personality type the final opportunity to change his mind before telling him that, in spite of his opinion, he must cooperate or leave.

A Sales Manager Who Confronted a Disruptive Personality

George Atar, a recent transfer to the Dallas office of a national sales company, was causing problems for the sales manager, Fred. George refused to fill out his sales report forms and encouraged the other salesmen to do the same. George often arrived to work late, failed to make all his calls and was argumentative with other employees.

Fred found that most of the problems with George resulted from his late arrival to work. George's customers would call before he arrived, and problems and pressure built up by the time George arrived. Fred decided to confront the "tardy" issue first.

When George came to work, late as usual, Fred called him into his office. Fred told George that he was concerned about his continual tardiness and would like his ideas on how to correct the problem. George insisted there was no problem. He made calls from home in the morning, he said and was not needed in the office as early as the other salesmen. Fred pointed out the problem with the early customer calls and mentioned the related arguments that arose with the other salesmen because of the calls. Fred listened carefully to George's responses but saw that George was unwilling to listen to reason.

Finally, he told George that he wanted him to be in the office at 8:00 A.M. each day, like the rest of the salesmen, and he, Fred, would decide if anything else needed to be done. George began to argue, but Fred stopped him. He reminded George that he had already listened carefully to what he had to say. He had weighed it carefully and had made his decision. He would expect to see George in the office at eight each morning. If not, he would know that George had resigned.

Confronting the Defiant Personality. The defiant personality may openly defy your instructions, or he may defy them secretly. If he openly defies them, deal with him as a destructive or disruptive type. If he does so secretly, you can only confront him when the defiance is brought to your attention.

Often, the defiant personality type will withdraw and refuse to participate in activities or discussion. In this case, you subtly confront the situation by asking for his opinion. If he says he has no opinion, ask what he thinks of your ideas or someone else's opinion. Continue asking questions based on suppositions or on other people's opinions until you get answers that reflect his opinions.

Often, the defiant personality type will answer questions but withhold much information. Confront the defiant type by asking if he has more information, if he has heard anything else, if there are any problems he hasn't talked about, if he can think of anything else and, finally, if he is certain that he has told you every single thing that applies to the problem.

If the defiant personality seems to still be secretive or withholding information, ask him if he has any reservations or concerns about the decision that you have just made. If he says no, then ask if he has any problem in performing his part of the required activity.

After going through this questioning process, there is no excuse left for the defiant personality type to defy your instructions. If he brings up any excuse or reason for not complying with your instructions, you immediately demand an explanation for his withholding information after you specifically asked for any problems or reservations he may have. Do not let him lead the conversation back to the excuse. Keep the conversation on his defiance of your request for the information he withheld. Demand his word that in the future, he will fully disclose his reservations or any problem areas he forsees. If he refuses to promise, give him his final choice to cooperate or leave.

Confronting the Dictatorial Personality. The dictatorial personality type requires earlier confrontation, which can still be done in a subtle way. When the dictatorial type tries to take over, bring his attention to your awareness of what he's doing by using some humor. You might say, "You're doing my job very well George, but I'll take over now unless you have a specific point to make."

Continue to direct him to make a point or provide information. You direct him away from dominating others by always asking him what specific point he wishes to make. When he tries to manipulate others, bring the question back to him. Ask for his opinion on the suggestion, idea or statement he forced out of someone else.

When the dictatorial person becomes demanding or assertive, subtly confront his behavior. Rather than discussing his demands, discuss the way he is attempting to force his demands on others. Say, "You must be tired, George. You seem to be demanding that we do what you want—or else." Or you might way, "This seems to be upsetting you, George. Would you rather be excused from the meeting and let us continue with the discussion?"

Confronting the Disorganized Personality. The disorganized personality type, because he has not learned to organize his thoughts, jumps from topic to topic, glosses over main ideas, introduces irrelevant information and wanders away from the main discussion.

The disorganized personality type can be kept on the track by the subtle technique of directing his attention back to the main discussion.

You might say, "George, do you agree with the first point (main discussion) that Paul made?" Or you might say, "We were talking about point A, George, can you handle that assignment?" This line of questioning is designed to keep the disorganized personality from leading you or others away from the main discussion.

How to Use Subtle Confrontation to Stop Subordinate Power Plays

A subordinate who is so inclined, and who sees an opportunity, may exercise a power play. He may give orders to others, usurp your authority and force compliance of others to his wishes, either to satisfy his ego or to lighten his own work load.

This situation is not only damaging to employee relations, it affects their productivity. They do his work because they feel bullied or unfairly forced to do more than their own share. In addition, obviously, the power grabber isn't doing his share. He may think he is, however, as he may believe his power tactics are getting better results from the other workers.

This situation must be confronted and the power tactics stopped. If not, he will eventually extend his power play into more and more of your responsibility and soon convince himself and others that you can't get anything done without him. Next, he'll believe and say that you do nothing, that he does your job for you.

The subtle confrontation approach is to call the subordinate in to review his own work. Ask him to report on his specific assigned duties. He will try to discuss how he has gotten others to do things. At that point, remind him that he is not responsible for the results of the other workers "which, incidentally," you may add, "are lower than they were previously."

Point out that you want to review his specific duties and assignments and that he can talk about other things later. It will very quickly become obvious that his own duties have been neglected. Once that is established, confront his interference with the performance of the other workers. Point out clearly and precisely that he is not to give orders or directions to others, that his job is to complete his own assignments and that he will be evaluated strictly on the basis of his own performance.

How to Use Subtle Confrontation to Stop Employee Intimidation

Intimidation is often used by one employee to control the behavior of other people. Intimidating people is obviously unethical and immoral. The new subtle confrontation approach to managing people provides a means of dealing with intimidators in all situations. The basic philosophy is to behave in ways that you plan in advance or in ways that you normally behave, rather than react to intimidation. In other words, don't let other people control your behavior.

If one person in an office refuses to say good morning to his fellow employees, for example, there is no reason for everyone else to stop greeting each other. If one person in an office uses profanity, there is no reason for everyone else to start using profanity. No matter what techniques are used by the intimidator, there is no reason to "buckle" under. The intimidator can be stopped quickly and graciously with the new subtle confrontation approach to managing people.

Techniques of Intimidation. Basically, intimidators play on the fears of others. They take advantage of the other person's fear of being made to look foolish, weak, disloyal, inefficient or unwilling to cooperate. Often, in childhood, the intimidator is larger or stronger than the rest of the children and uses his strength to intimidate them. In adulthood, we usually encounter a psychological type of intimidation, an intimidator who plays upon our fears.

One intimidator, whom I met while attending college, used big words to intimidate others into accepting his point of view or into doing things the way he wanted them done. We were working on a group project in a graduate business class and each member of the group had a specific area to work on. One member was assigned accounting, one finance, one marketing and so on.

Our group intimidator, by using words that the rest of the group didn't understand was able to manipulate us into doing the work while he merely presented the final results to the class. He counted on our not understanding the words he used, and he correctly assumed that we would not challenge him because of our fear of looking foolish for not knowing his words.

The same results are achieved by intimidators who play on our desires not to look weak, not to be disloyal and not to seem uncooperative. They present their material or ideas in such a way as to imply that a rejection is uncooperative, disloyal or weak. When someone starts challenging your loyalty, be careful.

Techniques that Neutralize Intimidation. Since intimidation is used to gain compliance without understanding, the way to block intimidation is to demand explanations that provide clear and complete understanding. For example, ask the intimidator who suggests disloyalty, "How can it be uncooperative to refuse to do something that will cause problems later?"

Or, you may simply ask for more details without challenging the intimidator. You might say that you need more information or a better understanding before you make a decision. In the case of the "big word" artist, simply ask for a definition of every word he uses that you don't understand. As he begins to define the words, he loses his power. When his ideas are restated in simple terms, he has nothing left to intimidate with.

In the earlier example of the "big word" user who intimidated our college work group, the intimidator failed when he presented our project to the whole class. The class instructor stopped the presenter every time he used an unfamiliar word and asked him to define it for the class. Stripped of his fallacious superiority, he came across to the class as the weak and ineffectual person that he was.

You can stop intimidators, whether they are trying to intimidate you or someone else. Simply call their bluff, because intimidation, by its very nature, is a bluff. People with real power don't have to intimidate. You call their bluff with subtle confrontation by simply asking for definitions, explanations, reasons, evidence and any other information you want. You have a right to a full understanding of the objective before you pursue it.

How an Operations Manager Used Subtle Confrontation
to Deal with the Frustration of an Overly Ambitious Worker

George Willis wanted to be a foreman. He had been on his current job eighteen months and felt he was ready to become a foreman. George decided to show the operations manager what he could do, so he began looking for opportunities to correct other employees' errors.

Soon, George had graduated from making friendly suggestions to employees who were making errors and began to tell everyone how to do things. He would show a worker a better way to do a job or a quicker way. Many of George's suggestions were very helpful. They made the men's work easier and saved money for the company.

But then, a slow change came over George. Instead of suggestions, he began to give orders. Instead of asking a worker to try something, George began to *tell* them to do it his way. Eventually, the workers began to complain to the operations manager, and he called George in for a conference.

The operations manager confronted George with the workers' complaints and said he would like to discuss George's productivity record at the same time. He then asked George to explain the complaints. George said they were probably the result of his showing the men better ways to do their jobs. John, the operations manager, then asked why they would resent being shown a better way to do things. George supposed they were jealous.

John then referred to the drop in George's own productivity record and asked him to explain it. George said it was the result of the amount of time he spent helping the other people in the plant. John then asked why George would let his own productivity drop to help others. George then expressed his desire to become a foremen, and said he was helping them to show what he could do.

John then laid out the records that showed an actual drop in productivity. George said he couldn't understand it. He knew the men were doing better using his techniques. John surmised that perhaps the men resented his method of telling them what to do. He pointed out that if he wanted to become a foreman he would have to win the men's support, not their resentment. George agreed to concentrate on his own job and establish good relations with the men rather than try to tell them what to do. John said he would look at George's work later to help him in techniques that would help his career.

USING THE NEW SUBTLE CONFRONTATION APPROACH TO SOLVE COMMON JOB PROBLEMS

Managers face three common problems that impact heavily on productivity. When changes are made that are frustrating to people their productivity usually drops. This drop in productivity results from indecision on the part of the employee. He is unhappy with the change and can't decide whether to rebel or commit himself to the job under the new circumstances.

Managers must confront the subordinate and reconcile the indecision. By using the new subtle confrontation approach to managing people, the subordinate is forced to think through his problem and make a decision. If his decision is to stay on the job, he must do so with conviction and commitment to the goals of the organization. Generally, once the decision is made, he performs with conviction.

Should he later change his mind and again become frustrated, he knows what his options are. He is again placed in the position of being forced to make a decision. The three problem areas that most commonly place an employee in a frustrating situation are:

1. Job reassignments
2. Job demotions
3. Job dissatisfactions

How to Deal with Job Reassignment Problems

Often, an employee must be reassigned to a new job. This may result from automation, from the old job being eliminated or from the employee's inability to do the job. In any of these situations the employee is likely to feel frustrated or insecure as a result of the change. These feelings may cause him to become angry and react with hostility toward management. There are three steps to go through in dealing with this situation.

1. Assure the employee of his security on the job.
2. Explain the procedures to be used in training him for the new job.
3. Confront his hostility or reluctance to accept the new job with subtle confrontation techniques.

Assure the Employee of His Security on the Job. It is important that the employee feels psychologically secure in order to prevent his worry from interfering with his work. He should be told that the new position is a permanent one and he will be trained to do the job. If there are any benefits of the new job that were not available on the old job, point them out. The working conditions might be better, or there might be an opportunity to socialize. Whatever the benefits are, point them out.

Explain the Procedures to be Used in Training Him for the New Job. If the new job is one that requires new skills, explain how the employee will learn the new skills. Again, it is important that he feels secure, because we must feel comfortable on the new job. To feel comfortable, the new skills must be made to look easy to learn.

Point out that the training will take place in small steps and he will only be required to learn one thing at a time. He will have an expert available to answer his questions and help him should he have any problems. He should be told that there will be no time pressures, and that he will be able to learn and practice at his own speed.

Confront the Hostility or Reluctance to Accept the New Job with Subtle Confrontation Techniques. If the employee still expresses hostility after he has been assured of security on the job and after having been told how he will be given complete training at his own pace, his hostility must be confronted. Ask him how his hostile feelings will affect his performance on the new job. If he says it will interfere with his performance, tell him that he will have to do something about his feelings, and that after he has been trained properly, you cannot accept low performance on the basis of angry feelings.

If he expresses reluctance to take the new job, ask him what he will do if he doesn't take it. If he begins to talk about some other job with the company, point out immediately that there is no other job. If he doesn't rapidly come to the conclusion himself, point out very clearly that his choice is one of taking the new job or of leaving the company.

Finally, when the new job is accepted, ask for his verbal commitment to do his best on the new job. Ask him to agree to put his resentment and angry feelings aside and commit himself to the new job. Those are the only circumstances under which he should be acceptable to you.

How to Deal with Job Demotion Problems

Every manger, at some time in his career, will have to demote someone. This may result from the closing of an office, the elimination of a job or the subordinate's inability to perform his duties. Regardless of the reason for the demotion, problems may arise because of the subordinate's reaction to the demotion. The subordinate may feel cheated or taken advantage of. It is very rarely that he will take the demotion without some bitterness and resentment.

Unless this resentment is neutralized, worked out and gotten out of the subordinate's mind, he will take out his resentment against the company in the performance of his duties on the new job. You can eliminate this problem by a simple two-step process. (1) Encourage the subordinate to ventilate his feelings of resentment and (2) confront his resistance to performing his duties on the new job.

Encourage the Subordinate to "Ventilate" His Feelings. Psychologists tell us that any emotional disturbance, such as anger, that results from frustration will peak out and subside if allowed to "ventilate." You can help the subordinate work out his resentment and expend his anger simply by encouraging him to talk it out. At first, he will be bitter, critical and possibly sarcastic. But after a few minutes of expressing these negative feelings, he will cool down and discuss the situation rationally.

You can expedite the process by using "reflective statements," a statement that deals only with the emotion, to encourage ventilation. You simply say, "I see this upsets you," or "I know this seems to be a very hard blow." Any statement or question relating to the anger or resentment is appropriate.

It is important to deal only with the feelings or emotion expressed by the subordinate and not the specifics of the demotion or the new job until all the anger and emotion has been expressed. Once the subordinate begins to talk calmly and rationally about the new job, then specific details may be discussed.

Later on, either days or weeks later, the subordinate may reflect back on what has happened and again become angry. If this happens, just repeat the process and let him ventilate his anger all over again.

Confront His Resistance to Performing His Duties on the New Job. Once the anger has been expressed and the subordinate is calm and rational, he must be confronted with his feelings about the new job. He may feel some resistance to accepting the new position. It is important to get the subordinate to accept the new job with a feeling of commitment.

If the subordinate is expressing reservations about the job, he must be directed to choose between accepting the job and the alternative—whatever that alternative is. The alternative might be a further demotion or separation from the company. You might ask, "Tom, now that you've had time to think it over, do you want this new job?"

If the answer is not strongly affirmative, explain that you sense some reluctance on his part to take the new job. Then explain that there can be no lack of commitment, because the person taking the job must put forth his best efforts. Make it perfectly clear that the subordinate can choose whether to take the job or leave the company. But if he chooses to stay, he must agree to put forth his best effort on the new job.

How to Deal with Job Dissatisfaction

Often, your subordinates will become dissatisfied with their jobs. Although job dissatisfaction may result from many different causes, it usually results from either the lack of a challenge or restrictions placed on the job by a superior. To deal with job dissatisfaction, confront the situation. Ask the subordinate what is specifically causing his dissatisfaction.

If the dissatisfaction is the result of restrictive policies, try to remove them. At least remove those that can be removed without causing problems to others.

If the dissatisfaction is the result of a lack of challenge, provide an additional assignment for the employee to work on. Often, there will be some aspect of the current job that can be expanded or some satellite element of the job that can be improved.

If there is nothing related to the current job that can be expanded or further refined as a challenging assignment, provide an assignment in some new area. Let the subordinate search for, develop, research or market a new product. There is always something challenging and new that can be assigned to the subordinate who feels he has no challenge on his current job.

How a Regional Manager Used Subtle Confrontation
to Improve Subordinate Relations

Jim Edmonds was promoted to regional manager of a northeastern distribution company. Just prior to Jim's arrival, a number of changes had taken place that left some employees with bitterness and resentment. These bitter feelings affected productivity, and the men were spending more time griping and complaining than they were working.

Jim developed a list of workers who were griping and talked to them individually in an effort to relieve their tension and improve relations with them. A typical confrontation is exemplified by one that Jim used with Ron Sims. Ron had been shifted to a new department as a result of a shift in production. Ron was complaining about everything from the work location to the number of hours worked and the new people he was working with.

Jim listened and discussed each point with Ron until he felt he thoroughly understood Ron's feelings. Jim explained to Ron that the major change taking place in the company's business necessitated changes on other levels, and he made it clear that there was no turning back. The company was committed to its new way of doing business, and each person would have to decide whether or not he wanted to continue with the company under the new conditions.

Jim then said to Ron, "I can see that you really resent this, Ron. How is it going to affect your work?" Jim was very friendly and made certain the question was a matter-of-fact request for information rather than a threat. Ron replied that his work was probably suffering. "After all," he said, "how can I work under these conditions?"

Jim said that in his opinion the conditions were good, but that Ron was comparing them to the old job that didn't exist any longer. Ron replied that he still didn't feel like working very hard. At this point, Jim asked Ron if he expected the same pay for a reduced level of work. Ron got the point. "Yes, I guess I get the message," replied Ron. "If I expect the same pay I should give the same work."

Jim went through the final phase of the confrontation with Ron and with the other employees. When each person voiced his complaint, Jim listened and discussed it. Then when the discussion was completed, Jim gave them a choice to make, either go back to work and earn the pay they were to receive or leave the company. Jim did not threaten or intimidate, he simply stated the facts in a friendly and businesslike way. Each employee then had to decide for himself whether or not he would accept the new conditions. In each case, Jim asked for that decision and asked them to commit themselves to doing a good job to earn the pay they received.

It took a few more days for the rumbling to quiet down. A few people left the company, but the ones that stayed improved their productivity and became satisfied with their new jobs.

◆ 8 ◆

The Managerial Hedge:
A New Approach
That Gets Results

◆ When a subordinate makes a mistake but believes his action was correct, you can use the managerial hedge to correct him without putting him down or appearing to criticize him. Some managers fear that correcting their subordinates will result in hard feelings or strained relations. They overlook the errors, hoping the subordinate will eventually learn to correct himself.

This fear of managers to confront their subordinates grew out of the old attempts at human relations in management during the fifties and sixties. In their attempt to show their concern for human feelings and needs, managers "overshot" and forgot their obligation to get the job done.

In the early and middle seventies, managers began to realize that this overconcern for people had to be blended with a concern for productivity. Once productivity was back in vogue, managers began to search for new ways to handle productivity problems without giving up their concern for the human aspects of supervision.

In this chapter, you'll see how the managerial hedge is used to resolve this problem. Managers learned that by hedging their criticism, they could show respect for their subordinates, gain their subordinates' trust and still confront the error. The hedge helps get the subordinate in a state of readiness and willingness to listen to corrective ideas.

HOW TO USE THE MANAGERIAL HEDGE
IN APPRAISAL SESSIONS

In appraisal sessions, the manager is generally eager to tell the subordinate the things he is doing wrong. The manager is anxious to straighten out the subordinate and tell him how to correct his errors.

There are two problems with this approach. One, the manager doesn't really get the subordinate's side of the story. If, by chance, the subordinate didn't make the error, the manager doesn't find out. He continues to waste his breath on a topic he is wrong about to someone who isn't listening. Criticism, even when warranted, has the effect of putting the subordinate on the defensive. If the subordinate responds to the criticism at all, he is being defensive. Defensiveness seems to be a confession of guilt to the manager. The subordinate begins to resent the manager and is less likely to cooperate with the manager in the future.

The manager can hedge by (1) holding back his point of view, (2) asking the subordinate to express his opinion first, (3) avoiding the use of argument or agreement, (4) summarizing the subordinate's implied points, (5) expressing understanding for the subordinate's position and (6) expressing his own view. You can develop the hedging technique by following these procedures.

1. Hold Back Your Own Point of View. The purpose of an appraisal session is to get the subordinate to recognize both his strengths and his weaknesses. If he is aware of his strengths (his behaviors that are successful) and his weaknesses (his behaviors that interfere with success), then he can continue to emphasize his strengths and concentrate on correcting his behaviors that are weaknesses.

Fortunately, only half this job has to be done. Many people easily recognize their strengths, although some don't, but are totally unaware of their weaknesses. The more unaware they are and the more weaknesses they have, the more complicated the appraisal session will be.

In order to determine the self-awareness of the subordinate, you should hold back your opinions and let him speak first. If you speak first, you create either a superficially positive framework or a superficially negative framework. In either event, the subordinate's response is a contrived answer. An answer designed to support your positive impression or an answer designed to defend himself against your negative criticism. If you express a more favorable impression than the subordinate holds, he is certainly not going to refute your position because everyone wants to look good to the boss. If you express an immediate negative reaction, then the human "fight or flight" motivation is triggered and the subordinate becomes defensive. He puts up a barrier against what you have to say.

2. Ask the Subordinate to Express His Opinion First. The correct approach is to have the subordinate comment on his own performance first. The subordinate will generally talk about his strengths and the good results he has gotten. In order to get him to face up to his weaknesses, you will have to ask more direct questions to elicit his appraisal of his actions in specific areas that reflect weaknesses.

For example, you might ask, "How do you feel you handled the problem with the union last week?" His answer may relate to the final solution. Then, zero in on the problem area with a more specific question. For example, you might say, "I am talking about the initial phase of the problem. How do you feel you handled Joe's complaint *before* he went to the union?" The idea is to get the subordinate to see for himself that his initial handling of the complaint resulted in the problem with the union.

3. Avoid the Use of Argument or Agreement. This is the basis of the managerial hedge. If you either argue or agree too early in the interview, you excite the psychological forces within the subordinate either to make him defensive or to cause him to hide his weaknesses in order to support your overly positive view of his strengths. The best thing to do is to hedge, to hold down your own comments and opinions, until the subordinate has begun to see and express the weaknesses himself.

If the subordinate offers an overly optimistic appraisal of himself, hedge. Say, "I don't see this yet," or, "I don't understand this yet," or "I haven't heard enough evidence to support that yet," or, "I can see where you played *a part* in that, but there are some other factors to consider."

The point is, don't argue but don't agree either. Try to hedge your comments until you have a good understanding of the subordinate's point of view. Then you can relate your ideas in a way that does not put the subordinate down.

4. Summarize the Subordinate's Implied Points. Often, a subordinate will imply more than he actually says. He may, for example, take total credit for an increase in productivity when, in fact, new machinery may be partly responsible. Or, a salesman may imply that he is solely responsible for sales increases that are partly due to a major price reduction.

In order to clarify these points, you must summarize what the subordinate seems to be implying. You might say, for example, "If I understand you, George, you feel you are solely responsible for our increase in productivity?" Usually this summary will be enough to bring the subordinate's attention to the fact that he is taking more credit than he deserves. He may reply, "Well the new machines made the increases possible, but I trained the people to operate them."

If you feel the subordinate is still taking too much credit, you may continue to summarize and question for the specific things the subordinate did. You might want to determine exactly what portion of the increase is the result of the actions of the subordinate and what portion is the result of other factors.

5. Express Understanding for the Subordinate's Point of View. Even though you may not agree with what your subordinate has said, you may be able to see the reasons he feels the way he does. Based upon the evidence or facts as he sees them, his opinions may be easily understandable. So, comment to the effect that, based upon the facts that he has presented, you understand his position. After you show this understanding, point out that there are some other factors that he may not have been aware of that you want to bring to his attention. This gives you an opportunity to express your point of view when he is more likely to accept it.

6. Express Your Own Point of View. By going through the first five steps, you have developed a state of readiness. You held back your own opinions so that your subordinate would not become defensive or unrealistic. You let your subordinate express his opinion first so that you could clearly understand his point of view and to show courtesy. You were also courteous by not arguing, and you showed empathy and interest by summarizing his implied points. You showed respect by expressing understanding and empathy for his point of view. These actions create a state of readiness. The subordinate is now obliged to return your courtesy and listen to you. He is ready and willing to evaluate your point of view as you did his.

At this point, you reintroduce the points you hedged earlier. You introduce your evidence and ask the subordinate how this affects his earlier belief that he alone was responsible for the increase in productivity. Or, you point out to a sales supervisor that a major competitor going out of the market had an impact on sales. Ask how much he thinks his sales were helped by the competitor withdrawing.

Educators tell us that self-discovery is the best and longest lasting type of learning. If you can use questions that result in the subordinate seeing his weaknesses for himself, while you hedge, the subordinate will grow from the appraisal session. If he does not "see the light," then you, of course, must forcefully express your opinion and point out those weaknesses. This may not always convince him, but at least he will know your opinion. He will not be able later to say that you agreed that he was doing everything perfectly. In a formal session, of course, you would develop some recommendations for improvement at this point.

A Performance Problem That Was Resolved With the Managerial Hedge

Charlie Sweetly was a 61 year old sales manager that everyone loved. Charlie was a nice guy who was always ready to help anyone who asked for his help. The problem was that Charlie spent so much time talking and helping other people that he was not getting his job done. Sales were down in his division and were getting worse. Sales were up in both other divisions, so only Charlie's division was keeping the plant from exceeding the previous year's sales.

Bob, the plant manager, called Charlie in for an appraisal session. Bob explained the purpose of the meeting and asked Charlie how he felt he was doing on the job. Charlie began by saying he was doing well. He proceeded to tell Bob how well he got along with everyone. He said all the salesmen liked him and knew they could count on him. Even people from the office came to him for help when they needed it. He was doing an excellent job, he concluded. "My good relationship with my people keeps them loyal and hard working."

"I know of your good relations with your salesmen. I'm not sure that good relations are enough to get the job done, however," Bob replied. "Why do you think your division's sales are down?" Bob paused and waited for Charlie's answer. Bob listened as Charlie talked about new competition, production problems and so on. Bob neither argued nor agreed. He listened, he questioned, he hedged, he showed understanding and empathy.

Finally, Bob felt that Charlie was ready to listen. He showed Charlie comparisons of the three sales divisions. He pointed out that these sales managers weren't nearly as popular as Charlie, yet they overcame production problems, new competition and problems with their sales personnel and were able to increase sales at the time Charlie's sales were dropping.

One by one, Bob had Charlie evaluate his excuses against the results of others. Even the office workers whom Charlie had befriended were doing more for the other sales divisions than they were for Charlie.

Charlie began to see the light. His people's results were lower because Charlie didn't set high enough standards. His people didn't see the importance of attaining new goals. Bob worked out new goals for Charlie.

Charlie agreed to check his sales results daily and make weekly reports to Bob.

Bob had to keep pressure on Charlie. In two cases, he forced Charlie to replace salesmen who were not making their objective. Slowly, Charlie improved his performance. As he spent more time improving sales results, he had less time to talk to others, and their performance also improved.

HOW TO USE THE MANAGERIAL HEDGE TO BREAK FIXED POSITIONS THAT HOLD DOWN PRODUCTIVITY

Often, productivity is held down simply because people take fixed positions and then refuse to budge. They refuse to evaluate the ideas of others because they believe their own methods are best. Since these people are often dedicated employees who otherwise conscientiously do their duties, it is desirable to correct them without a put down. The managerial hedge is useful for this purpose.

Using the Hedge as a New Approach to Eliminating Interdivisional Conflict

Often, production and marketing managers come into conflict over product specifications or quality. The production manager may believe his current specificiations and production procedures are the most productive. He will be able to show you strong evidence to support his point of view. Faced with all this evidence, you will be tempted to agree with the production manager. Don't!

This is the time to hedge. Point out that you understand and appreciate the fine system and good results he is obtaining, but you will have to weigh the final product against the objectives of marketing. By establishing the hedge now, you will have an easier time with any changes that may be required later. If the production manager sees, in the beginning, that there is a possibility of change required, he will be more easily persuaded later.

Take the same approach with marketing. The marketing manager will have market surveys, consumer reports and various product and marketing statistics that support the changes they want made. Again, your first impression will be to agree with the marketing manager. Again, don't!

First, use the hedge. Again, express your understanding and appreciation for the evidence collected and the proposed plan. But, state clearly that the proposal will have to be evaluated in relation to the costs involved in changes in production. The marketing manager will then be prepared should you not agree to all his recommendations.

A Competitive Challenge That Was Resolved with the Managerial Hedge

In the early sixties, a product marketing manager for a soft drink company decided to market his product in cans rather than bottles. He developed marketing plans for the new product and presented those plans to the president of the company. The president was impressed with the plan and called in the production manager to discuss the changes required to use cans instead of bottles.

The production manager began an immediate tirade against the cans. He said they were more expensive, caused more delays and required more expensive machinery than the bottles. The president listened carefully and then asked to see some of the figures that the production manager was basing his argument on.

As the production manager tried to support his argument, it became obvious that he did not have the necessary proof to back up his opinion. At this point, the president used the hedge. Rather than talking about the evidence required to support the production manager's opinion, he related to feelings the production manager was expressing. The president said, "You seem to have a lot of concerns about this suggested change Tom. Is there some problem here I don't know about?"

Tom then revealed that he had just ordered a large stock of replacement parts for the old machines. The company would lose thousands of dollars, as these parts would immediately become obsolete if they switched to cans. The president suggested that Tom check to see if the suppliers of the new machine would take the parts in trade. He assured Tom that no changes would be made until a solution for the problem was found.

Tom eventually worked out a deal whereby the original company took the parts back at a 10 percent discount. The new supplier paid the freight to return the parts and the 10 percent discount was capitalized as a cost of the new machine. Tom was credited with solving the problem and the marketing manager was credited with the new idea. The president's use of the managerial hedge turned a competitive situation into a cooperative one, and the conflict was resolved.

HOW TO USE THE MANAGERIAL HEDGE TO CHECK COMMITMENT TO ORGANIZATIONAL GOALS

You may occasionally doubt your subordinate's commitment to organizational goals. The reports you get may seem too flowery, or there may be too many excuses or explanations for the failure to reach company goals. The new approach to management requires that these situations be confronted. They are confronted, however, in a subtle way that leaves the subordinate's pride intact. As the manager, you hedge your remarks until the subordinate has a chance to state his point of view and withdraw gracefully.

How the Managerial Hedge Was Used to Resolve a Foreman's Conflict Over Worker Support vs. Accurate Reporting

Joe Hammerhill was an excellent foreman. He had twenty years' experience and knew more about an electronic assembly line than most people learn in a lifetime. Joe was proud of his record, and his line consistently had a better productivity record than any other assembly line in the plant. Joe made his bonus regularly and so did his men.

After an extremely successful quarter when new records had been set, old ones broken and higher bonuses earned than ever before, management began to suspect that Joe had begun to put speed ahead of quality. The salesmen had begun to complain that their dealers were making small repairs in their shops. The sets were coming in with loose wires, cold solder joints and, in one case, a missing condenser.

Joe insisted that his men were turning out the highest quality work. He had trained each and every man there and knew how skillful each man was. Chet, the plant manager, listened and did not argue with Joe. He simply told Joe that there was a quality problem somewhere and he would like Joe to find it.

He asked Joe to set up a quality check just before the sets were packaged and to make sure that not one set went out with a quality defect. Chet never accused Joe of faulty reporting or covering for his crew. He simply made Joe personally responsible for the quality of the products his crew produced.

Joe solved the problems. The quality check revealed so many defects that even Joe had to realize that his men were not performing at the professional level they were capable of. The repairs that had to be made on the line cut deeply into the line's productivity. Bonuses were lost, and the men saw the light. Soon, they were producing a quality product at a lower production level, but at a high enough level to earn a bonus again.

How Andy Johnson Used the Managerial Hedge to Build an Effective Sales Team

Andy Johnson took over a west coast sales team that was barely selling enough to keep the milk plant in business. The salesmen complained of private label competition, lower-priced competitors and late deliveries. Andy used the new managerial hedge approach to overcome these sales excuses and build an effective sales team.

Andy converted his defensive salesmen to offensive salesmen by using the managerial hedge. When a salesman complained about competition from private label brands, Andy listened carefully and expressed understanding. Then, he would ask the salesman what percentage of the business was left and how much of that was needed to reach his objective.

Finally, Andy would ask the salesman to develop a list of benefits for his product and work out a sales plan to appeal to the customers who would most likely buy those benefits. Through these hedging techniques, Andy led his salesmen to the realization that there was enough business left for them even after the competition made a sale.

Slowly, his salesmen began to pay less attention to the competition and concentrate on promoting their own product. As they did, their sales increased and they became more confident. Eventually, they became a professional sales force that consistently outsold the competition.

◆ 9 ◆

The New Subtle Approach
to Optimizing Results

◆The new approach to managing people for optimum results goes beyond the conventional pattern of management communications. Managers conventionally depend upon the organizational structure to provide lines of communication. Managers using the new approach go outside the formal organizational structure to gather information. A president, for example, goes below the vice-presidential level to gather first-hand information from lower level managers.

The new approach is based upon the belief that lower levels of management have valuable information and ideas that get watered down or sifted out during their transmittal up the chain of command. Business managers developed the new subtle approach to overcome this "sifting" effect.

A group of managers, attending a problem-solving seminar, tackled this communication problem and developed new techniques during the seminar. These managers reported at the seminar a year later that the new techniques had been successfully used on the job to optimize results.

You'll learn to use the new subtle techniques to optimize your results. You'll see, in this chapter, how to keep your subordinates from shifting their responsibility back to you and how to gather valuable information that will lead to optimum results. You'll also find examples of problems that have been confronted and solved with the new subtle approach to optimizing results.

HOW TO USE THE NEW SUBTLE CONFRONTATION APPROACH TO IMPROVE YOUR RESULTS

One way to improve your results is to subtly raise your subordinate's expectations. Research has shown that within reason a subordinate's performance expectations will rise to the level of his superior's expectations. If you want a five percent increase in productivity per year and your subordinates expect only a three percent increase, the first step is to convince them that you expect the five percent increase to occur.

One way to establish higher expectations is to work out the specific production or sales volumes the five percent increase would entail. Then, talk in terms of those total production figures rather than the percentage of increase. In this way, you subtly overcome your subordinate's psychological barrier involved with the three percent increase. As they become comfortable with the new figures, you can then subtly interject that the five percent rate will be continued over the next five years.

Another value of stating your goals in specific terms rather than in percentages is that each subordinate visualizes the actual number or volume that you are shooting for. This helps him develop plans and techniques to achieve the goal. The concept of five percent, on the other hand, is too general. It relates to doing more, rather than indicating a specific amount.

Once a person visualizes a specific goal, he develops a mental set that consciously and subconsciously seeks information related to that goal. Information that would normally be filtered out of awareness is now eagerly assimilated. Once a goal is visualized, the mind is subconsciously motivated to analyze and evaluate all information it is exposed to in relation to usefulness in achieving the goal.

You can raise your subordinate's expectations by following this system. Work out the results you want exactly and specifically, then begin a program of persuasion. Express your own desire and belief that the expectations can be achieved, then ask your subordinates to start working on ideas to achieve them. Institute new ideas and procedures as they are offered, and give feedback to all your subordinates on how the new ideas work. As your subordinates see progress being made, they will want to contribute to further improvement in order to share in the recognition for achieving the new goal. Soon, everyone will hold the higher expectations that you do and will achieve them if they are reasonable.

How to Dump the Monkey Off Your Back

An article in the November-December, 1974 issue of Harvard Business Review referred to the "Care and Feeding of Monkeys." Monkeys in this case was a reference to subordinates who impose themselves on management by demanding unwarranted time or by placing the responsibility for subordinate tasks upon the manager.

The following four steps will keep you in control and "dump the monkey" when one of your subordinates tries to "pass the buck" to you or tries to get you to take responsibility for something the subordinate should be doing. This procedure should be followed without sarcasm or hostility by subtly returning responsibility to the subordinate. The four steps are: (1) Don't take responsibility for someone else's problem. (2) When necessary to perform a function for a subordinate, let him know that you are doing him a favor. (3) When a subordinate imposes himself upon you, subtly remind him of your time limitations. (4) When a subordinate throws you the "monkey," throw it back.

1. Don't Take Responsibility for Someone Else's Problem. When a subordinate comes to you for help with a problem, by all means, help him. But, help doesn't mean taking the problem over, relieving the subordinate of the responsibility and taking the burden of solution upon yourself. Simply give the subordinate some suggestions or, perhaps, share a similar experience in which the process of solving the problem is revealed. Then, ask the subordinate if he has any ideas on how to approach the problem. Finally, make sure the subordinate realizes that he still owns the problem by asking him to report back in a few days to let you know how he's doing with it.

2. When Performing a Function for a Subordinate, Let Him Know That You Are Doing Him a Favor. Occasionally, a subordinate will ask you to do something the he can't do and, perhaps, only you can. It may be a meeting with a higher executive that he can't get to, or it may be a function of a specialized nature that only a person with specific skills can perform. These things must be done, but the subordinate must be made aware that you did it to help him complete his job and that you are not taking over the job.

Occasionally, a subordinate may ask you to come to his office. You should do this only after determining why it can't be handled in your office If a project or display is laid out in his office of if he has customers in his office, it may be necessary to go to his office. The mere fact that you question his inability to come to your office subtly lets him know that you are doing him a favor by coming to his office because of the special circumstances that exist. This cuts off attempts by subordinates to manipulate you, as they see that you are aware of what is going on.

3. When a Subordinate Imposes Himself Upon You, Remind Him of Your Time Limitations. Many people have no respect for, or are unaware of, the time constraints of their superiors. They pop in and out of their boss's offices as though they were public phone booths. When this happens, tact is required in order not to cut off the necessary communications that require this inner-office contact.

One way to subtly cut down unnecessary office intrusions, is to use every intrusion as an opportunity to challenge your subordinates for concrete proposals and results. Ask how they stand on specific results, what they did yesterday, what they're doing today, what will be done next and when they will have specific results. Get the message across that every time they come into your office they are going to be questioned and expected to discuss hard business problems rather than social issues.

4. When a Subordinate Throws You a "Monkey," Throw It Back. The humorous visualization of a monkey jumping back and forth from one shoulder to another underlies the importance of a subordinate passing the responsibility for a task up to you. If you let your subordinates pass the work up to you, you'll be overworked, you'll have no time to supervise and the subordinate won't learn to handle his job.

If, for example, a subordinate comes up with the idea that you should write a letter, talk to a foreman, prepare a report, start a project or call a meeting to straighten out his peers, you simply assign him the task. Again, be sure that when he leaves your office, he understands that he is the one to do the job. Don't let him toss the "monkey" back on the way out the door.

How to Make a Managerial End Run and Improve Your Results

Most organizations block the flow of upward communications. Men on the assembly line or at their office desks know ten times more than the information that is passed up the line. Each department head or supervisor filters out much of the information he receives from his subordinates before he talks to his boss. This filtering process is not intentional, it is a normal psychological function.

We all filter and interpret information in a way that meets our own needs and expectations. If we think our current procedures are best, then we filter out the incoming information that challenges this assumption. We also filter out information that seems threatening to our position or information from what we consider an unworthy source. In other words, we often filter or evaluate and reject information, not on the basis of the value of the information for improving results, but on the basis of personal feelings.

You can compensate for this problem and improve your results by making a managerial end run. Go below the level reporting to you and have informal discussions about improving results. Establish a reputation for talking to everyone up and down the line. As you talk, ask questions that bring out their ideas for improvement.

Ask every subordinate you talk to if he has any ideas on how to improve results. They often won't, but you'll usually find more ideas to listen to than you can implement. I worked for one manager who started each day by visiting for a few minutes with each department head. He went to their offices the first thing each morning (that also stops anyone who wants to monopolize your time the first thing in the morning) and chatted with each.

The first time he made the rounds there was just a little friendly socializing, but he very quickly began to ask for ideas and suggestions, and he got them. Many of those ideas resulted in changes that substantially improved his results. You can use this new approach to improve your results also.

How a Marketing Executive Used the New Subtle Confrontation Approach to Correct an Employee Who Used Profane Language in the Office

Kent Morrison, a newly appointed vice-president of marketing for a midwestern canning company was disturbed by the X-rated language one of his subordinates used. Kent was no prude, but Rick Skay's language was foul and embarrassing to many of the office employees. Kent decided to confront Rick immediately, so as not to seem to condone the language.

Kent called Rick into his office and said he wanted to talk to Rick about a social problem in the office. "What have I got to do with any social problem?" Rick asked. "Well, as a matter of fact, it's your problem that I want to talk about," said Kent. "Have you had any complaints about your profanity?" Kent continued. "Hell no! Who is going to complain about a little manly language?" replied Rick.

Kent explained that he had overheard some pretty rough language, more than just manly language and had noticed that the girls were embarrassed. "Since you've been here a long time I thought someone might have said something to you," Kent concluded. Rick answered, "Once in awhile, some 'silly sister' makes some 'crybaby' remarks but if they are going to work with men, they have to get used to it."

"Well, how do the men in the office feel about your language?" Kent asked. "Men don't give a damn," Rick replied. "Have you asked them?" Kent pressed on. "What's to ask? What's the big deal?" Rick retorted. "The deal is this, Rick. I think you have hurt your reputation very badly by insulting and embarrassing the women in this office. I want you to ask some of the men in the office how they feel about your language. You might ask some of the women, but that's up to you. Then come back and talk to me," Kent ordered.

"I want you to see for yourself the results of your language in this office," continued Kent. "Then, I will help you work out a program to correct the problem. I think that together we can solve the problem and restore your reputation."

At first, Rick resisted the idea that there was a problem, but Kent stood firm and insisted that he ask his co-workers. Rick even complained that his co-workers were sissies when they verified Kent's claims about his language. But, finally, Kent convinced him that he had to change.

Kent provided professional help for Rick, which was not made known to the office workers so as not to embarrass him. In a few months, Rick overcame the problem. His co-workers were amazed at the change and actually respected Rick for the effort he had taken to change his behavior.

HOW TO USE SUBTLE CONFRONTATION
IN PERSONNEL ADMINISTRATION

Whether you hold a staff or line position, at one time or another you have problems with people. Some of these problems will be minor in nature and will require very little thought or concern. Some, however, will be complicated, important to your success and may best be resolved with the new techniques of subtle confrontation.

Determining When to Use Subtle Confrontation
in Personnel Administration

Subtle confrontation, very simply, should be used only where it can be effective. That is, use it only in situations where you have some control. Things that you have no control over need not be worried about. If a subordinate has a problem with his wife, you may offer advice if he asks for it, but the resolution of the problem is out of your control. You won't be there to see what happens or hear what is said, so you won't be able to control the outcome.

If his work suffers as a result of his problem with his wife, you may need to use subtle confrontation techniques to correct the work problem. You can relate to his loss of proficiency and demand that he bring his work back up to standard. You can't say "Make up with your wife," but you can say "Your drop in productivity is about to cost you your job."

Of course, you'll want to help if a subordinate asks for help or advice with a personal problem. Any help you give may result in better work performance. But remember, the problem is his, not yours; you can advise, not solve. Your problem is the work situation, and the work situation is what you must concentrate on.

You use subtle confrontation to bring a work problem into the subordinate's awareness. Once he's aware of the problem, he may automatically correct it. If he doesn't, he must then be made aware of the consequences of not correcting the problem and given a choice between the two courses of action—correcting the behavior or taking the consequences.

How Subtle Confrontation
Can Improve Your Effectiveness With People

Subtle confrontation is a new system of management that brings a subordinate's personal problem into a confrontation atmosphere. A manager confronts a subordinate with a problem and a behavior change that the subordinate is required to make. Unless the subordinate can convince the manager that the manager's information is wrong (and some part of his information is nearly always wrong) the subordinate must either choose to make the required change or accept the consequences.

You can improve your effectiveness with people by confronting small problems before they become big ones. If a man comes to work late five minutes every day, confront the situation before it becomes fifteen minutes, or one-half hour or an hour. As a person continues to get away with a bad habit, he becomes more comfortable with the habit and slowly extends the bad behavior until the consequences become extreme. These extreme "make or break" confrontations can be avoided if the small "seeds" of a problem are confronted before they grow into extreme situations.

A word of caution: Make sure that the situation deserves confrontation before you take action. Don't act on someone else's say so. Make sure, in your own mind, that there is a job-related problem before you act, and remember that some part of your information is almost always wrong! Question your subordinate to find out what part is wrong before you demand that he make a decision.

How One Manager Reduced His Work Load
and Simultaneously Improved His Results

Hugo Spokes, general manager of a West Coast vegetable canning plant was an easy mark for his subordinates to throw the "monkey" to. Whenever one of his subordinates had a problem that required effort beyond their normal routine, they threw the problem to Hugo. Hugo finally got tired of being pushed around by his subordinates and decided to make some changes. Hugo called in a management consultant who specialized in just this type of problem.

The consultant watched the interaction between Hugo and his subordinates for two weeks. During that time, he got a pretty good feel for those who really needed help and those who he suspected were just taking advantage of Hugo's good nature. He then worked out a procedure for Hugo to follow in dealing with his subordinates.

First, if a subordinate came to Hugo with a problem, Hugo would ask how much work the subordinate had done to solve the problem. If nothing had been done, the subordinate would be sent back to work out the preliminary details before Hugo would look at the problem.

If the preliminary work had been done, Hugo would review the details in the presence of the subordinate and then ask the subordinate what specific area he wanted help on. Unless the help was needed in an area that only Hugo had expertise in, Hugo would send the subordinate to someone else on the staff who had the expertise and suggested that the subordinate make the decision. If he still needed help, of course, he was invited to return to Hugo.

When the subordinate returned with the completed details and recommendations of other staff members, Hugo would place responsibility squarely on the shoulders of the subordinate. He would tell the subordinate, "Your decision on this project will have a major impact on our profits." If the subordinate didn't get this subtle hint and make the decision himself, he was told to. Hugo would merely say, "You handle it."

In all cases where the initial problem was one that the subordinate should be able to handle, given his current level of expertise, he was simply told, "You handle it," or "You decide." Soon, the subordinates were making all the low-level decisions without discussing them with Hugo. The more decisions they made on their own, the more proficient they became.

Hugo had more time to give help and guidance to those that really needed it. He became a more effective manager, gained the respect of his subordinates and his results improved rapidly.

◆ 10 ◆
The New Subtle Approach to Negotiation

◆The new approach to negotiation is a subtle one. Rather than trying to overpower or overwhelm your negotiating opponent, you make your points in a calm and subtle way. Research has shown that this new management approach is more effective than an aggressive approach. By conducting your negotiating in a calm and rational manner, your opponent is less likely to take a stubborn position.

The old hard-line approach to negotiating often created animosity and resulted in stubborn positions being taken by negotiators simply because they resented the tactics of their opponents. A person who felt he was being bullied got tough to show that he couldn't be bullied.

The manager who uses the new subtle approach in negotiation wins the respect of his opponents. If he is courteous, his opponents will return courtesy. If he listens carefully to his opponents, they will tend to listen more to him. If he really tries to understand his opponent's point of view, they will be more likely to try to understand his point of view.

In this chapter, you'll see how to use subtle negotiating strategies to make better bargains. You'll learn the three steps of successful negotiation and how they can help you get a better deal. You'll also learn in this chapter how to deal with emotional outbursts and sarcastic remarks. The techniques in this chapter will help you "keep your cool" no matter what your opponent does.

THREE STEPS IN SUCCESSFUL NEGOTIATION

You can be more successful in negotiating by using the following three-step approach. The first step is to determine the real issue. Often, your opponent will use a ploy or talk about a minor issue first. Bargaining hard against these minor issues may put you in a position of vulnerability when the main issue surfaces.

The second step, which is tied closely to the first step, is to determine just how important the issue is. If it isn't important, you won't have to waste any concessions on it.

The third step is to deal with the emotional reaction of your opponents. By handling their emotional outbursts in a subtle restrained way, you develop a harmonious climate for negotiation.

How to Determine the Real Issue

One way to determine the real issue that the other party is concerned with is to watch for nonverbal clues. The way a person sits, stands and moves provides information about his level of interest and concern about the point being discussed. A person is not likely to be slouched over or looking away from you when discussing a vital point. When a real issue is at stake, the following indications of interest will be apparent:

1. An erect stance with a slight tilt toward you
2. Hands on hips with feet spread apart
3. Head cocked slightly to the side
4. The use of vigorous gestures
5. Menacing gestures
6. Tightly drawn facial muscles
7. A scowl
8. Narrowing of the eyelids
9. Dilated pupils of the eyes
10. Excitement in the voice.

The ten listed clues which indicate interest, excitement, dominance or anger, depending upon the situation and the verbal remarks that accompany them, are tip-offs to the sincerity of the negotiator. His interest and sincerity tip you off that he is discussing the real issue.

All the clues listed may not be in evidence, but the more of them you see, the more likely the real issue is being discussed. If, for example, your negotiating opponent has been calm and casual when discussing previous points but begins to express excitement in his voice, his pupils begin to dilate and his facial muscles begin to draw tight, you can be sure the topic is more important to him than those previously discussed. The fact that his behavior changed at all is an indication of a different feeling about the current topic.

Once you are aware of the importance of the various issues being negotiated, you have an advantage over your opponent. You can then subtly suggest that these "minor" issues are interfering with the more important issues. Once your opponent realizes that you recognize the unimportant issues, he will be less likely to waste time on them.

A Negotiator Who Dug Out the Real Issue

Bill Devereux was chief negotiator for the Willard Company, a manufacturer of home hardware items. Bill had worked his way up through the plant and knew all the men by first name. Bill had been in charge of negotiations for three years. He had been promoted to chief negotiator just after the currently expiring contract had been signed.

The policy of the Willard Company was to promote good relations with the workers, and this had been effectively accomplished. There had been a few rumbles of dissatisfaction lately but nothing of consequence. Negotiations had just begun on a new contract, and Bill was surprised at the hostile union attitude.

The union negotiator, Al Bottoms, opened the meeting by saying "The day of the sweetheart contract has come to an end at Willard." He proceeded to enumerate a list of seventeen demands and threatened a strike if they were not all met. Al was gruff and emotional and Bill felt that it was not the time to respond. He quietly stated that he could see that Al felt very strongly about the issues. He further commented that he was surprised at the long list of demands and would like to recess immediately in order to study them. He suggested they regroup in the afternoon.

When the meeting resumed, Bill opened the meeting by saying he needed some information about each of the demands and would like to ask some questions about each of them. Bill's strategy was to get the union negotiator to talk about each one so that he, Bill, could evaluate the nonverbal clues of the union negotiator in order to determine the issue that was most important to the union.

Bill began by asking about the wage demands. Al responded with a string of statistics supporting the union case for the increase. Bill noticed that Al was generally calm and businesslike. There were no nonverbal indications of excitement or anger, so Bill decided the issue of wages was not the highest priority item on the list. Bill continued to question Al about each item on the list.

Al showed no signs of unusual interest until the productivity fund was discussed. At that point, the pupils of Al's eyes began to dilate, he straightened up and leaned toward Bill. Al began to use vigorous gestures and emotionalism in stressing his points. Bill got the (nonverbal) message. The crucial point in the negotiations was the productivity fund. Bill continued the questioning on each point, but he knew what the union considered most important.

At the next recess, Bill thoroughly researched the details leading up to the demand for the productivity fund and how much the fund would cost the company. By evaluating the costs of the other demands, Bill worked out a strategy that would be least costly to the company.

When negotiations began again, Bill had the upper hand. Knowing what was most important to Al, Bill was able to win concessions that were important to the company in exchange for establishing the productivity fund. Bill also insisted that the productivity fund was to be used only for payments to people who were laid off due to productivity increases.

How to Determine the Importance of Each Issue

In addition to developing an understanding of the real issue, you can determine the importance of each issue by the same techniques used for determining the real issue. By watching for the number of nonverbal clues that the negotiator expresses you can guess the relative importance of each issue.

In addition to observing non-verbal clues, you can listen to words your opponent uses. He may say, "This is important," or "This is a crucial issue." Also, you can question him directly by asking, "How important is this issue?" or, "Which of these two or three issues is most important?" You might be more subtle by asking such questions as, "How do the men feel about this issue?" or, "What do you think about dropping this issue?"

Again, once you determine the importance or value of each issue, you are in a better bargaining position. You can weigh the value to you of these minor issues against their value to your opponent. Perhaps you can trade a number of these "no value" issues in order not to concede on a more important issue.

The opposing negotiator may wind up caught in his own trap. If you offer to concede on these minor issues that he was only using for "bargaining chips," you put him on the defensive. He must either reveal his strategy, by admitting that some other issue is more important, or he must make some concession in return for these minor issues.

Often, union negotiators use these minor issues to win larger more important concessions. When the major or most important issue is too difficult to negotiate, they agree to "back off" on the minor issues in return for the major one. There is no reason you can't reverse this procedure. In effect, give them something other than their major demand to take back to their members. They save face, and you save money.

How to Deal with Emotional Outbursts

Often, during negotiations, one of the negotiators may become upset or angry. The angry person may then make sarcastic or emotional remarks. These emotional reactions usually result in a counterargument from other negotiators. These angry counterarguments may develop into a situation that establishes a disharmonious climate, which negatively affects the balance of the negotiations.

The New Five-Step Approach for Dealing with Emotional Outbursts

There are five basic steps that you can follow in dealing with emotional outbursts that will keep the negotiations on the issues and keep them from being settled on an emotional basis. The following five steps should be followed in the order presented.

1. Maintain a harmonious climate.
2. React empathetically to emotional outbursts.
3. Present your own position as though the outburst had not occurred.

4. Do not make concessions under emotional pressure.
5. Seek the removal of a negotiator who continually employs emotional outbursts.

1. Maintain a Harmonious Climate. A sudden outburst or sarcastic remark is usually unexpected and will throw you off guard. Some negotiators purposely engage in sarcasm or emotional outbursts just for that purpose. They try to catch you off guard and make you think you have done or said something to incur their anger. You are then supposed to feel guilty for causing the outburst and become more willing to make concessions to atone for your error.

Don't fall for this trap. Recognize sarcasm and emotionalism as a possible ploy to win concessions. Keep your cool. Don't react in anger. Look questioningly at the associates of the negotiator who made the outbursts. Look at them as if to say, "Are you going to be associated with this?" Often, this quizzical look will draw a comment from one of his associates.

In any event, remember that you need to keep things on a harmonious level. Don't express any criticism or anger yourself. If the associates of the offending negotiator say nothing then let it pass. It's OK to show surprise, but not anger. Don't act in the least as though you believe you caused the outburst.

2. React Empathetically to Emotional Outbursts. Dr. Carl Rogers, a prestigious modern psychologist, developed a system for dealing with emotionally upset people that can be used in the negotiating situation. Dr. Rogers suggests repeating back to the emotionally upset person the words used in expressing the emotion.

For example, if the opposing negotiator blurts out, "You have been taking advantage of our people." You would repeat the phrase. You would say, "You feel we have been taking advantage of your people?" This system shows the other person that you heard and understood what he said and, at the same time, that you are willing to listen to a further explanation. This system was called "empathetic listening" by Dr. Rogers.

To listen empathetically, you try for a complete understanding of the other person's position. You try for an understanding of why he is upset and then for an understanding of the evidence he supports his opinions with. As you gain understanding, you gain respect from the other person. He sees that you are really trying to understand his position rather than argue and respects you for that. The understanding also puts you in a better bargaining position. You can negotiate better when you understand the feelings and opinions of the other person. By following this procedure you "turn the tables" on the negotiator who uses emotion to manipulate. You wind up with valuable information about his opinions, tactics and feelings, which you can use to your advantage.

3. Present Your Own Position as Though the Outbursts Had Not Occurred. It is very important to present your position without giving any consideration to the emotional outburst. After having shown understanding for the other person's feelings, you must then show that your feelings and understanding for another human being have no bearing on your job as a negotiator. If you give the impression that you will soften your position simply because someone is emotionally upset, the tactic will be used against you again and again.

Present your position with cold calculated logic. Give facts, figures and statistics in support of your viewpoint. Make it perfectly clear that you are dealing with logic, not emotion. It is extremely important to deal strongly at this point, in order to dispel any doubts about your ability to deal with emotional outbursts.

4. Do Not Make Concessions Under Emotional Pressure. Should an air of emotionalism or less-than-harmonious conditions prevail, refrain from making any concessions. You can do this by dealing with the emotions rather than the content. Either repeat the phrases to express understanding as proposed by Carl Rogers or relate directly to the emotion itself.

Drs. Buzzotta, Lefton and M. Sherberg in *Effective Selling Through Psychology* relate a system of drawing out the emotionally upset person by relating to the emotion while ignoring the content. You say, "I see you're upset," or, "You seem to be angry about this." You redirect the conversation to the emotion, which keeps you from negotiating under pressure.

If these procedures fail to eliminate the emotional actions of your negotiating opponents, call for a recess. In the morning, you might recess until after lunch. In the afternoon, you can recess until the next day. Normally, when the session reconvenes, your opponents will have gotten the message and will negotiate without emotional pressure. If not, simply repeat the procedure.

5. Seek the Removal of a Negotiator Who Consistently Employs Emotional Outbursts. Occasionally, you will encounter a group of negotiators in which one member will consistently employ emotional outbursts. This may be either a fake negotiating technique or a personality problem. In either case, after reasonable attempts to deal on a rational

basis, ask the head of the opposing negotiating team to remove the negotiator from the bargaining group.

Should you encounter any resistance from the chief negotiator,
simply stand your ground, and point out that you have shown courtesy,
consideration and understanding for the emotionally violent negotiator,
but that nothing has helped. Explain that you will not be able to negotiate
until this problem personality is removed from the negotiating team.

Once the chief negotiator sees that you mean business and are willing
to negotiate seriously, and once the problem personality is out of the way,
he will rectify the situation. Whether the emotionalism was an act or real
will be of no consequence at this point. He will have to be removed to save
face for the other negotiators.

How Harold Colter Lost a Battle and Won the War

Harold Colter was the chief negotiator for Colter Industries, a
machine tool manufacturer. Harold was cool-headed and a reasonable
negotiator. He was concerned with the welfare of his employees and was
known for agreeing to reasonable union demands. Harold paid his
employees slightly more than the industry average and received better than
average productivity in return.

A new union negotiator had been appointed to represent the plant
workers at this year's negotiations. Harold greeted the new representative
warmly and began to build the harmonious relations that had existed
between himself and previous union representatives.

To Harold's surprise, George, the union representative, began an
emotionally laden attack on the company. He yelled about unfair wages,
working conditions and the inability of the men to earn overtime compensation as did others in the industry. Harold empathetically responded by
repeating George's concerns and asked George what, specifically, he had
in mind.

George unveiled a package demand that called for a wage increase, a
piecework incentive and a double-time rate for overtime. Harold sensed
that the overtime provision was a phony issue, and verbal and nonverbal
actions of George's seemed to play down this issue.

Harold offered a three percent salary increase and agreed to the
double-time provision provided the piecework incentive was dropped.

This, of course, was not what the union wanted, as there was hardly ever any overtime worked.

George argued that this was completely unsatisfactory and demanded the whole package. Harold refused and George began his emotional attack again. This time, Harold simply said he would have to recess for the day and suggested they meet again the following week. George, visibly shaken when his plan had not worked, blurted out that they would meet tomorrow or not at all. Harold agreed.

For the next three days, Harold bargained calmly and reasonably. Each time George put on his emotional act, Harold simply said, "You seem to be upset, George. Would you like to take a recess?" This usually brought George back to a calm discussion.

Harold gave in on the piecework incentive plan (lost the battle) but did not agree to the overtime penalty provision and established the wage rate at the same level as that paid by the rest of the industry. Harold got a provision tied to the piecework agreement that permitted the men to work overtime at straight time plus the piecework incentive they would earn (won the war). For the first time, the men were not paid a higher rate than others in the industry. They were able to make more money on the piecework agreement, however, and Harold felt that this was fair, as he would get extra productivity for the money.

USING THE NEW APPROACH TO GET A SETTLEMENT

The new approach to negotiating differs from the old "battle of wills" approach in which issues were settled by strikes or lockouts. The new approach is intended to find a rational solution that is beneficial to both parties. You can't expect a union negotiator to go back to the members without any benefits for them, but you don't have to accept an agreement that makes you vulnerable to competition. The agreement should be of value to both management and the employees.

How to Add Appeal to Your Offer

The way to add appeal to your offer is to play up the face-saving aspects of your offer. The most successful international negotiators are the ones who find a way for both parties to save face. You will always get a better deal if you can find a way for the other party to walk away looking good.

Show the opposing negotiator how certain aspects of your offer will make him look good to his men. Throw in some inconsequential concession that he can show as something extra he gained that had not been asked for.

In cases where the negotiator has taken a strong stand which is wrong or incompatible with your position, do not belittle his position. Find excuses for him. Blame people who worked up the material for him. Say, "I can see why you would take that position based upon the evidence 'they' have given you. But it seems 'they' have erred in developing the evidence." Always find an excuse that saves face for the negotiator and your offer will be more appealing.

How to Get a Settlement

A settlement doesn't usually come all at once. It comes in small steps. Unions learned long ago to get company representatives to agree to small concessions, one by one, until only a major issue was left. No one could expect the union to forego it's major issue and, at this point, management had nothing left to bargain with.

In the new approach to negotiating, you withhold concessions until you get something in return. Sometimes the "something in return" is simply a substantial watering down of some other demand. So, hold back and make concessions only when you clearly see a concession in return.

To get a final settlement, hold out on three or more issues. It's easier to negotiate concessions from a package of three or four issues than it is from one or two. One of the final three or four issues might be extremely important to the union, important enough to strike for. All three, however, are not usually that important, and substantial concessions may be negotiated from issues "two" and "three" to keep "one" intact.

How a Tough-Minded Negotiator Won a Favorable Contract

Clark Morgan, the chief negotiator for a southwestern clothing manufacturer, scheduled early negotiating sessions. It was only 8:00 A.M.

on the fourth day of negotiations on the new labor contract and negotiations had been going on for two hours. Clark believed in getting down to hard bargaining early, while the mind was fresh and sharp.

Many minor issues had been settled, and the bargaining was coming rapidly to the final critical issues. The critical remaining issues were wage increases and the question of who would determine work schedules, the union or management. Clark had wisely held three minor issues in abeyance to use as bargaining power. The three minor issues were vacation time, night shift differential and Saturday starting time. The minor issues were relatively inexpensive, as compared to the major critical issues.

Facing Clark's final offer of a five percent wage increase, the union representative informed Clark that unless their demands for an eight percent increase and job section seniority rights were met, a strike would be called at 8:00 A.M. the following morning.

At 6:00 A.M. the next morning, Clark proposed a face-saving offer that would permit the union negotiators to face their members. Clark offered to concede on the three minor points and job section seniority, provided the union accepted the five percent wage offer.

The union presented the offer to the members, who rejected the offer. A new meeting was scheduled and a final settlement, which was accepted by the members, was worked out. A six percent wage increase without the job section seniority provision. Clark paid one percent extra in wages and retained the right for management to schedule the work gangs in the company's best interest.

Clark negotiated this favorable contract at a time when his competitors had been bullied into eight to ten percent wage increases. Clark was successful, because he kept minor issues alive to bargain with and because he used them to help the union negotiators save face.

◆ 11 ◆
Applying
The New Approach
to Supervisory Training

◆ Research in the sixties and early seventies showed that traditional approaches to supervisory training were not working. Many supervisors were voicing agreement to use a more personal, rather than authoritarian, managerial style but were not doing so in actual practice on the job. Their behavior was quite different from their descriptions of what they believed to be appropriate supervisory behavior.

The new approach is based upon subtle psychological techniques that utilize the supervisor's own attitudes and opinions to learn to actually perform the new more participative supervisory skills. In this chapter, you'll see how the supervisor's own desire to contribute to his and his co-workers' personal development is utilized to teach, support and utilize the new skills on the job.

In this chapter, you'll see how adult learning principles were used to provide the initiative and responsibility that lead the individual supervisor to develop new attitudes, change to a more participative management approach and still retain supervisory control.

The "task-force" approach to group training is covered in this chapter as a new method to utilize the basic adult learning principles that adults learn best by doing, are problem oriented, are motivated to learn skills that are helpful to them and learn best when they can relate the new material to prior experience and are free to make mistakes.

A FOUR-STEP STAFF DEVELOPMENT PROGRAM

The old mundane management approach to staff development which left training to chance has been replaced by a systematic approach to human resource development. Today, managerial training programs are a continuing part of every manager's career. In addition to drawing upon his past experience to solve current management problems, today's manager is expected to keep abreast of the latest management and training techniques as well. The following four-step approach provides a guide for your staff development.

The Development of Constructive Attitudes

Although you will usually find that most of your staff will have positive, profit-oriented managerial attitudes, they may not hold attitudes that motivate constructive action. The development of constructive attitudes should be a top priority, as it is the first step in the development of an effective and productive staff.

Research has shown that attitudes are most likely to be changed if people are exposed to writings, opinions of influential people and statistical evidence without the pressure of an attitude being forced upon them. If they are exposed to these forms of evidence in a casual atmosphere and allowed to reach their own conclusions, they will be more likely to change their own attitudes.

One manager, who made a great effort to convince his foremen that giving their gang feedback on production results would increase productivity, made personal appeals with prepared speeches to three of his four plants. Because the fourth plant was located out of the state the other three were in, he simply mailed his supporting material to the foremen and asked them to read through it.

As productivity picked up at the fourth plant, the manager decided to investigate. He found that the foremen at the fourth plant who had only read the mailed material, had changed their attitudes about giving their men productivity feedback while the three plants where the foremen had been lectured had not accepted the new attitudes.

The Development of Specific Supervisory Skills

Although the new approach to training relies on the supervisor's own initiative and internal desire to succeed, the new knowledge and/or skills must be presented in an understandable way. The "buddy system" or peer group discussions have been found most effective in training supervisors to use new skills. These cooperative study methods result in feed back and support for the new skills when they are tried on the job. The following presentation techniques have been found most effective in skills training.

1. Explain to the trainee how the knowledge or attitude being taught will affect his results.
2. Cover one point at a time when explaining the skill.
3. Demonstrate each step.
4. Question the supervisor to make sure each step is understood.
5. Repeat the instructions for any unclear area.

It is important to permit questions to be asked freely during all stages of the presentation. If the supervisors don't feel free to ask questions at any time they feel it necessary, they may try to save the question until the presentation ends. Questions that are saved, however, are usually forgotten. The best way to prevent this is to encourage questions throughout the presentation. Once the supervisors see that questions are welcome, they will question areas that are unclear and their training will be enhanced.

The Application of New Skills

The best way to learn a new skill is, of course, to practice it. The new approach to training is to provide as many alternate ways as possible to learn the new skills. By assigning the supervisor a number of different jobs that require the new skills, he will develop expertise and confidence. As he becomes confident, he will use the new skills more freely, and they will soon become habit.

Although the supervisors should be left to work on the new skills without having you look over their shoulders, you should check frequently to make sure no mistakes are being made.

Correct any errors that are being made and then leave immediately so that the supervisor will see that you have confidence in him. Always check before leaving to see if the supervisor has any questions. There may be some specific question that he will need an answer to in order to perform his job effectively.

The Reinforcement of Skilled Performance

The retention of a new skill is dependent upon some reward being received by the performer of the new skill. The reward creates a feeling of self-satisfaction which motivates the performer to continue using the new skill. Reinforcement of rewards may be monetary or complementary; a few pats on the back supported by adequate pay will reinforce the new skill until it becomes habit.

A new skill becomes habit through repetitive use. During the reinforcement period, a supervisor begins to see that he is getting better results with the new skills. He thus develops attitudinal support.

How a Skillful Manager Improved Supervisory Attitudes with Reinforcement

Ken March, operations vice-president of a midwestern trucking company, was concerned about the attitudes of the terminal managers. The company had 47 terminals spread over the midwestern United States. In all but a few of the terminals, the managers were hard-boiled, hard-working loyal men who believed the best way to manage was by threat.

Although profits were high, absenteeism and turnover rates were also high. Ken knew that, eventually, these problems would result in poor service and a loss of business. As a matter of fact, some decline in business was now evident.

Ken knew how hard attitudes are to change, so he decided to utilize some form of training that would expose the men to new attitudes about supervision and reinforce behavior that supported the new attitudes.

Ken enlisted the training department to do the job. The training department conducted a number of supervisory workshops for the terminal managers. The training was devised so that through reading, role play and discussion the men would develop attitudes toward a more employee-centered approach to supervision. Games were devised that could only be won by the elimination of threats and the introduction of measures of trust and concern for the employees.

The games and role plays were repeated over and over until each manager was comfortable with the new techniques. The games were continued by mail after the managers returned to work. Ken, the vice-president, wrote letters of commendation to the winning and high-scoring managers.

It soon became evident that the new techniques were being used on the job. The managers had made the transition from class to the job. Ken watched the absenteeism rates and turnover rates and, at the slightest improvement, called the terminal manager and complimented the manager on the improvement.

Ken never mentioned the new techniques as being responsible, but he kept the managers aware of their improvements. Occasionally, the managers would mention the new techniques as being responsible for the improvements. When they did so, Ken would compliment them on how well they were using the techniques and how well they had learned them.

By continual reinforcement, Ken was able to keep the new techniques in operation until they became habit. The men eventually used the new supervisory techniques as naturally as they had used the hard-line approach in the past.

The absentee rate dropped to normal and turnover was practically eliminated. The managers began to take more pride in their work and raised their expectations of what their subordinates could accomplish. The employees responded to this new level of confidence by becoming more productive. The company's profits increased, and what started as an attempt to correct one poor attitude resulted in a broad-based attitudinal change that eventually made the company one of the most productive in the industry.

How to Use Participative Techniques in Training Supervisors

The business world is filled with stories of people who were outstanding workers that failed after being promoted to a supervisory position. Management has learned the hard way that outstanding salesmen aren't necessarily good supervisors and that the most productive machinists aren't necessarily the best foremen.

The problem, of course, is that supervision requires special communications, an understanding of how people learn and an understanding of the conditions that promote high productivity. These skills, quite different from work skills, require special training.

The New Task-Force Approach to Supervising Training

One of the most effective methods of training supervisors is the task-force approach. Supervisors are grouped in teams of two or more members to form a task force for the specific purpose of learning supervisory methods and techniques. The task force is usually limited to five members but as many as seven or eight may be effective if they are people who usually work together and are known to be productive working as a group.

Research has shown that when teams are responsible for the learning of the individual team members, there is more learning. Not only do the team members help each other, they keep all team members aware that they are expected to learn in order to support the image of the group.

The task force must be given some basic material for initial study to bring them up to date on the state of the art. It has been found that people who study available research information in written form will accept the information and alter their attitudes about supervisory practices that they reject when given the information verbally. The opportunity to discuss the information with their peers in the task force setting generally develops a group consensus favorable to the new attitudes.

The following research material provides a sound basis for use in the initial attitude-formation stage of supervisory training. This material should be presented to the task force to study and discuss as a first step in developing their own supervisory training program.

A REVIEW OF WORKER MOTIVATION THEORIES
—THE THREE STUDIES

Motivation studies were initially concerned with the physical environment, working conditions and hours people worked. The purpose was to determine if changing these factors would increase productivity. It was thought that rest periods at fixed or alternating intervals might reduce fatigue and thus elicit better productivity. It was postulated that a reduced work day might even improve production.

The three most important research projects, the Harvard, the Michigan and the Pittsburgh studies, have been named after the universities that conducted the studies. A preponderance of the literature on motivation is based on these studies and the rest either refers to them or to the authors who reviewed them.

This review concentrates on the Harvard, Pittsburgh and Michigan studies while emphasizing the contributions of the prominent researchers and writers involved in these studies to the field of motivation.

The Harvard Studies

Elton Mayo, professor of Industrial Research, Graduate School of Business at Harvard, first studied the group work situation in the mule-spinning department of a textile mill near Philadelphia, between 1923 and 1924. The turnover rate was high, four different incentive schemes had failed and one hundred men per year were hired to keep forty working.

Mayo's (1945) group instituted ten-minute rest periods and instructed the men in the best methods of relaxation. Although the men had been involved in scheduling their own work periods, the significant results were, in Mayo's view, attributable to the personal interest shown by the supervisors in the men and to the social contact developed between a previously isolated group of men. The results lowered labor turnover, reduced melancholy and improved morale.

Mayo's second study concerned small groups in experimental situations. This study covered a period from 1927 to 1932 at the Hawthorne works of the Western Electric Company and became famous as the Hawthorne Experiment or Hawthorne Study.

At Hawthorne, two groups were separated who performed the same kind of work in rooms that were initially equally lighted. Light in one room was diminished in ordered quantities, while no change was made in the light intensity in the second room. Even though the light was diminished to a very low level, there was no reduction in output.

A second test was made in a room separated from the main assembly room to assemble telegraph relays under vaying conditions to see whether changes in lighting and rest periods would improve productivity. Changes were made periodically in rest period schedules, and at various times refreshments were served. After enough time had elapsed for the group to forget the earlier rest schedules, the same ones were used again. *No matter what changes were made, productivity improved.*

Even when changing back to a previous rest period schedule, productivity again increased. Any change, no matter how small or insignificant, again resulted in improved productivity. *This constantly improving reaction to change became known as the now famous "halo effect."* The reason for this effect was that the group felt it was a select group, singled out by management as the elite. Mayo (1933) found that these people developed a feeling of freedom from interference and control as a result of the special attention given them. They ceased to regard the man in charge as a boss and began to see him as an advisor and helper. (p. 66)

The Hawthorne study also provided the first suggestion of productivity being related to personal problems, such as lack of communications and poor supervision. It was discovered that workers tended to cluster in groups that functioned as informal organizations, which acted as stabilizers on the level of production. The small groups taking part in the test were not subject to these pressures because of their separation from the main shop.

From Mayo's study of the "halo effect" at Hawthorne came the insight that led to the development of human relations programs. Man's reaction to special treatment and to participation in the management process concerning his own work led to the belief that man could be motivated to greatly improve his productivity if treated with dignity and as an individual.

Mayo's third study was made of three companies with an absentee problem. The study found that the most productive group was the one with a high team spirit. This group had a good attendance record and wanted to keep the good reputation they had earned. Foremen of these groups had been trained by insightful management *to be patient, to listen, to avoid emotional upsets when dealing with the men and to preserve the dignity of the individual.* These foremen had been trained in handling people for twenty years. The company utilizing this policy had only 1/2 to 2 percent absenteeism, while Company B had 2 to 5 percent and Company C had 2½ to 10½ percent absenteeism during the study period, 1942 to 1943.

Further insight into social effect on productivity emerged from Mayo's southern California study in an aircraft plant. Three types of groups were encountered. The first was the very small two to seven-man group. The small size lent itself to the development of intimacy and group expectation of all members performing as a team, and each member was expected to be at work each day to hold up his share.

The second group consisted of a large group of participants who were led by a central core of highly motivated regulars. These highly motivated workers set the pace for the group, as they were respected through social contact.

The third group, Mayo (1933) found to be the best or most productive group. It came into being as a result of management's efforts to create it. This group had a high team spirit as a result of their supervisor's concern with the human aspects of administration. *These supervisors used job skills to make the work easy for the men and acted as go-betweens for the men and higher management.* These supervisors were confident that absenteeism and labor turnover would not become a problem for them. (p. 104)

Mayo (1933) speculated "Man's desire to be continuously associated in work with his fellows is a strong, if not the strongest human characteristic." (p. 111)

Roethlisberger and Dickson (1946) in *Management and the Worker*, covered the human relations aspect of the Hawthorne study. They wrote a detailed account, in chronological order of all events in the Hawthorne experiments, including the preparations made for the study. In their book, the function of management was defined as an effort to keep the social system in a state of equilibrium, so that the purposes of the organization are realized. They proposed a human relations type counseling program for industry, to find and alleviate employee discomfort. (p. 603)

The Michigan Studies

The University of Michigan's Institute for Social Research conducted a series of studies of first-line supervisors to determine what effect the behavior and attitude of supervisors had on their subordinates.

The Michigan researchers studied twenty-four separate groups of supervisors and their workers. They found that there were twelve high-producing and twelve low-producing groups, all of which were about equal in ability and background.

Each supervisor was rated on whether he put emphasis on people or on the job. If the supervisor's attitude indicated he was primarily concerned with the supervision of people, he was rated "employee-centered." If he considered his main job to be production expediting, then he was rated "production-centered."

Saul W. Gellerman (1969) reports that the conclusions of this study at the Prudential Insurance Company indicated that the employee-centered supervisors got the best production out of their subordinates. *The employee-centered supervisors laid out a general outline of how the work was to be done and left the details up to the workers themselves.* The employees of six out of the nine supervisors identified as employee-centered, seemed to flower under this system. They were cheerful, wasted less time, got more done and were stimulated as a group to better performance. (pp. 34-35)

Seven of eight groups classified as having production-centered supervisors were low-producing groups. *Evidently the emphasis on production was made at the expense of the worker's dignity. The production-centered supervisors tended to be defensive, authoritarian and arbitrary.* The study indicated that workers responded negatively to this type of supervision.

Although employee-centered supervision is more productive than production-centered supervision, other studies and analyses of those studies concluded that a combination of employee-centered and production-centered supervision is still more effective. One Michigan study indicated that, in the short run, production-centered supervision was more effective but thereafter production reverted to a lower than previous level.

Vroom and Mann (1964) found, in a trucking company study, that employees working individually liked authoritarian direction and responded better to it, even in the long run.

Daniel Katz, a former Program Director of the Human Relations Program at the University of Michigan, conducted a study to examine the extent to which the level of productivity depends upon the characteristics of supervision and upon those employee attitudes which constitute morale. Katz's (1951) findings in this study, the Chesapeake and Ohio Railroad study, are summarized in the introduction to his book (pp. xi-xii) as follows:

> The high-producing supervisor appears to regard the attainment of productivity as a problem in motivation and sees his role primarily as

one of motivating workers to achieve a goal, or creating conditions under which the goal can be reached. He differentiates his role from the workers themselves, he clearly perceives and accepts the responsibilities of leadership.

Rensis Likert, in reviewing eighty Michigan studies, found that the high-producing unit was one where there was group participation in setting goals, improving methods and appraising progress toward those goals. There was much information flowing in both directions, resulting in supervisors knowing and understanding problems of subordinates. There was extensive friendly interaction with a high degree of confidence and trust. Most of the technical and professional knowledge was readily available in the organization and the informal and formal organizations were one and the same. Control data was issued for self-guidance and for coordinated problem-solving and guidance, not for punishment.

Likert (1967) said that a properly led group would generate satisfaction for its members in pride and accomplishment and that this would overcome any tendencies to restrict production. He proposed full control of the specific fragment of the job a worker is doing be passed on to the worker himself. (p. 4-10)

Victor Vroom found five motivational determinants of effective job performance in reviewing five hundred research investigations. He found that the level of performance would be higher for achievement-oriented people:

1. If the work was represented as challenging or difficult.
2. If the workers believe they are being overcompensated for their job.
3. If the workers believe the task requires special skills they value and believe themselves to possess.
4. If feedback is given concerning their performance level.
5. If they are given an opportunity to participate in decisions that may affect them in the future.

The Pittsburgh Studies

Frederich Herzberg (1959), Research Director, Bernard Mausner, Research Psychologist and Barbara Synderman, Research Associate at the

Psychological Service of Pittsburgh, conducted a study of the attitudes people held toward their job. These studies were interpreted by Herzberg to indicate that some job factors affecting attitude were satisfiers and others were dissatisfiers. The implication was that factors of dissatisfaction could only be improved to the degree necessary to alleviate dissatisfaction. From that point upward, different factors came into play to create job satisfaction at a level above toleration.

Herzberg's study was designed to examine the factors- attitudes-effects as a unit. The approach used was to obtain an account of a worker's periods of high or low morale, to find out what incident happened to cause it and what the worker felt and to determine the result or effects of the incident, or the resulting morale state.

Herzberg concluded that *achievement, recognition, work itself, responsibility, advancement,* and *salary,* in that order, plus ten other factors were the factors responsible for the highly motivated producers.

The lowly motivated workers' bad feelings seemed to have resulted first, and most importantly, from *company policy and administration.* Low motivation *was described as resulting from ineffective administration and unfair personnel policies. The second most important reason for bad feelings was supervision, salary was third, work and interpersonal relations with supervisors tied for fourth, advancement was fifth and working conditions sixth.* Workers had more often complained of too little rather than too much work. (p. 267)

Herzberg found that the basic satisfiers: achievement, recognition, advancement, responsibility and work itself appeared "with significantly greater frequencies in the highs (highly motivated) than they did in the lows (lowly motivated)." (p. 80) Recognition, advancement and work did appear in the responses of the lowly motivated, but only infrequently. Herzberg concluded that these factors were important as job satisfiers but were not effective in overcoming job dissatisfaction.

He defined company policy, administration, supervision and working conditions as major job dissatisfiers, as they had led to bad feelings in the lowly motivated. Improving these dissatisfiers did not lead to positive attitudes about the job any more than the absence of the satisfiers led to job dissatisfaction.

Salary was found three times as often in the responses of the lowly motivated and was believed to be a job dissatisfier. Where salary was mentioned by the highly motivated, it was viewed as a sign of achievement or a form of recognition.

Herzberg, in discussing the effects of job attitudes, concluded that improved performance occurred as a result of improved job attitudes, and that decreased performance occurred as a result of a negative change in job attitudes. He reasoned that favorable attitudes were more dynamic causes of change in performance than were unfavorable attitudes. (pp. 83-87)

Herzberg summarizes with the opinion that the dissatisfiers are like hygiene. Hygiene is a preventive measure, not a curative one. The satisfiers or factors that lead to job satisfaction are motivators because they satisfy the individual's need for self-actualization. He is thus motivated to positive behavior as opposed to the avoidance needs of preventive factors.

He found it especially important to eliminate the dissatisfiers in situations where the job is routine and offers little opportunity for responsibility, achievement or self-actualization. He speculated: "The profoundest motivation to work comes from the recognition of individual achievement and from the sense of personal growth in responsibility." (pp. 114-15)

Conclusions

The Harvard studies revealed the power of group associations on productivity. Group membership was found to be the employee's first concern. The group's attitude about production was assumed by the individual as a condition of group acceptance.

The Michigan studies pointed out that the attitude of first-line supervisors determined, to a significant degree, the level of productivity of the group. The employee-centered supervisor obtained better productivity than did the work-centered supervisor.

The Pittsburgh studies examined the effect of employees' attitudes about their jobs on productivity. Herzberg classified job factors affecting productivity as satisfiers and dissatisfiers. The implication was that factors of dissatisfaction could be improved to the degree that dissatisfaction would be alleviated, but no higher. These factors, the major job dissatisfiers, were company policy and administration, supervision and working conditions.

To get to a level above the alleviated dissatisfaction level or to a positive job attitude level, a set of factors called satisfiers are required. Herzberg identified these positive factors as achievement, recognition, work itself, responsibility, advancement, and salary, in that order. Those and ten other factors were concluded by Herzberg to be responsible for the highly motivated producer. He further concluded that improved performance resulted from improved job attitudes and that a decrease in performance was due to a negative change in attitude, but the favorable attitudes were more dynamic causes of change than the unfavorable.

The literature covering these three studies as well as other literature, such as the work of Chris Argyris on organization, McGregor on management, Gellerman on morale, H.J. Leavitt on organization, McClelland on achievement, White on competency, de Charms on self-actualization and Maslow on basic need, all indicate that work motivation can only be accomplished by satisfying the workers' needs.

The Training Program

Once the task force has completed its initial study of the basic research material, have it develop a list of supervisory skills that its members want training in. Most people eagerly seek advanced training in order to feel more comfortable on the job they are doing. In this situation, the supervisors are doubly motivated by the knowledge that they will be able to improve their work skills and by the motivational effect of being involved in the development of the training program.

Once the list of skills is prepared, it is time to bring in professional training programs. If possible, the programs should also be conducted by professional trainers. The supervisors know best what they need to learn, but professional trainers know best how to present the material so that it can be most easily learned.

Retain the task force management of the group so that the group will continue to cooperate and encourage each other to learn.

HOW TO USE THE NEW APPROACH TO DEVELOP CONSTRUCTIVE SUPERVISORY BEHAVIOR

Once the supervisory task force has completed its initial study of the research training needs and a program has been set to train the new skills, the new approach to managing people can be used to develop constructive supervisory behavior. The supervisor's environment must be manipulated to support the use of the new skills. The system of rewards must be altered to reinforce the new behavioral skills rather than continue to reinforce the old supervisory methods and practices.

Provide Rewards Only for the Use of New Techniques

The most common problem in the implementation of new skills has been found to be *the lack of a reward system that supports the new techniques*. In the past, management has continued to base job recognition and monetary rewards on traditional management techniques. Supervisors learned very quickly to put the new skills aside and continue the traditional techniques in order to earn promotions and salary increases.

The way to insure that the new techniques are rewarded is to include them in all job evaluation forms. They should be listed on the job description form, the performance appraisal form and the salary review form. Then, make it very clear that the new techniques are the primary job elements that will be considered in promotion and salary review.

How a New Manager Used the New Approach to Correct a Problem Supervisor

John Tipton was promoted to plant manager of a New England electronics firm. John was anxious to develop cooperation between management and the workers but knew that a problem existed with one foreman. George Paley, the night shift production foreman, was egotistical and harsh in dealing with his subordinates.

George had been trained along with all foremen in the plant in new supervisory techniques that treated the employees as team members rather than subordinates. George had ignored the new techniques and his gang's productivity had fallen behind all other departments.

John called George in for a job description review as a means of drawing George's attention to the new techniques listed on the job description form. After a thorough discussion of each of the new techniques, John explained how he would use the job description.

The new techniques listed on the job description form would be the criteria he would use for performance appraisal and salary review. When George left the office, he was fully aware that the only way he would ever get another raise would be as a result of using the new supervisory techniques listed on the job description.

George slowly changed from a harsh, sarcastic supervisor to a more polite and considerate one. John worked with George and gave him daily feedback and ideas on how to change. One by one, George overcame his problems and, through the use of the new supervisory skills, built up his gang's productivity.

◆12 ◆

Applying
the New Approach to
Performance Counseling:
A Key to Getting
Better Results

◆During the "human relations" oriented sixties, managers began to see a common problem in appraising subordinate performance. The appraisal session gave the manager and the subordinate an opportunity to discuss the subordinate's performance, but it did not provide an "action model" for the subordinate to use to improve his performance.

Often, the appraisal session became a gripe session. The manager criticized the subordinate for his past errors, and the subordinate complained about unfair management practices or unusual constraints that had interfered with his productivity. Both the manager and the subordinate felt better because they got their gripes off their chests. The subordinate's productivity did not increase, however, because no real coaching or counseling occurred.

Slowly, articles began to appear in the literature criticizing performance appraisal. One well known author expressed the opinion that performance appraisals were a waste of time. Many new methods, based on the "human relations" approach were then tried. Concern for the subordinate, as opposed to concern for productivity, became the basis for the employee-centered revolution in all phases of employee relations.

This employee-centered approach to dealing with all employee problems was based on the belief that the solution to all problems with employees should come from within the employee. If productivity was low, if there was a skill deficiency, if there was an absentee problem, if the employee's morale was low—no matter what the problem—the solution was to be found by simply asking the employee. After years of fumbling, management fed a new finding back to the researchers and theorists. The employees very often didn't have the answer, couldn't solve the problem, didn't really want to correct their own absentee problems and didn't care about improving their productivity.

Finally, managers who had experienced both systems began to realize that performance appraisal and performance counseling were two different functions. Performance appraisal could be used to identify problem areas and to secure the subordinate's agreement to take improvement actions. Performance counseling, however, must include a coaching function. The manager would coach the subordinates by teaching them specific ways to overcome their problems.

In this chapter, you'll learn a new approach to productivity counseling that blends the best of employee-centered appraisal sessions with action techniques that improve productivity. You'll see how to break through employee resistance, neutralize conflict, handle work stoppages, deal with hostility and correct an uncooperative subordinate, and you will learn a new six-step coaching program to improve employee performance.

NEW SOLUTIONS TO PERFORMANCE COACHING PROBLEMS: A SIX-STEP COACHING PLAN

Recent research has shown that to be effective in counseling subordinates, the manager must develop trust and a cooperative working climate. Many employees look at a counseling session with suspicion. They remember the threats and criticism of past appraisal sessions and expect them to be repeated. These negative expectations that people bring to the counseling sessions create problems that the manager must overcome in order to develop a cooperative employee attitude.

Performance coaching includes two counseling steps and four coaching steps. The first step, establishing an effective counseling climate, and the last step, reviewing and evaluating results, are counseling steps. The second through fifth steps: developing the job position image, providing step-by-step instruction, conducting practice sessions and making progress checks are the four coaching steps.

1. Establishing an Effective Counseling Climate

An effective counseling climate encourages the cooperation of the employee. By creating a trustworthy climate in which your subordinate feels free to discuss performance problems without reprimand and to establish improvement procedures without feeling incapable of doing his job, the subordinate will be motivated to make the necessary improvements. The following methods can be used to create an effective counseling climate:

Conduct the Meeting in a Casual Atmosphere. If a neutral ground away from your office is available, use it. An informally decorated meeting room or a restaurant that affords privacy provide good alternatives to a formal meeting in your office. If you have used your office for informal get-togethers in the past and your subordinates visualize your office as an informal meeting place, then it may be appropriate for use in a counseling session. The key is to make the subordinate feel at ease. Some employees can never feel at ease in the boss's office, so watch for signs of tension and move to a new meeting place when an employee seems nervous or tense.

State the Purpose of the Counseling Session and Specify How the Subordinate Will Benefit. Many subordinates feel apprehensive when called into a private meeting with their boss. To dispel any fears, immediately tell your subordinate the purpose of the meeting. You might say that the meeting is a *regular quarterly counseling session*, in which the two of you together will review his performance level and establish specific goals for the future (next quarter).

Point out specific ways in which the subordinate will benefit from the counseling session. By mentioning benefits, you remind your subordinates that they will gain something of value from the session. These reminders also trigger the subordinate's subconscious motives to learn. For example, an employee who believes that mastering a higher skill level will earn the respect of his or her peers will be motivated to attain the higher skill level.

Some benefits that might be mentioned are: recognition, advancement, prestige, preparation for the future, self-satisfaction with personal improvements, job-security, easier work, lack of confusion on the job, a sense of accomplishment, a feeling of pride and a sense of mastery of the job.

Demonstrate Faith in Your Subordinate's Ability. Show that you have faith and confidence in your subordinates by giving them the chance to talk first. Keep the conversation on the subordinate's performance, however, by asking performance-related questions. Ask the subordinate if there are any particular performance areas he needs help with. If the subordinate can't think of any, then turn to specific areas and ask the subordinate to evaluate his or her progress in that area. Then, ask the subordinate how he can improve in those areas.

By asking the subordinate for his or her own ideas on how to improve, you have demonstrated faith in the subordinate. If the subordinate does have ideas that will improve his or her performance, make sure those ideas are included in the goals for the next period. It is important that the improvement goals be mutually developed by you and the subordinate so that they are supported by the subordinate as well as you.

By letting the subordinate decide upon or "come up" with his own improvement recommendations, you clearly demonstrate your faith in him. In addition to demonstrating your faith in the subordinate, this technique usually results in more effective improvement goals. Research has shown that subordinates generally set tougher goals for themselves and are more likely to select the specific improvement areas that result in the highest increase in productivity.

Occasionally one of your subordinates will be unable or unwilling to come up with any areas that need improvement. Your first reaction may be to "tell him a few things" that he needs to know. This may result in defensiveness and destroy the possibility of an effective counseling climate. The best approach is to point out that there are a number of improvement areas that have been suggested by his co-workers. Point out that you will be glad to go over those suggestions and help him select those that might be helpful to him. Usually, the most reluctant employee will come up with at least one improvement area when faced with the alternative of having someone else's recommendations imposed upon them.

Place Responsibility for Achieving the Goal on the Subordinate. You obviously can't spend all of your time helping all your subordinates achieve their goals. But, someone must be responsible, or nothing will get done. Let the employee know that your part is to help him or her overcome any problems that interfere with their reaching the established goals.

Point out that improving productivity is a joint responsibility, with the subordinate holding primary responsibility for his own improvement and the responsibility for making you aware of problems or opportunities that require changes in procedures or methods or physical rearrangements. Your responsibility is to discuss these changes and facilitate their implementation where possible.

2. Developing the Job Position Image

This second coaching step is really the motivational step. Here, you begin a process of meshing the subordinate's identification of self with the job position image. The more highly perceived the job image, the more rewarding the meshing of the individual and job identification will be. If the job position can be described as one that is highly beneficial to the organization in either economic or moral value, the subordinate can identify himself with this value. The pursuit of this value then leads to the fulfillment of both personal and organizational goals.

For example, a job that contributes to productivity increases benefits for every member of the organization and the public at large. The idea that a worker can participate in and identify with these improvements forms the motivation for meshing the images of the worker and the job position. This meshing of a worker's image with a highly productive job image is one of the best ways to develop long-term motivation to constantly increase productivity.

Prepare the Subordinate for the Coaching Process. After discussing the value (image) of the job, the subordinate should be prepared for the actual improvement steps that he or she must go through. This can be an overview of the process that clearly illustrates how the subordinate will go through a step-by-step improvement procedure until the previously established goals are met. These steps should be described in accurate and simple terms that the subordinate can easily understand.

Each step should be related to the subordinate's current work process, and the value of changing should be clearly pointed out. Continually point out the benefits of any change in procedure or work practice, and provide the subordinate with an opportunity to ask questions to satisfy any concerns he may feel. This procedure should be followed throughout the coaching program.

Plan All Aspects of the Coaching Program in Advance. The plan must take into account what the subordinate already knows about the job and the specific areas in which he needs help. This can be determined from a supervisory evaluation and from the list of improvement areas previously developed by the subordinate. The following check list may be of value in preparing your subordinates for a coaching program:

Coaching Preparation Checklist

1. What is the objective of the coaching program?
2. What does the employee currently know about this job?
3. What is the gap between his current knowledge and the objectives of the program?
4. What other experience does the employee have?
5. Can the program be related to this experience?
6. How will the employee benefit from this program?
7. How can the employee's interest in the program be developed?
8. How can I put the employee at ease when correcting his actions?
9. What questions will the employee most likely ask?
10. What aspects of the job will provide an interesting story?
11. What aspects of the job are important to increasing productivity?
12. What aspects of the job are important to the employee's success?

By answering the questions presented in the "Coaching Preparation Checklist," you can develop the information needed to prepare your subordinates for the coaching plan. By discussing the gap between an employee's current skills level and the skills level objective, for example, you can prepare the employee for the specific coaching to be expected. Or, you might point out that his past experience is relevant to the new skills he will be learning. All of the information developed from the "Coaching Preparation Checklist" will help make the employee receptive to a coaching program.

3. Providing Step-by-Step Instruction.

Psychologists have discovered and educators have demonstrated that learning occurs in small steps. If coaching or other training proceeds in small steps, the instruction will be consistent with what the employee can most easily learn. Therefore, all instruction should be given in small sequential steps. Another advantage of the step-by-step process is that it is easily adapted to employees who are at various skills levels. The beginning employee can start with the first step and the employee with advanced skills can start with an advanced step near his level of expertise.

Job Component Break-Down. In order to coach on a step-by-step basis, a job must be broken down into its smallest component steps. A machine operator's job must be broken down into the smallest movements of the hand, the direction of movement, forward, backward, around, over or under. These movements must be recorded in minute detail if they are to be taught with any expectation of success. If a job is being studied for the first time, it is best to study a number of different operators in different plants. It may be that one operator will be utilizing a more efficient method than the others. The most efficient method, of course, is the one you want to break down and teach others.

Explain the Improvement Step. Begin the actual on-the-job (or classroom) coaching by explaining very carefully what the improvement step is, how it will affect productivity and what the employee will have to do to master the step. Make sure the employee understands the objective of the step by having him or her summarize or repeat back to you what the change is and what the results will be.

Demonstrate the Improvement Step. Go through the procedure very slowly, exaggerating each movement and verbally describing the importance of each movement. Ask for questions as you proceed. Often, an employee will have a question but will fear interrupting you. By showing early that you expect questions, you will overcome this problem.

After going through the procedure in an exaggerated fashion, go through it at the normal working speed so the employee can see the normal method of operation. Then, repeat the step at both the exaggerated and normal speed again. Repetition is the key to learning.

Question the Employee for Understanding. After the demonstration, question the employee to make sure he or she understood what you were doing. Ask questions to determine whether or not each movement was observed and understood. Find out if the employee wants you to repeat some part of the demonstration. Ask "what," "why," "how" and "when" questions to test the employee's understanding. You might say, "What did I do first? Why did I move to the side when performing the second step? How are these two pieces joined? When do you reverse the procedure?" Any question that requires an understanding of some part of the operation will be helpful.

The following instructional checklist will provide a means of insuring that you use good training principles throughout the coaching process.

Step-by-Step Coaching Checklist

1. How can I best relate the new skills to the trainee's background and experience?
2. Can I briefly explain the new skills in clear and precise terms?
3. What visual aids will best demonstrate the new skills?
4. What questions can I ask that will test the trainee's understanding of the material presented?
5. Have I broken the skill down into single-step sequential learning units?
6. What steps are likely to be confusing or difficult for the trainee to understand?
7. How can I encourage questions from the trainee?
8. How can I make the training interesting to the trainee?
9. What examples will best point out the reasons for learning the new skill or technique?
10. How can I best *stress* the key elements of each step?
11. How much can I reasonably expect the trainee to learn in this session?
12. How should this session be presented to a beginner?
13. How should this session be presented to an experienced person?
14. Have I allowed for discussion time?
15. How can the trainee be provided a practice session?
16. What are the most common errors that occur in a practice session?
17. How will I correct these errors?
18. Can the trainee explain the new skill to me (or someone else) after he completes practicing this step?
19. Can the trainee tell me what he learned, why he learned it and how the new skill will benefit him and the company?
20. How can I be sure the new skill is used immediately and continuously on the job?

The twenty-question "Step-by-Step Coaching Checklist" will keep you aware of the techniques that have proven successful in training others. Reproduce it or refer to it regularly when coaching a subordinate.

4. Conducting Practice Sessions

Often, elaborate training programs fail because practice sessions are not provided. The employee watches and listens and thinks he learns the new skills. Without practice, however, he finds that, back on the job, he is unable to remember the new techniques. He feels uncomfortable trying to use a skill he doesn't remember very well or isn't sure of, so he reverts back to the more comfortable old way of doing the job. The skill is lost, and the training has been wasted.

You can avoid this problem in a coaching program because you are there on the job scene, not in a training room away from the actual work situation. You can make sure that your subordinate practices the new skill three times before being left to use the new skill on the job.

The employee must practice the new skill immediately in order to retain it. Have your subordinate (or trainee) go slowly through the procedure and explain to you (or the instructor) exactly what he or she is doing and why. This explanation will bring out any misunderstandings if there are any, and if there are none, it will reinforce the learning. The verbalizing of the procedure and the acknowledgement by you (the coach) that the description is correct also gives the employee confidence in performing the new skill.

Usually, the employee will make mistakes during the practice session. He may even correctly perform the skill the first time and then make an error the second or third time. Completing three practice sessions, according to psychologists, is the key to effective learning. If the employee performs the skill correctly three times, he will remember the correct procedure. If he makes an error at any point, correct the error immediately and start a new series of three practice sessions.

Some instructors will have the trainee practice three times to correct the error. Then, after the error has been corrected, the instructor requires the trainee to practice the entire skill three times. This gives the trainee the confidence that he or she can get by the problem area without repeating the error. Once the employee gets through three practice sessions, he is ready to use the new skill on the job.

5. Making Progress Checks

This step is the one most commonly associated with coaching. You go to the subordinate's working location, look at what he is doing and, if any error is being made, correct it on the spot. Once the correction is made, watch your subordinate do it correctly and then go away.

Normally, you do not stand and watch an employee perform. Although certain occasions such as the demonstration of new machinery or the demonstration of the employee's special skills will require an audience, the usual procedure is to *teach a skill, have the employees practice it* and then *leave them alone.*

For example, after teaching employees a new system for grinding drill bits, let them practice under supervision, then get them started grinding bits by the new system. Once all the employees are using the new system, walk away and leave them alone.

Periodically, return and examine the results, look at the drill bits and check the system being used. If everyone is using the new system and the bits have been properly ground, go away. If any problems are found, correct them, get the employees who are making errors aside for close supervision and stay with them until all errors are corrected.

6. Reviewing and Evaluating Learning

To evaluate the learning that took place during the coaching program, we need something to measure against. Since the initial objective was to improve productivity, we measure the increase in productivity against the improvement goals established in step 1. If the productivity increases were met, then, of course, the major objective has been achieved. The specific skill learning should still be evaluated as the objectives may have been met in spite of skill deficiencies.

The evaluation of a skill, obviously, must take place through observation on an individual basis. You simply watch each step very carefully and determine if each step is correct. Once an incorrect step is observed, that step, as incorrectly executed, must be compared with the same step being correctly executed by someone else. The incorrectly executed step may have resulted from an improvement made by the employee. You certainly would not want to correct a more efficient step and stifle innovation.

Incorrect execution of the new skills that results in productivity lower than established objectives will require retraining. Since the employees who are making errors have been through the training once and have failed to learn the new skills, they will require close supervision during and after the retraining period.

Prior to starting the retraining, the problem employees should be questioned to determine what special problems they have in learning the new skills. Often, the employee is aware of specific factors that interfere with his learning. Once these factors are known, a new training effort can be made to overcome them. Special factors or obstacles should always be looked for when dealing with people who have previously been instructed and who you thought were well trained. The following checklist will be helpful in evaluation and retaining problems.

Evaluation and Retraining Checklist

1. Have the training objectives been met?
2. Are there special factors that were obstacles to the learning of some employees?
3. Did an innovation occur that rendered the new skill obsolete?
4. How did the employees with skill deficiencies pass the initial performance tests?
5. How much additional training is needed?
6. How long must the retrained employees be given close supervision?
7. What special help will be required to keep retrained employees from slipping back into their old habits?
8. How often should retrained employees' performance be checked?
9. At what point does the cost of retraining exceed the value of the new skill?
10. At what point should the employee be considered untrainable, and should he be removed from the job?

*How a Plant Foreman Used the Six-Step Coaching Plan
to Get Better Production*

The Lincoln Hand Tool Company, after four years of steady growth, had experienced sales declines for three months in a row. A survey by the Market Research Department revealed that a new line of lightweight hand tools produced by a competitor was replacing Lincoln's hand tools in the western sales region.

The market research manager reported that the new line was rapidly replacing Lincoln in hardware and discount stores. He believed the initial success of the new lightweight line would encourage the competing company to expand nationwide, eventually replacing Lincoln throughout the United States. He recommended an immediate investment in modern machinery to produce a new lightweight inexpensive line of hand tools to undercut the new competition.

The board of directors voted to move into the new line of lightweight tools but decided to make the change in four steps. One division or one-quarter of the production facility was to be changed every other month until the job was completed. The plant foreman would be required to train the men to use the new machines. He was sent to the machine manufacturing company to learn the operation of the new machines in advance of their installation in the plant.

Don, the foreman, called the men together and explained, in a casual way, the problem the company was experiencing and how the new machines were necessary to produce the lighter weight tools. Don told the men how they and the company would benefit by their learning to operate the new machines without error as rapidly as possible. Don encouraged questions and answered them candidly and honestly. He assured them that there was no reason to be worried about lay-off. "The market studies have shown that we can recapture our share of the market once we get the new lightweight tools in production," he concluded.

Don next expressed confidence in the men's ability to produce a substantially large number of tools with the new machinery. The increased production, he pointed out, would keep the company competitive with the new company that had been taking their customers, and their jobs would be insured. Also, there was a definite possibility of increased compensation. Management had promised a bonus if all departments were above the new standards by the end of the year and the company was profitable. Having operated the new machines himself, Don said he was sure they could easily surpass the new standards. Don explained how he had gone to the factory and had been trained to operate the new machines. They were easier to operate than the old ones, he told the men.

Don next pointed out that improving productivity would be a joint responsibility between the men and himself. They, of course, would have primary responsibility, but he would provide training and help them solve any problems that came up. He encouraged them to help each other. If one person found a short-cut, he should share the short-cut method with the other employees. By sharing with each other, soon they would all be producing at a much higher level.

Next, Don began developing an image for an employee operating the new machinery. He developed a picture of a highly skilled employee operating the latest in machine technology. The upgraded job, he told them, was one the men could be proud of. The new machines would be the lifeblood of the company. Without the new machines, he explained, there was no way for the company to stay in business.

When the new machinery arrived, Don was ready. He had developed a sequential training program that permitted the men to learn the new machinery in small steps. Don rotated the men on the new machines until everyone in the plant had experience on the new machines. That way, the second, third and fourth stages would be more easily implemented. Don used the twenty-question checklist to make sure the employees were properly trained.

Don continued to conduct practice sessions for the men scheduled for stages two, three and four, so the men would be ready and comfortable with the new machinery when it arrived.

Don made extensive checks to see that the men were operating the new machinery properly. If an error was found, it was corrected immediately. A few problems developed with the machinery that was installed in stage two, but the earlier practice sessions paid off. The men recognized the improper operation and immediately called for the engineers to make the necessary corrections.

By the time the machines arrived to be installed in the third stage, the men were ready. When the third stage machines were installed, the men on the first and second stage operations were already exceeding standard.

Don measured the productivity increases at this point and reviewed the operating procedures that were being followed. This review resulted in further increases in productivity, as the men working the machines had developed short-cuts and improvements in the operating procedures that were more productive than the ones recommended by the manufacturer.

Finally, the fourth stage machines were installed. A faulty motor kept the fourth division crew from making standard the first month, but the results of the other three divisions were so much above standard that the results of the total plant were well above standard.

HOW TO BREAK THROUGH RESISTANCE TO COUNSELING

Resistance to counseling usually results from uncertainty as to what will happen during the session. The fear exists that a demand will be made that the employee will be unable to meet, or it will not be met simply because the subordinate is an argumentative personality type who resents any change he doesn't initiate himself.

The first fear can be overcome by very clearly stating the purpose of the meeting in specific terms. The second fear can be neutralized by stating early in the interview that the employee will not be asked to do anything without help. Point out that in the case of productivity increases, training and guidance will be provided.

The third counseling problem, that of the argumentative employee, can be dealt with by a candid expression of the exact requirements the employee must meet. Research has shown that the argumentative stance does not keep the employee from following directions. After he has expressed his hostile reactions, he proceeds to perform his duties.

He will try to convince you with argument not to proceed with the planned change. If you weaken, he will press on. If you stand firm, he will finally agree to do as you ask. In extreme cases, or in cases where the employee has gotten his way in the past, he may actually refuse to cooperate.

When an employee refuses or states that he will refuse, you must immediately confront this problem in a courteous but firm way. Simply tell him he has two choices, to obey your instructions by cooperating or be taken off the job.

HOW TO DEAL WITH SUBORDINATE CONFLICT DURING PERFORMANCE APPRAISAL

One objective of performance appraisal is to bring your subordinate's attention to performance weaknesses that need improvement. If you let your subordinate bring up the weaknesses as a result of your questioning, there will be no problem. Often, however, an employee will miss the point. You must then bring up the performance weakness yourself.

Conflict often occurs when a manager brings a performance weakness to a subordinate's attention. The conflict develops from the subordinate's hostile or defensive reaction. In either case, you can avoid becoming engaged in conflict by simply refusing to argue.

If your subordinate becomes defensive and reacts with denials or excuses, you simply ask him to explain the situation he is basing his statements on. Be understanding, show that you are not being critical and explain that you are just helping him prepare to make some improvements that will benefit both himself and the organization.

If your subordinate reacts in a hostile way by becoming argumentative, stating that you've got the wrong information or making sarcastic remarks, you can still avoid argument and get your point across. Be firm but polite, and ask him to examine the information with you to see if together you can find some performance areas which need strengthening.

This approach will usually bring him around. He may continue to try to bluff or argue with you, but don't let him lead you into an argument. Show understanding and listen patiently. He will eventually agree to do what you want. Recent research has shown that the argumentative personality is just as susceptible to persuasion as anyone else. He expresses his argumentative disposition and then proceeds to obey orders.

Again, in extreme cases, be prepared to give him a choice between working on the improvement areas, being reassigned to another job or leaving the company.

How an Engineering Executive Dealt with a Hostile Subordinate

Lloyd Wilton, a hard-working energetic young man, was transferred from engineering maintenance, at his request, into the planning department. At first, Lloyd was cheerful and friendly, got along well with his fellow employees and was a very productive worker. After several months, however, Lloyd's work began to slip. He became very gruff with fellow employees, he was actually sarcastic with a foreman and his productivity dropped lower and lower every week.

Bill Talmadge, the engineering vice-president called Lloyd in for an appraisal of his performance for the six months he had been in the planning department. Lloyd immediately became hostile, asserting that he did his job and saw no reason for performance appraisals. "All you have to do is look and you can see me working," Lloyd said.

Bill asked Lloyd to compare his own productivity today with what it had been the first day on the job. After three attempts to get Bill into an argument, Lloyd finally agreed that his productivity had dropped. When Bill pressed for a reason, Lloyd finally stated that planning was not what he had been told it would be, and there was no longer any reason for him to "break his back" for nothing.

With a few more questions, Bill found out that Lloyd transferred into planning expecting to get a new supervisor's job, which he heard was to be filled in three months. When the job didn't materialize, he became dissatisfied.

Bill explained that the new supervisory position had been delayed as a result of a general reorganization of the department. He very candidly told Lloyd that he would not now be considered for that position, as his recent behavior didn't warrant it.

Bill then elicited an improvement plan from Lloyd to bring his performance back up to an acceptable level. Bill assured Lloyd that once he corrected his performance slump, he would again become eligible for promotion should an opening occur.

◆ 13 ◆
Using the New Approach to Solve Performance Problems

◆ **R**ecent attempts to solve performance problems by involving the employees in work design, paying piecework incentives and the use of flexible working hours, although somewhat successful, have not resulted in the wholesale solution to performance problems that had been initially predicted. No matter how far we advance, problems seem to keep pace.

A new approach that evolved from a training principle has recently been used successfully by a number of public and private organizations. The learning principle that adults are problem-oriented suggested that performance problems on the job should be posed as problems for the employees to solve themselves. The idea was tried and found to work remarkably well by a number of companies.

Further research in these companies demonstrated that once employees were given responsibility for solving their own problems, they did solve them within the limits of their expertise.

Under the old system, they had used their best efforts to "beat the system" or "cheat the clock." Now they worked to "beat the problem."

In this chapter, you'll see how the new problem-solving approach actually works to elicit a number of motivating forces from within the employee. These forces move your employees to continue increasing their productivity even after their problem is solved. You'll see how to add the guidance and challenges that keep those forces working, how to increase productivity and how to solve performance problems.

HOW TO USE ACHIEVEMENT MOTIVATION
TO SOLVE PERFORMANCE PROBLEMS

At one time or another, every business faces performance problems. Perhaps people slowly lower their productivity over time, or perhaps they fail to utilize new equipment or new techniques that were designed to improve productivity. Since it is not reasonable to expect a foreman to stand and watch every move workers make or a manager to stand and watch every move his subordinates make, a motivational approach is helpful.

One motivational approach, based on the work of David C. McClelland of Harvard University, could be called the "achievement-motivation approach." McClelland led a group of psychologists in the study of the achievement motive and very quickly discovered the importance this motive played in economic success. His group identified a number of factors that characterized achievement-motivated people, people who achieved a higher standard of excellence, were more productive and achieved much more than the average person. An experiment conducted at the Institute of Human Resource Development proved that group productivity could be increased by artificially stimulating the achievement motive on a group as well as an individual basis. The following synthesis of this work with the findings of Dr. McClelland and other research forms a concrete approach to resolve performance problems.

The Achievement-Motivation Approach to Performance Problems

From the finding that highly achievement-motivated people demand more from themselves and the knowledge that everyone is motivated to some extent (it may be a very low level) by achievement needs, the achievement-motivation approach to solving performance problems evolved. You can use this new approach to resolve performance problems of your subordinates, whether they are problems with supervisors or workers themselves.

Slight alterations will be necessary in dealing with line workers who are represented by unions or with workers who are resisting the introduction of new machinery that they feel will eliminate jobs. They must be convinced that no one will be laid off, or alternately, that unless productivity is increased, everyone will be laid off.

The following steps will provide the proper framework and attitudes necessary to implement any productivity program and include the specific factors that will *excite the achievement motive into emergence, nourish it into a higher level of prominence and utilize it in the solution of productivity problems.* The steps are:

1. Establish a highly principled goal.
2. Set specific performance improvement guidelines.
3. Solicit participation by those who must make the improvements in setting those guidelines.
4. Build moderate risks into the guidelines.
5. Prepare a schedule of times or dates to appeal for performance improvement.
6. Establish small-step improvement targets.
7. Present immediate candid feedback on the degree of target accomplishment.
8. Provide some form of reward as progress is made and a larger reward when the productivity goal is reached.

Establish a Highly Principled Goal. People respond to higher goals that have moral, ethical or social value. So, in developing the overall improvement goal, develop one that can be justified in terms that will provide value to your subordinates. For example, the goal might be a cost reduction of ten cents a unit that will generate enough business to reschedule the night gang. The goal, obviously, will be stated differently for management records. The concern here is to state the goal in terms that appeal to the men's need for security. They'll feel more secure with all employees called back to work.

Set Specific Performance Improvement Guidelines. Many programs fail because the goals are not specific or there are no specific guidelines to reach the goals. Previously mentioned research found that highly productive groups resulted when supervisors made work easy for their men. One of the things they did to make it easy was to clearly describe exactly how each improvement step was to be accomplished.

Achievement-oriented people are especially responsive to clearly established guidelines. This gives them an understandable way to improve and to achieve more. The guidelines also offer an easy way to determine the progress that is being made. This excites the achievement motive within the worker, and he strives harder to achieve the established goals.

Solicit Participation by Those Who Must Make the Improvements, in Setting Those Guidelines. The importance of gaining participation in setting the guidelines is that participation generates commitment. People who help establish their own goals are more likely to work toward them. Remember your overall goal, however, and make sure the individual's guidelines are congruent with the overall goals. If necessary, simply tell him that the guides must be more stringent in order to achieve your overall goals. He will still feel committed, as he participated as far as was possible under the circumstances.

Build Moderate Risks into the Guidelines. If at all possible, write the guidelines so that your subordinates are free to make minor changes or experiments. Obviously, an experiment or change will have some risk involved. Make it clear to your subordinate that he will not be criticized for minor losses resulting from change or experimentation. The absence of criticism for losing small amounts of productivity will encourage your subordinates or employees to take these small risks. As they begin to feel comfortable taking small risks, they have, in effect, developed an achievement-motivation characteristic. The greater number of achievement-motivation characteristics assumed by the worker or subordinate supervisor, the higher his level of achievement motivation becomes.

Prepare a Schedule of Times or Dates to Appeal for Performance Improvements. One of the most useful aspects of the highly achievement-motivated performer is that he or she responds to appeals for improvement. Again, you can develop this characteristic in the group by scheduling improvement appeals at times when improvements are most likely to occur. Obviously, some of these times would be when improved equipment is introduced, when new skills are taught and when the performers have practiced new systems or skills just long enough to become comfortable with them.

By scheduling appeals to coincide with times when the potential for improvement is highest, you make improvement easy for the performer, and the performer is gratified with his success. The success, of course, reinforces the response to the appeal. The performer (worker or supervisor) internalizes another characteristic of achievement motivation.

Establish Small-Step Improvement Targets. People who are highly achievement motivated limit their failures by progressing in very small steps. By achieving one step, becoming comfortable with it and then advancing an additional step, they progress rapidly and surpass those who attempt to move in larger steps.

A side benefit of this characteristic is that it is a safe way to get improvements from those who are not achievement motivated and are afraid of change. Those who are afraid to change, to try more difficult assignments or to work at a faster rate can be helped to improve by moving them in very small steps that they feel comfortable with.

The small-step approach is ideally suited for both individual and group work. Since small steps are usually acceptable to everyone, it can be used with a large group to increase productivity and establish this as another characteristic in the "family" that makes up achievement motivation.

Present Immediate Candid Feedback on the Degree of Target Accomplishment. From reinforcement theory we know that feedback must be immediate to be effective. McClelland also found that people who are highly achievement motivated like this feedback to be candid and precise. In order to improve, they need to know precisely how well or how poorly they are doing.

By getting feedback of a candid and precise nature, they know the specific areas that need to be improved and the specific areas that should be strengthened. So, again, you can encourage the development of this characteristic in all your subordinates. Provide the feedback to your subordinates and then follow up to see that they make an effort to improve. Eventually, this characteristic will be internalized as it becomes habitual performance.

Provide Some Form of Reward as Progress is Made and a Larger Reward When the Productivity Goal is Reached. Experiments in behavior modification have demonstrated that rewards for small improvements, or even rewards for close approximations to the desired improvement will result in the performer learning the improvement and continuing to perform at the higher level. In addition to the rewards for the small progressive steps, a larger reward should be given when the major productivity goal is reached. The rewards may be in the form of some type of recognition or they may be monetary. In each situation, determine rewards that are appropriate, but not overdone, for the progress made.

Motivating Older Employees with Achievement-Related Goals

Older workers often slow down as a result of boredom with their work. They can be encouraged to regain their former levels of productivity by giving them new achievement-related goals. These goals must be more than just a speed-up in routine duties. There must be some way in which the older worker can receive recognition for his often overdeveloped skills. One way to do this is to give longevity rewards and rewards for exceptional quality work.

Awakening the older workers' interest by giving special awards must be followed up by giving them an assignment that permits them to demonstrate their skill. This might be a special project, or it might be an assignment for the older worker to train a new worker. Anything that will demonstrate respect and recognition for the older worker will help generate his desire to uphold his reputation, and he will become more productive.

How a Personnel Manager Got an Older Employee to Improve Her Performance

Miss Wilson was an older employee who had been with the company 27 years. Over the last two years, she had become progressively slower. Her files were not organized and her reports were never in on time. Sid Watson, the personnel manager, called Miss Wilson in, discussed her problem with the work and invited her to join him in establishing some improvement goals.

When Miss Wilson saw that Sid meant business and that she had no choice but to improve her performance, she helped establish the new improvement guidelines. They set dates and a schedule for review and discussed how Miss Wilson might make improvement experiments on her own. Although Miss Wilson was defensive during the meeting, she took the new goals seriously on the job and began making progress very soon.

Sid watched Miss Wilson very closely at first, and complimented her regularly on her steady progress. Within a few weeks, Miss Wilson's performance was up to her old standards. At that point, Sid called her in and told her he was very satisfied with her performance and was going to give her a special assignment that would gain her the credit she deserved for the skills and effort she put forth.

By appealing to an older worker's desire for recognition, Sid rekindled the need to be competent. Miss Wilson was soon taking pride in the quality of her work and became especially proud of completing her special assignments ahead of schedule. She earned, and was given, a salary increase which reinforced her newfound desire to be a productive worker.

Most older workers can be remotivated to do the same or better quality work than they did when younger. But they need recognition and challenging work, just as young people do. The usual work for them, however, is routine because they have developed such a high level of skill. It often takes a special project to reintroduce challenge into their jobs. Then they will again become productive.

THE NEW WAY TO BREAK THROUGH ACHIEVEMENT BARRIERS

Every work group, sooner or later, reaches a plateau which becomes a barrier to further achievement. Many organizations introduce special training programs, incentives and contests to motivate the group to break through the barriers. All of these are valuable techniques and can result in the breakthrough. One motivator is especially useful, when tied into these techniques, in motivating the group to continue at the higher "breakthrough" level. I call this motivator the productivity support-facilitator.

The Productivity Support-Facilitator

The productivity support-facilitator is a simple feedback system that keeps the work group constantly aware of how they are doing in relation to a specific goal. This can be done by using a chart in which two chart lines are used. Line "A" represents the goal and line "B" represents the actual work level. Line "A" is laid out over a month's period. Each day, line "B" is plotted to show exactly what the group accomplished that day. The work group can see exactly how close they are to the goal at any time by looking at the chart.

By checking their progress each day the group can see the small improvements they are making and this feedback supports their efforts. It proves that the extra effort or trying the new skill paid off. The chart becomes a reward in itself. In effect, each time a member of the work group looks at the chart, the chart says, "You're doing better" or "You've dropped off a little."

This constant reminder for all to see keeps the group on the track. It's an encouragement to try harder and a reward for achieving success. Especially for achievement-oriented people, it provides the candid feedback they need to improve their performance.

Many breakthroughs have already been made using this system in industry. The productivity support-facilitator has been found to be effective even without new training, incentives or contests. Used alone, it has been responsible for productivity increases. By using it in conjunction with training programs, incentives and contests, it can get outstanding results.

How to Develop Superior Team Performance

Another way to increase a work group's productivity, is to set a superordinate goal. Research has shown time and time again that teams do better if they shoot for a higher than usual level of productivity. If, for example, you normally run a contest or a work improvement project and shoot for a 10 percent increase in productivity, set a higher one. You might shoot for a 20 or 25 percent increase. The important point is that everyone knows that they have to do much better than they normally do.

Once they start performing, give them immediate feedback and point out how much farther they have to go. Ask them what help they need on a continual basis, and continually ask for improvement ideas. For the term of the project or contest, keep the team aware that new ideas are needed and that you welcome them.

Finally, encourage cooperation. Competition between outside groups may be motivational but competition within a group is debilitating. When cooperation occurs, reward it, and point out the benefit that resulted from the cooperation.

How an Inter-Divisional Contest Was Used to Set New Performance Records

Bill Diegin, the sales supervisor for the eastern division of a California printing firm, was a capable natural leader. Bill held an M.B.A. from a well-known university, was intelligent and a good worker. Bill seemed to have far more potential than he used. Although he got the job done, Bill never had outstanding results. He seemed to be content to let things drift along.

Tom, the general sales manager, decided to try a sales contest to appeal to Bill's achievement motivation, or, as Tom said, "to find out once and for all if this guy has any motivation." Tom established a contest between the four divisions and offered an all-expense paid trip to Hawaii to the winning sales supervisor and four salesmen. Tom knew Bill was anxious to go to Hawaii and hoped this motivation would bring out Bill's real potential.

Bill did respond to the Hawaii offer and began to put out additional effort to win the contest. Tom began an immediate feedback program to let Bill see how he was doing. He also brought to Bill's attention the fun involved in doing a better job, the feelings of self-satisfaction that resulted from a job well done. Tom pointed out the admiration and respect that Bill's men began to show him. Tom slowly laid a foundation for Bill to take pride in working toward his potential.

Tom developed a feedback chart and charted out a goal for Bill to shoot at. He gave the chart to Bill and suggested that Bill record his own progress on the chart each day. Bill recorded his division's results each day, and Tom made a point of commenting on those results each day. Tom never related to the contest, although he knew that was Bill's motivation. Tom related only to the goal on the chart and how Bill was doing in relation to the goal.

Tom's plan was to excite Bill's achievement motivation so that Bill would continue to work towards his potential after the contest was over. Tom's plan worked. As Bill began to experience the pleasurable feelings that come with competence, growth, improvement and achievement of goals that once seemed far away, he developed more productive work habits. He slowly developed the achievement-related characteristics that helped him win the contest, and he became a more professional supervisor.

HOW TO DEVELOP CREATIVITY
TO REACH DIFFICULT GOALS

You can tap the hidden creativity of your subordinates and develop creative solutions to your most difficult problems. By establishing the solution you want as a goal to be achieved and then employing your subordinates in a group exercise to develop creative ways to achieve the goal, you can develop new creative ways to achieve your most difficult goals. First, you must establish a framework of positive thinking and then apply creative problem-solving techniques.

How Positive Thinking Promotes Creativity

Thinking positive will not get you anything you don't work for. And even if you do work for it, if you don't have the skills or the ability to do what you want, you still won't get it. Positive thinking doesn't get things for you. What positive thinking does is permit you to ignore the negative things that might interfere with your progress, so that you can work consciously on only those positive things that may lead to success.

This is the way positive thinking works in creativity. You establish a framework that requires each group member to treat each statement or idea as positive. No one is allowed to criticize any statement that is made. This way, a negative remark that might stifle a group member's creativity is not allowed in the conversation.

In this positive framework, positive thinking pays off. Everyone is encouraged to try new ideas on the group without fear of ridicule. Each group member builds on the idea of the previous speaker without criticizing any part of what was previously said. The previous speaker may later add another building block by adding to some part of what the new speaker says.

Within each speaker's comments there are elements that are new, old, good, bad, relevant or irrelevant. Succeeding speakers simply tie into the new, good or relevant elements of the previous speaker's comments. These positive elements, theoretically, will evoke new or more relevant comments as each new speaker's ideas are triggered by the comments of previous speakers. This process leads to creative solutions of the problems being discussed.

How to Get Creative Solutions From Your Subordinates

Creativity evolves in an atmosphere of friendliness, courtesy, understanding, permissiveness and challenge. A creative challenge obviously calls for a more creative solution. It is your job as a manager to make the challenge and then provide the creative atmosphere that is conducive to creative solutions. The following eight points, synthesized from various research findings, will help you get more creative solutions from your subordinates.

1. Establish a clearly defined challenging goal.
2. Provide a positive framework.
3. Instill a high-level success expectation.
4. Encourage idea clarification.
5. Pursue a thorough evaluation of irrelevant ideas.
6. Ask for various alternatives.
7. Provide a break time.
8. Ask for solutions.

Establish a Clearly Defined Challenging Goal. To bring out creativity, a goal must be challenging. It should be something new, something never done before or something that current techniques won't accomplish without some alteration. In addition to being challenging, the goal must be clearly defined. A clearly defined goal is one that is stated in specific terms, with enough detail to permit a picture to be formed in the individual's mind that will guide him to the correct solution. By stating the goal in picture-clear detail, you keep the group from getting off the track and misdirecting their efforts at the wrong goal.

Provide a Positive Framework. As mentioned earlier, creativity evolves from a combination of positive elements. As one positive element is synthesized with another, a new idea is triggered and, eventually, a creative solution evolves. Your job is to prevent negative remarks from stifling other people's ideas and blocking the creative process.

Dr. Carl Rogers (1961) developed a system to overcome these "blockages" and keep the discussion on a creative track. Dr. Rogers had group members restate the previous speaker's remark or idea before stating their own. As a matter of fact, to clarify understanding, the second speaker was required to get a release from the first speaker, before making his own statement. The first speaker only released the second speaker when the second speaker had a clear understanding of what the first was trying to say. In addition to creating a lot of laughs, this system promotes thorough understanding.

Instill a High-Level Success Expectation. When people hold a high expectation of succeeding, they work harder, accomplish more and are more creative. Research has shown that this holds true even when there is no reason on which to base the expectation. The best way to develop this expectation is to express it verbally. People tend to assume the expectations of their peer groups and superiors.

Recent research has shown that people tend to perform much beyond their general level of productivity when their bosses express a higher level of expectation. Within reasonable limits, the higher the expectation level of the boss, the higher the performance of the subordinate.

Encourage Idea Clarification. Misunderstanding is so common that it is best to stress idea clarification. Encourage members of the group to ask questions after they express an idea to make sure it's clear. It is always best to have someone else summarize the idea so that the speaker can determine whether or not his idea has really been understood.

Pursue a Thorough Evaluation of Irrelevant Ideas. Most often, creativity evolves from an irrelevant idea. When initially expressed, these irrelevant ideas are usually blocked out by other members of the group. In one experiment, psychologists disguised a creative solution to a problem in irrelevant statements. The irrelevant statements were presented by a group member who continually "horsed around" and often irritated the other members of the group.

Although the creative solution was presented thirty-four times in a two-hour session by the unpopular group member, the other members of the group failed to notice the connection. They effectively closed their minds to anything the unpopular member said. Only when the psychologists restated the message did the group members see the connection.

Obviously, a person's popularity should have no effect on how ideas are evaluated. To foster creativity, encourage a thorough evaluation of all ideas no matter how irrelevant they seem.

Ask for Various Alternatives. One element of creativity is the synthesis of various ideas into one idea that surpasses the ideas from which it evolved. By asking your subordinates to develop various alternatives you encourage the development of alternatives that can be synthesized into a more creative idea. As the group develops the alternatives, they will hopefully weigh them against each other and, in the process, see the more creative solution. If not, they can be directed to do so later.

Provide a Break Time. The latest research into problem-solving has unearthed some interesting approaches to creativity. A break time has been proven most productive in reaching a creative solution after a concentrated discussion period. Researchers found that the most productive creative results occurred when a group worked on a problem from two to four hours and was then dismissed with instructions for each group member to return to their regular duties for an hour and, thereafter, to write out their individual ideas on how to solve the problems.

This system has been very productive, but other systems have been found productive by other researchers. One system keeps the group in session but provides a diversion at break time. During the break time, an irrelevant topic is discussed with care taken not to tie into the problem subject. After the diversionary break, correlations are drawn between the problem subject and the diversionary topic. Insights usually occur from this activity that provide creative solutions to the problem.

Ask for Solutions. Whether solutions are solicited on an individual or a group basis, they should be asked for. Often, group members have solutions partly formulated and need the direction of being required to speak to crystallize their ideas. The request for a solution also directs the members' attention to the various alternatives and encourages them to evaluate the various alternatives in relation to their objective. This process often results in a number of creative solutions to the problem.

A Quarterly Meeting That Keeps a Midwest Manufacturing Company Ahead of Competition

Tim Anderson, president of a midwestern manufacturing company, was faced with inflationary cost increases, drops in productivity and a lackluster approach to problem-solving. Tim believed a new creative approach was needed in order to avoid eventual bankruptcy.

Tim formulated a problem-solving group drawn from his top executives. His first goal was to reduce costs to the previous year's level. He instructed the group in creative problem-solving approaches and scheduled weekly meetings. At first, the group was unwieldly and spent more time criticizing each other and talking about things out of their control than they spent working on the problem.

Slowly, however, the group began to jell. Tim developed a positive framework and encouraged exploration of the wildest idea. One person came up with a new processing system, another with a method of sharpening cutting tools automatically as they were used, a new distribution system was developed and a new inventory control system was designed.

This early success gave Tim something to relate to. In future months, he stressed the value of the early accomplishments and made it clear that he expected even more success in the future. Tim scheduled these meetings every three months. In the interim, each member was assigned specific areas to investigate for further possible productivity gains.

Tim attended all the quarterly meetings but did not dominate them. He played the role of a referee. He kept the team members on the track and followed the eight steps previously listed to evoke creativity from his subordinates.

By the end of the first year, productivity had increased by 14 percent, more than twice the rate of inflation. For the first time in a number of years, prices were not increased. New orders began to come in, which resulted in an even more profitable position. This company continues to follow this plan and has reduced costs in two out of the last three years. They are determined to reduce costs further in the future.

◆14◆

How to Use
the New Approach
to Develop
a High-Performance Team

PROBLEM/SOLUTION INDEX

In this chapter, you will find new solutions to the following managerial problems:

◆The old system of calling in all your subordinates and saying, "Here is what I want done, now go out and do it," left a lot of problems for those required to do it. If they just happened to be especially skilled in the problem area and had a thorough understanding of the problem and of the possible consequences of various actions, they got the job done. Most often, however, the understanding and the necessary skills did not exist. The order, obviously, could not be carried out.

This system was replaced, fortunately, by the "human relations" oriented system which eventually went too far the other way. Today, we have many managers spending so much time caring for the human aspects of administration that they fail to firmly establish the goal or job that is to be done.

The new approach to managing people crosses both bridges. Problems and anxieties are explored, information is gathered, understanding is stressed, support and encouragement is provided *and then results are demanded.*

An experiment one company made in two flour mills conclusively demonstrated the advantage of the new approach. One flour mill was staffed with executives who had been specially trained to take a "results-minded" approach. The other mill was staffed with executives who had been thoroughly trained in the human aspects of management, but not in the tougher confrontations and high-productivity techniques that the executives of their sister mill employed.

The results over a two-year period developed into a wide gap between the two mills. Although both mills progressed for about three months at an equal rate, the results-minded mill far outpaced the other mill from the fourth month on. In the fourth month, the mill workers managed by those executives without the results-minded expectations became complacent. The other mill workers continued a gradual improvement over the two-year period.

Obviously, the problem was not that the manager's concern for the human aspects of administration kept the men from progressing. Rather, it provided support for what the men thought management wanted. Since no new goal or higher expectations had been proposed by management, the men believed the productivity level reached in three months was high enough. Consequently, they worked to achieve that goal. There was no reason for them to do more.

DEVELOPING RESULTS-MINDED MANAGERS

A high-performance team must hold an attitude conducive to exceptional results. They must be results minded. High performers see themselves as being an elite group with special skills and they expect to do better than the average team. They work harder, challenge each other and take pride in their outstanding results. To take advantage of these highly motivated efforts, a framework conducive to exceptional results must be available. The following ten-step plan was designed specifically to provide a framework for high-performance results.

A Ten-Step High-Performance Profit Plan

In an analysis of high performers in the organizations I have worked for and in a review of the major research on high and low performance in industry in this country covering the last fifty years, I have found a common set of high-performance determinants. The use of these ten steps, designed to provide a framework conducive to exceptional results, will result in outstanding profits for your organization.

1. Set super goals for the organization.
2. Determine the accounts that are the most likely sales targets for the expanded production.

3. Assign people who are most qualified to initiate the high performance program.

4. Determine which people are best qualified to take over and follow up after the initial thrust.

5. Develop a list of products for promotion that offers the best chance of success and the least chance of failure.

6. Specify any training that may be needed to sustain the program.

7. Set up a training schedule to qualify the follow-up people as soon as possible.

8. Establish a time-oriented action plan to achieve the super goal.

9. Identify behavioral weaknesses that may interfere with the plan and tie them into individual objectives.

10. Assign a three-man group to expedite the program.

Set Super Goals for the Organization. To develop high performance, you must establish very high goals, super goals. These goals should be enhanced by colorful descriptive words. For example, you might set a goal of "Double the Budget." "Double the Budget" becomes the rallying call that acts as a reminder and stimulator. Everyone wants to be a member of an elite group, and a group that intends to double its budget would certainly be elite. Everyone will put forth extra effort to achieve the super goal and at the same time win membership in an elite group.

The super goal will be more effective as a motivational framework if it is tied into a strong moral or logical argument. The argument that productivity increases will protect jobs and expand the business should add logic to the goal. If costs can be reduced to a point that prices can also be reduced, you have moral persuasion also.

Determine the Accounts That Are the Most Likely Sales Targets for the Expanded Production. In every business, there are large volume accounts that can and will respond rapidly to a good offer. In the retail business, for example, many accounts schedule their sales promotions as far as six weeks to six months ahead, depending upon the industry and the lead time required to get merchandise. Most of these accounts, once they set their schedule, refuse to change it even for a good deal.

There are a few accounts, however, that will change their scheduled promotions if a better deal comes along. These are the accounts you need to identify in advance. Once they have been identified, check with them to see if they are susceptible to a special deal on your particular product. The information gained from them will help you determine which products will provide the highest possibility of success.

Assign People Who Are Most Qualified to Initiate the High-Performance Program. The people most likely to get a high-performance program going are people who are themselves high performers. These are achievement-oriented people, people who take pleasure in achievement. The people who have consistently turned in good results in the past will continue to do so in the future. People who seem to get the job done, no matter how much work is piled on, are most likely to get the program off the ground. Give the assignment to them.

Determine Which People Are Best Qualified to Take Over and Follow Up After the Initial Thrust. People who have a good reputation for handling details are best for the day-to-day routines and follow-up production schedules. These people may be less aggressive in initiating a program (this is not always so), but once the program is in operation, they will keep it going. People who have done neat and orderly work, and especially those who always have their work done on time, without strain or stress, are best for follow-up assignments.

Develop a List of Products for Promotion That Offers the Best Chance of Success and the Least Chance of Failure. In selecting the products that are most likely to be successful, care should also be taken that the chance of failure is not high. In the fashion world, for example, a new creation may be an outstanding success, or it may be a complete failure. This risk is too great when trying to develop a high-profit plan. To insure success, choose those products that have been successful when promoted, without even occasional failure.

Specify Any Training That May Be Needed to Sustain the Program. Training may be needed by production, management, marketing, distribution and sales people to support the higher level of activity. Unless each of these groups is aware of the additional activity required to support the high-performance plan, they will continue to operate at the old activity levels. Each of these groups should be presented with the new requirements and should have their activities analyzed to determine what, if any, training is required to support the high-profit plan. Training should be implemented immediately where needed.

Set Up a Training Schedule to Qualify the Follow-Up People as Soon as Possible. A training schedule should be set up that gives priority to normal problem areas. If you normally have problems in production, they will intensify during the increased production program. If your sales program is weak, it will buckle under the strain of the high-performance profit plan.

Wherever the weaknesses exist, set up a training program to overcome them. Training must start early and continue throughout the improvement program. The major problems will be obvious, and training can be planned in advance to overcome them, but unexpected problems will develop as the production levels increase. These problems must be watched to determine if further training is required or if normal problem-solving methods are required.

Establish a Time-Oriented Action Plan to Achieve the Super Goal. An action plan must be established that covers all details of achieving the super goal. The plan should be time oriented in terms of individual phases of the plan as well as a date to have the plan 100 percent operational. Some phases of the program may take longer to get started or longer to build up to a high-performance level. These phases should be started earlier than the others, so that all phases of the program can be coordinated to achieve the operational goals at the same time.

A list of the various elements that must be coordinated in the total program should be developed. Another list of people or departments that will be needed to support or implement each phase of the program should also be developed. These lists can then be used to develop a diagram illustrating what is to be done by whom each step of the way and by what date. You should set up a calendar of events by listing the months across the top of a page of paper and listing the people or departments down the left margin. Enter the activities that each department or person is to perform under the appropriate month. The following simplified calendar will serve the point.

ACTION PLAN

	JAN.	FEB.	MARCH
Engineering	New Designs		Check Opns.
Operations		Install Machinery	Check Start-up
Manufacturing			Start-Up
Marketing	Research Market	Devise Plan	Begin Advertising
Legal	Check Constraints		Legal Review
Accounting	Establish System	Analyze Costs	Profit Projection
Sales	Dev. Sales Plan	Train Salesmen	Start Sell

Identify Behavioral Weaknesses That May Interfere with the Plan and Tie Them into Individual Objectives. Many of the problems that delay a program result from personality problems or behavior by one individual that is irritating to another. Generally, the quarrelsome or argumentative individual is known. Therefore, this problem can be resolved by establishing written objectives for everyone and should include the behavioral problems in the objectives.

The quarrelsome individual may be given an objective that requires him to keep warm friendly relations going between his department and other departments. If he is generally argumentative with one specific person or department, emphasize the necessity for him to keep good relations with that particular person or department. You should follow up very early on behavioral problems by calling the individual in and asking for a progress report. Remind him that his objective is to develop warm friendly relations, not to bring in reasons for failure.

Assign a Three-Man Group to Expedite the Program. Three people of calm resolve, people who are achievement oriented but who are understanding and empathetic to the problems of others should be assigned to this job. They should be given time to meet alone, away from the job or on the job in a location free from disturbance. In a quiet environment, they can reflect on the purpose of the program and discuss ideas that will expedite it.

I have found that three people are best for a group intended to solve problems and expedite a program. Two people often lock in disagreement, while a third can stimulate a solution or move the group to a new area of discussion. Four or more people become too burdensome a group, and too many extraneous topics will emerge that deter the group from its purpose.

This group of expediters should be required to prepare and present weekly progress reports. When the project falls behind, it is their job to develop and implement plans to get the program back on the original schedule.

A Marketing Manager's Success with the Ten-Step
High-Performance Profit Plan

Ed Chambers, the National Marketing Manager for Bright Leaf Processors Inc. (BLI), had been asked to develop a product marketing plan to accommodate a 25 percent increase in production. BLI, a well-established vegetable processor and canner, wanted to expand into the canned fruit market. Start-up expenses were very high, competition was aggressive and the president of the company wanted a well-developed plan to insure the sale of the production.

The operations vice-president projected 30,000 cases per month of the new canned fruit could be produced at a production cost that would be about 10 percent lower than the cost of producing vegetables. Although some fruit which required "pitting" incurred more direct expense, the fixed overhead charged against the new fruit-canning lines was considerably lower than the charges being assessed against the vegetable line. All production estimates were based on straight-time cost projections.

Ed analyzed the data and found that production costs were about 15 percent lower than competition. If production could be increased to 40,000 cases per month, costs would be 25 percent lower than competition. Ed decided to set a super goal for the organization, produce the 40,000 cases per month and use the cost advantages to fight competition. He decided to use 20 of the 25 percent cost reductions to fund the marketing program.

Ed decided to use 10 percent of the cost savings as a trade discount and 10 percent in other promotional activities. He dubbed the program "The 10 Percent Solution." This descriptive phrase caught the imagination of the sales force and generated enthusiasm throughout the organization. The new investment was publicized as an expression of management's commitment to increasing production and jobs in the local area.

Next, Ed had a survey done by market research to determine what large accounts would be the most likely targets for the new production. Large volume buyers and promoters were identified and scheduled for sales calls. Two buyers who were not in the local sales area were identified as possible prospects for surplus production if the local area could not absorb all the production.

The most highly successful salesmen were selected to carry out the assignment. Those salesmen who had successfully introduced new products in the past were selected to sell the top volume accounts in the area. These high performers were then to help train the regular salesmen to follow up after the initial sale had been made.

Ed selected two products for special emphasis. Canned peaches and canned pears were both popular items with consumers in the area and Ed wanted to tie into these preferences. He believed that the fact that people liked peaches and pears would result in an early identification with BLI as a fruit supplier if the two were promoted together.

Next, Ed established a list of training needs to sustain the program. The men had to be trained to operate the new machinery, production scheduling had to be arranged to provide alternate service during machine breakdowns and the marketing and distribution personnel would need information on quality, sizes, quantities and availability lead-time requirements.

The training program was established as an on-going program to train, inform and solve problems throughout the first year of production.

Ed established a time-oriented action plan to insure that sales and production were coordinated. The plan revealed an early problem that resulted in rescheduling a sale for which the product would not have been ready. Overtime had to be scheduled to get the production necessary to reach the 40,000 case per month goal by the end of three months after the machines were installed.

Only one personality problem existed, that of a foreman who thought he knew too much to listen to directions. A production order form was developed for work given to this foreman. His objectives were rewritten and he was required to use the production order as a check-off. He was required to turn the form in with the production checked off on the form each day. When the form was not complete, he was sent back and asked to work until the required production was reached.

Finally, Ed selected a three-man group to expedite the program. Ed's assistant, the controller and the plant superintendent were selected as the expeditors for the program. Early in the program, the controller found an error in the original proposal. The cost reduction would be 15 percent, not 25 percent as initially estimated. Problem-solving meetings were established and new techniques were worked out that recovered part of the cost savings. By using less space and more overtime, the savings were increased to 20 percent, which was enough to fund the marketing program.

The expediters kept records, investigated snags that occurred, prepared weekly reports and conducted problem-solving meetings in order to keep production on schedule. Many unforeseen difficulties occurred but the expediters kept them under control and resolved them as they occurred. The plan worked and 90 percent of the plant's production was being sold within the planned three-month introductory period.

DEVELOPING RESULTS-MINDED PERFORMERS

There are three different situations that provide an opportunity to develop results-minded performers. Each of these situations requires a slightly different approach to achieve the same result. The first situation is related to a new employee and the techniques that establish his identification with the organization in a results-oriented way. The second situation is one in which a new program or a new business phase is begun, in which the current employees who are performing satisfactorily are given higher goals. The third situation is one in which people are operating at substandard levels. Each of the three will be discussed separately.

Establishing Results-Minded Images for New Employees

Generally, new employees are like five-year-old children entering kindergarten. They are moving into a completely new world. They don't know what to do, what to say, how to act or what to expect. They are very susceptible to any attitude or action they are exposed to. They determine by the attitudes they encounter whether they are expected to coast, work at a leisurely pace or be high producers.

I know one manager who always interviews a new employee on the employee's first day of work with the company. This manager opens by saying, "We want results here. We want everyone to be a results-minded high-performance employee. You may get the impression during your first few days that there isn't much to do. That's only because we want you to become well acquainted with our organization. You will move slowly until you have mastered your job. So don't be fooled by the slow pace. We're high performers and we want results."

This manager sets the stage. If the new employee encounters any contrary attitudes, he'll know them to be of an individual nature and not what is expected by management.

The new employee will imitate the behavior of his boss and peers. Just as a little child imitates his parents, siblings, teachers and other children to develop a self-image, the new employee imitates his boss and co-workers to develop an employee-image.

The new employee, naturally, is not competent when he begins his job. He is motivated to become competent, however, and will attempt to become competent through imitation. He should be assigned to work with the most productive results-minded employees during his first six months. As he assimilates their attitudes and work habits, he will develop the same results-minded orientation that they have.

Using New Programs to Develop a More Results-Minded Attitude of Employees Who Perform Satisfactorily

Employees who are performing at a satisfactory level, but who could perform at higher levels need a reason to do so. They need a higher goal or important reason to change. One way to do this is to establish a new productivity improvement program. Explain the need for and the rewards of achieving the new levels of production and begin the program.

Feedback must be provided so the employees can see the new levels they are achieving. A large wall chart or graph would be very useful for this purpose. Once they see that the new higher standards can be met, they will become comfortable with them and a new, more results-minded attitude will develop.

Motivational Techniques That Develop Results-Minded Performance from Substandard Performers

Motivation results from tension. If we are hungry, we begin to feel tense and this tenseness soon brings our hunger into our awareness and motivates us to find food. If we are left alone without people, the same thing happens. We soon become tense and are motivated to find people. Often, these motivations do not come into our awareness. We are simply motivated at a subconscious level to take actions to relieve the discomfort caused by the tension.

Substandard performers can be developed into more results-minded employees by creating some tension for them. By creating some mild discomfort, you evoke their own internal motivational drives to eliminate the discomfort. One way to do this is to use comparison charts. Let the substandard workers see the improvements being made by other workers compared to their own continued low level.

The fact that others do better may not bother them, but the fact that everyone else is increasing, while they are staying at the same rate, will create a mild discomfort. Change is discomforting, and they are in the midst of change. This or any discomfort that you introduce, will soon have them increasing their own productivity.

Once they begin to improve, support their efforts. Compliment, encourage and provide feedback. They can make more progress than others because they have farther to go. Help them, train them or provide any support they need. Once they feel the pleasure of becoming high performers, they will begin to become more results minded about all their work and will continue to perform at the new higher levels.

How Tom Baker Set a Pricing Trend
That Improved Profits for the Whole Division

Tom Baker was a well-liked, results-oriented, distribution center manager. He was friendly with his subordinates, empathetic to their problems and concerned with their results. Tom had recently lost two major product lines that had previously contributed significantly to his results. The current period's results were in and Tom's division had incurred a loss for the first time.

Tom called his people together and explained the situation. The loss of the two product lines had resulted in a net loss in the entire division. Tom wanted to reduce costs, so that a lower price could be charged to gain the additional business needed to put them back in a profitable position.

Tom developed a list of target accounts and began selling at the new price. Soon, he had replaced the lost volume with new orders and new business continued to come in. The extra volume caused a cost reduction and the employees became excited about the productivity increases they were making.

Tom's success resulted in a request from the division manager for a plan the whole division could use. Tom used the figures for his various production levels and established percentages for costs and volumes that could be expected with the program. He then developed the following four-step plan to build new sales volume.

Volume-Building Sales Plan

1. Establish unit costs for current production levels.
2. Determine unit costs for a 20 percent production increase.
3. Sell large-volume orders to select outlets based on the lower unit costs.
4. Establish a new price list based on the new lower costs when the new volume levels are firmly entrenched.

You can use the "Volume-Building Sales Plan" in your own organization if your product's sales respond to price changes. If you can reduce costs by increasing volume and a price reduction will increase your sales, this system will work. You might want to test it with a sales promotion rather than a general price reduction to see what the results would be.

◆15◆

The New
Behavioral Approach
to Deal with
Employee Grievances

◆The old approach to dealing with employee grievances was to try to get the employee to forget it or at least shut up about it. The foreman would argue, cajole or threaten the employee. If that didn't work, he would try to smooth things over by treating the grievance as something that only happens occasionally. This approach led to long drawn-out negotiations with union representatives or sometimes strikes.

A new approach to dealing with grievances grew out of unnecessary strikes. Strikes that neither the unions nor the businesses wanted. The new system is a step-by-step procedure, beginning with the foreman. The foreman tries to resolve the grievance to the satisfaction of both the employee and the company. If the foreman can settle the grievance at the first step, a lot of money and time is saved.

Recent psychological research has shown that the approach used in dealing with a grievance is more important than the grievance itself. The way the employee is treated has a greater impact on how the grievance is settled than the conditions of the settlement.

This research found that approximately 50 percent of all grievances could be eliminated simply by using an empathetic, rather than a hostile, approach when discussing the grievance with the employee.

HOW TO ELIMINATE 50 PERCENT OF ALL GRIEVANCES

By listening carefully to the employee's grievance, by trying to understand his point of view, by being empathetic, by trying to see just how much of a problem the grievance causes the employee, you can eliminate it. Often, an employee just wants someone to listen. Once he gets the complaint off his chest to a sympathetic "ear," he is satisfied and will drop the grievance. He will most likely carry the grievance forward only if the foreman argues with him.

How to Deal with Minor Grievances

Of the 50 percent of grievances that cannot be resolved by listening and showing empathy, most can be resolved with minor concessions. One employee who complained that a foreman had performed a task prohibited by the union contract agreed to settle the grievance for five minutes off the job to compensate for the time the foreman had worked. In another similar situation, the employee who complained, when asked what concession he wanted in return for the work offense, replied, "nothing." He just wanted it known that he had seen a violation.

By researching the interactions between foremen and workers who initiated a grievance, a system has been worked out to stop grievances, in most cases, before they go beyond the first or second step. This approach is intended to cultivate good relations with the employees. It assumes an attitude of trust and cooperation on the part of management which, in return, should lead to trust and cooperation on the part of the employees.

Be Cheerful and Courteous. An atmosphere of friendliness is crucial in dealing with a grievance. If the employee gets an initial feeling of antagonism, he will begin to fight rather than explain his point of view. Once an argument starts, it's too late for logic. An argument can be avoided, however, by using words like "thanks," "I see," "I understand" and "please." Simple courtesy will create a friendly climate, conducive to the friendly settlement of the grievance.

Show Concern for the Employee. Let the employee see that you really are concerned. Ask questions to determine how important the grievance is. Find out how much of a problem it caused the employee. Once you understand how much trouble or injury the employee suffered, you will better understand the importance he places on the grievance. You are then in a better position to determine what concession is reasonable under the circumstances.

Express Regret for the Problems the Employee Suffered. Let the employee know that you regret any hardship he has suffered. Tell him that, under the circumstances, you understand his feelings. Summarize what he has told you to make sure you clearly understand what happened and how important it is to him. After the summary, ask him if you have expressed it correctly.

Ask What Concessions He Would Like from the Company. Negotiators who are accustomed to the often unrealistic demands of union negotiators are surprised at the small logical demands made by employees. Usually, they ask for less than an appropriate award. In the few cases where they have asked for too much, a realistic suggestion from the foreman has been accepted.

Make the Concession Immediately. Once the employee has agreed to a concession that is reasonable in relation to the grievance, make the concession immediately. If he takes time to talk it over with other people, there is always the chance that a troublemaker will encourage him to demand a larger concession.

I know of one case, which did not involve the unions, where the employee's initial request was reasonable, but the foreman was ordered not to make the concession, as it was at odds with company policy. The employee went to court and won a much larger award. As a result of the court decision, the company not only incurred large expenses for the court costs, but had to change policy affecting all employees. The first small concession is usually the best one.

How a Minor Grievance Grew into a Major Problem

A recent change from a 22-pound to a 30-pound motor assembly in an electric motor manufacturing plant resulted in a minor grievance. The pack-off man at the end of the assembly line complained that the new motors were too heavy and that he needed to switch back and forth with one of the other workers until his arms built up enough strength to handle the new heavier motors.

The foreman laughed at the complaint and told the worker to just keep plugging away, "Your arms will strengthen without being relieved."

A few hours later the foreman came back, and the whole line had stopped. The shop steward was there and informed the foreman that a formal grievance had been filed and there was a work stoppage in progress until a provision for rest periods was made.

The foreman was surprised. No one had asked him for a rest period. The shop steward informed the foreman that the new motors were too heavy for the pack-off man, and a rest period must be provided. "But the work is no heavier on the rest of the gang," the foreman protested. "Why do they need a rest period?" The shop steward told the foreman, "You can't give just one person a rest period. They all work together so you must give them all a rest period."

This grievance was finally resolved in favor of the union. Fourteen people who didn't need them, were given five-minute rest breaks every hour, to cover one person who did. The employee's original minor grievance would have been a lot simpler to resolve. The employee only asked for a "change-off" with another worker. That simple change would have avoided the expensive rest periods now given to the whole line. By simply rotating the pack-off position between the two men on either side of the end position, no one would have grown overly tired and the minor grievance could have been resolved.

By showing concern for the employee, by expressing regret for any problem the employee suffers and by asking what concession the employee expects, minor problems can be handled inexpensively. An immediate small concession brings good will and higher productivity. Ignoring a legitimate complaint leads to major problems and grievances.

How to Deal with Conflict-Based Grievances

Often, grievances become conflict laden. The employee is angry over some real or imagined injury and presents his case in a very hostile argumentative fashion. In this situation, research has shown that the anger must be dealt with separately. The emotion must be separated from the grievance. First, deal with the emotion, then deal with the grievance. Recent research in the sales situation has shown that the boisterous or argumentative customer can be persuaded, in spite of his outbursts, if he is not argued with.

The same principle applies to an employee, so don't argue. The following six steps were devised to separate the argument from the factual grievance and reach a quick settlement.

A Six-Step Grievance Procedure

This new approach to dealing with grievances is based on Dr. Carl Roger's "Active Listening" approach to helping people clarify their thoughts and ventilate their emotions. Remember to clear the emotion or argument out of the way first and then deal with the content.

1. Separate the Emotion from the Grievance. When the employee expresses emotion or anger in relating his grievance, separate the emotion from the content of the message and deal with just the emotion. For an analogy, you might think of a two-way mirror, you reflect back the emotion but let the content go through. Dr. Carl Rogers (1950) suggests parroting the words of the angry person. If the angry employee remarks, "I'm tired of being cheated," you simply respond, "You feel you are being cheated?"

The employee then concentrates on telling you about being cheated. In the process, he ventilates his anger, works off the emotional head of steam and is ready to talk about the problem in a rational way.

Another approach, taken by Dr. Robert Lefton (1970), is to encourage ventilation by stating to the angry person that you are aware of the anger. If the employee remarks, "I'm tired of being cheated," you respond by saying, "I can see that you are upset." This draws the employee's attention to his anger and again he ventilates by telling you how upset he is. When he has finished ventilating his anger, as before, he is ready to discuss the grievance in a rational way.

2. Determine How Significant the Grievance is. To determine the significance of the grievance, ask the employee how much of a problem it caused him. Ask him to tell you about it in detail. Find out how he suffered, how strongly he feels about it and just how important he thinks it is. Don't disagree with his explanation, just listen. If you argue, he becomes more angry and stubborn. If you listen, he continues to work off his anger.

3. Summarize Your Understanding of the Grievance. Ask the employee to listen to your summary to make sure you understand the grievance. Repeat what he told you factually. Do not relate to the emotions or anger he previously expressed. If he brings up the anger or feelings, just state that, based on the way he felt, you can understand him becoming angry. This doesn't mean you agree, it's just that you understand.

After your summary is complete, ask the employee if your understanding is correct. Clear up any misunderstandings at this point and summarize again to be sure you understand the grievance.

4. Apologize for Any Inconvenience the Employee Has Suffered. Research has shown that when a sincere apology has been made, the employee feels less aggrieved and often drops the grievance. If the grievance isn't dropped, he is usually willing to settle for a much smaller concession. People feel at least partly repaid by the apology.

5. Ask the Employee What Concession He Would Like From the Company. Care should be taken in how this question is asked. You might say, "Do you want the company to do anything?" or, "What do you think the company should do?" Generally, the employee will express the desire to have the condition corrected. Occasionally, they will ask for compensation.

When an employee asks for compensation, a foreman should ask if the employee will settle for a little free time or some other favor. It's best to avoid paying for grievances if possible. You don't want to establish a reputation for paying cash where it isn't necessary. Most people will settle with the foreman on reasonable terms rather than face higher management with a negotiation.

6. Make the Concession Immediately. Once a concession has been made, get it off the books. Give the employee immediate time off or whatever special treatment he has agreed to. If cash compensation is to be awarded, make sure its included with the next payroll check. The faster it's handled, the more quickly it fades from memory. The less it's thought about, the less effect it will have on productivity.

How a New Plant Manager Reduced Grievances at a Troubled Plant

Fred Hindley was resented even before he got to his new assignment as plant manager of a midwestern pharmaceutical plant. The previous manager had not been able to solve the plant problems, and the employees had heard that Fred was a tough manager who was sent in to straighten them out.

One of Fred's foremen explained the situation to Fred on his first day at the plant. Fred responded, "I want to develop good relations here. If someone resents me for something I've done, its my problem. But, if they resent me for something they think, it's their problem, so I'll ignore it.

Fred called all the foremen together and explained his philosophy on grievances. "Settle them on the spot." He gave the foremen the six-step guideline and explained that he was not to be brought in unless an employee specifically requested that he attend. Fred emphasized that the foremen had the authority and were to settle immediately where possible.

Next, Fred called all the employees together and told them that he believed they could work together in a cooperative way. He mentioned the backlog of grievances and said the foremen would begin working on them immediately. The men would be called in one at a time and all grievances would be processed as rapidly as possible.

In a few months, all the grievances had been handled and the plant was operating smoothly. Fred said that he believed "the most significant part of the program was the apologies. When the men deserved and received an apology, they quickly dropped the grievance." Fred had significantly reduced the number of grievances at the end of six months and had practically eliminated them by the end of one year.

HOW TO DISCIPLINE WITHOUT CREATING RESENTMENT

There is always the possibility of some resentment from a person being disciplined. Many people honestly feel there is never a justification for discipline. Some feel discipline is ineffective and offenders should be fired without a second chance. Some feel offenders will correct their own offenses once they are confronted with them.

The only way to keep unacceptable offenses from becoming widespread is to use discipline. If one employee gets away with breaking a rule, other employees will begin to imitate the offender. I know a salesman who used to continually show up late for work. He did his job well, so his boss let him get away with the tardiness.

Slowly, other people began to come in late. Eventually, none of the salespeople came to work on time, and the office workers began to come in late also. At this point, the manager came to his senses. He put out a new set of rules and policies and stated very clearly that any infraction of the rules would result in disciplinary action. After two salesmen were disciplined, the practice stopped.

Clearly State the Offenses That Will Be Disciplined

Punishment, of course, is the least desirable method of changing behavior. The change in behavior resulting from punishment is usually short lived and is often accompanied by undesirable side effects. Some offenses, however, must be punished. Willful destruction of property, negligence that results in damage to property or harm to people, physical violence and theft are offenses that should be punishable.

The rules relating to these offenses should be very clearly stated, and their purpose should be explained. The discipline for each offense should be stated clearly so there will be no argument over the discipline when it is administered. The person breaking the rule knows what discipline to expect and is less likely to resist the administration of the discipline.

Discipline should always be administered in private. It is less likely to evoke an argumentative reaction in a private setting, especially if discipline is administered fairly. If you reduce the discipline for one person, the other employees lose trust in management. Resentment will then be felt when the next employee is disciplined in line with policy guidelines. The most effective policy is to administer discipline equally and fairly in all cases.

How to Deal with an Employee Who Won't Accept Discipline

Occasionally, an employee will refuse to accept the discipline. You may order a day off without pay for example, and the employee will refuse to take the day off. You would prefer to keep the employee, because he is a well-trained worker. But if you back down, all discipline will lose its effectiveness. When an employee refuses to accept discipline, you have no choice but to fire him.

First, you offer him the choice of either accepting the discipline or resigning. Make it clear that discipline for a rule violation is a substitute for discharge. Explain calmly and carefully that, normally, a rule or policy violation requires discharge, but that the disciplinary actions have been worked out to avoid discharging a good employee. If he refuses the discipline, your only other way out is to let him resign.

Firing a person is very difficult for any manager. No one wants to see another person lose his means of livelihood. There is also the possibility of anxiety and depression for the laid-off employee, especially in times when the economy is slow and reemployment is difficult. It is very difficult for most managers to face the prospect of being involved in firing an employee, knowing these adverse effects may occur.

It is easy at this point to shift an employee to another job or to another division rather than fire him. This makes sense when dealing with a person who is not qualified for, or has some problem with, the current job but is capable of doing a different job in another division. But, to transfer a troublesome or disciplinary problem employee to another division is unfair. You merely give the problem to someone else.

When the logical solution to a problem is to fire the employee, it should be done immediately. There is no reason to beat around the bush. Tell the employee very candidly precisely what offense he committed, and, in a very businesslike way, inform him that he is fired. It's a good idea to let the employee know that you've already talked to higher management and that they agree with your decision.

You're not trying to pass the buck to higher management, you take full responsibility for the decision but let the employee know there is no higher appeal. This saves you both a lot of time. As soon as you've told the employee that he is fired, give him all the details that he needs to collect any pay or compensation for benefits that he has coming. Make the collection as easy as possible. It would be best to have the check there for him if possible. Once he's fired, he probably won't want to hang around very long.

Firing, as well as any disciplinary action should be done privately. A man is more likely to accept discipline in a private setting. He may feel that his ego is threatened if he is reprimanded in front of the other employees. He may react argumentatively in front of the other employees to protect his ego but accept the reprimand calmly when it is conducted in private.

How a Strike Over a Disciplined Employee Was Avoided

Mel Stevens, a precision machine operator, has worked for the company for over 20 years and was a valuable well-liked employee. Recently, however, Mel had begun to present a problem to the company. His work quality had dropped, and his productivity had dropped and was continuing to get lower every month.

Bob, the foreman, found the answer. Mel had a bottle hidden at work and had been drinking on the job. Bob took Mel to the general manager and the three of them discussed the problem. Mel discussed his problem openly and promised not to drink on the job again. Mel was given the rest of the day off and reported to work sober the next morning.

Mel's work improved for a few weeks, but then the old problem occurred again. Bob caught Mel drinking again, and this time, Mel was fired. Thirty minutes later, the local union representative called, saying the employees would strike if Mel were not allowed to return to work the next morning.

The settlement was negotiated. Mel was given a week off without pay and allowed to return to work the following week. Part of the settlement provided for a list of rules that were given to the employees along with disciplinary actions that would be taken for violations of the rules. Drinking on the job was covered as an offense that was punishable by a week off without pay for a first offense and discharge from the company for a second offense. Mel, shortly thereafter, was caught drinking on the job again. He was discharged from the company without resistance from the union.

A FINAL NOTE FROM THE AUTHOR

This book was meant to bring the details of a new successful approach to managing people to the awareness of managers who are dissatisfied with their results and their subordinates' productivity. The approaches described in this book do work. They have been tried and found successful over and over again.

This new approach to managing people can work for you. If you use the easy-to-follow "Problem-Solution Indexes" at the beginning of each chapter, you can quickly find an approach for dealing with your current problem.

If you use this new approach, your results will improve, your productivity will increase and your profits will soar.

Suggested Further Readings

Breger, Louis, *From Instinct to Identity. The Development of Personality*. Englewood Cliffs, New Jersey: Prentice-Hall, Inc., 1974.

Donaldson, Les, *How to Use Psychological Leverage to Double the Power of What You Say*. West Nyack, New York: Parker Publishing Co., Inc., 1978.

Feinberg, Mortimer R., Robert Tanofsky and John J. Tarrant. *The New Psychology for Managing People*. Englewood Cliffs, New Jersey: Prentice-Hall, Inc., 1975.

Freud, Sigmund, *Psychopathology of Everyday Life*. Trans. A.A. Brill. New York: The New American Library, Inc., n.d.

Gellerman, Saul, *Motivation and Productivity*. New York: American Management Association, 1963.

Georgopoulas, Basil. S., Gerald M. Mahoney and Nyle W. Jones, Jr. "A Path-Goal Approach to Productivity." *Journal of Applied Psychology*. Vol. 41, 1957.

Hertzberg, Frederick, et. al., *The Motivation to Work*. New York: John Wiley and Sons, Inc., 1959.

Hovland, C., I. Janis and H. Kelley, *Communications and Persuasion*. New Haven, Conn.: Yale University Press, 1961.

Janis, Irving L., *Victims of Groupthink*. Boston: Houghton Mifflin Co., 1972.

Jay, Anthony, *Management and Machiavelli*. New York: Holt, Rinehart and Winston, 1967.

Karrass, Chester L., *The Negotiating Game*. Cleveland, Ohio: The World Publishing Co., 1970.

Katz, Daniel, et. al., *Productivity, Supervision and Morale Among Railroad Workers*. Ann Arbor, Michigan: Survey Research Center, University of Michigan, 1951.

Leavitt, Harold J., *Managerial Psychology*. Chicago: The University of Chicago Press, 1964.

Lefton, R.E., Ph.D., V.R. Buzzotta, Ph.D. and Mannie Sherberg, *Dimensional Management Strategies*. St. Louis: Psychological Associates, Inc., 1970.

Lickert, Rensis, *The Human Organization. Its Management and Value*. New York: McGraw-Hill Book Co., 1967.

Mager, Robert F. and Peter Pipe, *Analyzing Performance Problems*. Belmont, Ca.: Fearon Publishers, 1970.

Maslow, Abraham H., *Motivation and Personality*. New York: Harper and Row Publishers, Inc., 1954.

Mayo, Elton, *The Human Problems of an Industrial Civilization*. New York: The McMillan Co., 1933.

Mayo, Elton, *Social Problems of an Industrial Civilization*. Boston: Harvard Graduate School of Business, 1945.

Miles, Matthew B., *Learning to Work in Groups*. New York: Teachers College Press, 1970.

Minnick, Wayne C., *The Art of Persuasion*. New York: Houghton Mifflin Co., 1968.

Nadler, Leonard, *Developing Human Resources*. Houston: Gulf Publishing Co., 1971.

Nirenberg, Jesse S., Ph.D., *Getting Through to People*. Englewood Cliffs, New Jersey: Prentice-Hall, Inc., 1963.

Porter, Lyman and Edward E. Lawler, *Managerial Attitudes and Performance*. Homewood, Ill.: Irwin Dorsey, 1968.

Roethlisberger, F. J., and William J. Dickson, *Management and the Worker*. Cambridge, Mass.: Harvard University Press, 1946.

Rogers, Carl R., Ph.D., *On Becoming a Person. A Therapist's View of Psychotherapy*. Boston: Houghton Mifflin Co., 1961.

Vroom, Victor H., *Work and Motivation*. New York: John Wiley and Sons, Inc., 1964.

Index

A

B

也許也事不盡如人意，
也許剛好少了一份運氣……

但是，風水總會輪流轉，
總會從落葉蕭瑟到繁華盛開！

對自己好，讓幸福降臨，
這一切，都靠妳自己。

做個好命女

吳淡如

Contents

Contents

Contents

Contents

Contents

Contents

自序

妳是命運路上的好駕駛嗎

——從一個遊戲開始，和自己對話

如果命運是一條車道，我們來玩一個開車的遊戲，請「不假思索」的回答下列問題，如果…

① ▼如果妳有一個家財萬貫的情人，決定送妳一輛車當生日禮物，妳會（已婚的也請回到未婚的時代吧）：

Ⓐ。拒絕。表示自己不是愛他的錢，或不想欠他人情。

B。當下很愉快的接受他的好意，問他是什麼車。

C。半推半就的接受他的好意，日後會想要做等值的回報。

②▼假如妳個人名下有一部車，在不考慮車價因素，妳希望它是：

A。敞篷跑車

B。大型休旅車

C。雙B房車

D。一般平價的房車

③▼如果妳一個人開車上路，忽然車拋錨了，妳第一個電話會打給：（請假設以下四個關係妳都擁有）

A。男友

B。家人

C。某個可能知道如何幫妳解決問題的友人

D。特約拖吊廠

④▼萬一妳隨著一大群車陣紅燈右轉，別人都很順利，卻只有妳被交警攔了下來，妳會：

做個好命女

A。跟警察辯論，為什麼你不抓別人只抓我？

B。跟警察道歉，乖乖受罰

C。企圖以撒嬌來免罰

D。沈默以對，覺得自己很倒楣

⑤▼週休二日時，如果妳和男友第一次要開這部車出去玩，妳會希望怎麼玩：

A。兩人一起到人跡罕至的山林間探險

B。兩人一起到知名風景區做一日遊

C。直駛外縣市的五星級飯店度假

D。呼朋引伴，希望有親朋或好友同遊，去哪兒都好

來看解答吧！

①▼家財萬貫的情人，送妳一輛車當生日禮物，妳的選擇代表的意義是：

A。拒絕。表示自己不是愛他的錢，或不想欠他──妳是個受了傳統家教的女孩，

妳的尊嚴重於一切。然而，久而久之，妳很可能讓男人覺得妳並不需要他。妳很難從兩性中得到男人給妳的好處。

B。當下很愉快的接受他的好意——妳向來天真活潑也很討男人歡喜，習於接受男性的幫助，在兩性關係中從來不吃虧。萬萬不要以為自己會有為了愛情不要麵包的一天。

C。接受他的好意，但日後會想要在精神上有等值的回報——在妳的觀念裡，精神和物質的界線是很模糊的，只要男人一對妳好，或曾經對你好，妳就會對他死心塌地。

A。敞篷跑車——妳最愛的是自由，自認為與眾不同，應該擁有不平凡的人生。

B。大型休旅車——妳喜歡所有實用的東西，平常對美食與外表的重視，遠遠超過精神上的成長。

C。雙B房車——妳最愛的東西是面子，永遠跟隨主流社會的價值觀。

D。一般平價的房車——覺得良人是妳人生中最重要的目的。妳認為，如果沒有圓滿的家庭，其他的成功對妳都沒有意義。

③ ▼妳一個人開車上路，車拋錨了，妳第一個打電話的對象，表示妳的獨立性：

A。男友——獨立性五十分。在妳的內心中，妳覺得男人該幫妳解決一切大問題，什麼事妳也都會先找自己的男人商量。妳想要一個能扛起妳的天空的男人，不過，即使妳的男人很有責任感，妳的依賴性也會讓他傷腦筋。非不得已，妳才想要靠自己。

B。家人——獨立性三十分。由於妳在幸福家庭中長大，與家人關係密切，妳心中一直有個沒長大的小孩。妳無法跟任何家人反對的對象交往太久。但因為妳較無主見，在婚姻中常會被家人的意見弄得失去自己，也會讓另一半覺得困擾。

C。某個可能知道如何幫妳解決問題的友人——獨立性七十分。妳擁有良好的人際關係，個性十分的「四海皆兄弟」，很容易在事業上獲得成功。但那也可能是因為家庭從來不能提供妳庇護，而男人也多半讓妳失望。

D。特約拖吊廠——獨立性九十分。妳是個明快果決很有處理困境能力的女人。請多期許自己一些，大才小用就太可惜了。

④▼妳隨著一大群車陣紅燈右轉，別人都很順利，卻只有妳被交警攔了下來，從妳的作法可以看出妳會不會為自己爭取權利：

A。跟警察辯論，為什麼你不抓別人只抓我？──這是很不智的作法，因為雖然外界環境對妳不公平，但妳常常採取莽撞衝動的方式，使自己在不公平的環境中更陷於不利。

B。跟警察道歉，乖乖受罰──其實妳知道這樣做還有機會將損失降到最低，妳是個理智而正直的人，很懂得如何察言觀色、化險為夷。吃虧後妳雖然不太會反擊，但永不忘記前車之鑑。

C。企圖以撒嬌來免罰──妳總是沒忘了利用女性的特質來享受特權。外柔內剛，遇到不公平的環境，也會讓自己的損失降到最低。

D。沈默以對，覺得自己倒楣──當環境不公時，妳逆來順受的能力超強，遇到命運不公時常以自責取代行動力，但可要小心火山爆發哦！

⑤▼週休二日時，妳和男友第一次開車出去玩，妳希望的玩法代表妳對婚姻的期

做個好命女

14

望：

A。兩人一起到人跡罕至的山林間探險——妳對婚姻有憧憬，但只想到要享受兩個人的生活，不想跟任何長輩同住，有沒有小孩無所謂，兩個人能夠互相需要。

B。兩人一起到知名風景區做一日遊——妳渴望婚姻，但想得很簡單，只要能夠找到一個妳可以接受的男人就好，妳對婚姻品質的要求並不特別。

C。直駛某個五星級飯店度假——妳渴望過著舒服的生活，對生活的品質要求很高，如果結了婚後妳過的日子沒有未婚時舒服，妳會很失望。

D。呼朋引伴，希望有親朋或好友同遊，去哪兒都好——妳最不喜歡孤單，可以接受大家庭的熱熱鬧鬧喳喳呼呼，較能適應傳統家庭的結構。妳一進入家庭就會變成「人生以服務為目的」。

※　※　※

以上是「好命女」的趣味暖身操。

《做個好命女》，是一本寫給想要好命的女人的書，寫給覺得自己還有好命可能的女人。

如果命運是一條車道的話，我們都在不一樣的車道上。有的人的道路比較平坦，有的人的道路比較顛簸難行，而每一條道路也不總是一直如此，有時路段平坦到可以讓妳風馳電掣，有時總會遇到馬路施工，有時還有鐵釘埋伏讓妳冷不防爆了胎呢！

雖然剛開始我們駛在不一樣的路面上，但好在：車道不會一直固定在那裡，人生路處處有匝口。有時，妳的一個漂亮選擇會讓妳從石子路開上高速公路。

當然，也有可能是相反的，一個不太美妙的選擇對妳的耽誤遠超乎想像。

開車的人，技術很重要，識路很重要，迷途能知返也很重要。知道我們該在下個路口迴車，該往哪個方向才能到我們要到的地方，是一個好駕駛的必備條件。

《做個好命女》，不能算是一本萬無一失的開車指南，卻是一本人生路、愛情路的開車小偏方。

每個女人都有資格做個好命女！

【寫給妳的第一個故事】
公主整夜不能睡

公主整夜不能睡

一個公主的愛情歷史

　　我寫過的許多愛情故事，都是在不眠
的夜晚裡有了頭緒，因而我分不清失眠是
利是弊。

　　有人因為擔憂人生而失眠，有人因為
趕工而失眠，有人因為失戀而失眠。

　　我都不是。我總是莫名其妙便偶爾失
了眠，也許也許，冥冥之間有個精靈，喚
我起身，別懶別懶，好為它寫個故事。

這個晚上，涼風習習，而我，竟然無法入眠。

無法入眠，依我的經驗，與其待在床上數羊，承受那種近乎坐以待斃的感覺，不如抖擻精神起床。

我決定給自己好日子過。

我好久不知道酒味了吧！從我的珍藏中，摸出一瓶法國大香檳區的頂級XO，金黃色的液體一滴一滴流進白蘭地杯之後，我微微轉動酒杯，大口吸進它濃郁的香氣。

我十分珍貴上等的烈酒，能以口舌感受它的芬郁，且無條件服膺酒徒們的格言：這些佳釀是上天賜予人們最好的享受。

但請放心。我是個有節制的愛酒者。

因我明瞭：再甘美的酒也禁不起貪杯、狂飲、隨時都能喝則與水無異；再好的東西，若眞成了由你吃到飽的自助餐，必然招致味覺的厭煩。

譬如愛情。

☆☆☆☆☆

譬如愛情。

我寫過的許多愛情故事，都在不眠的夜晚裡有了頭緒，因而我分不清失眠是利是弊。

有人因為擔憂人生而失眠，有人因為趕工而失眠，有人因為失戀而失眠。我都不是。我總是莫名其妙便偶爾失了眠，也許也許，冥冥之間有個精靈，喚我起身，別懶別懶，好為它寫個故事。

當我失眠，當我喝著如我個性一樣不溫吞的烈酒，我總會發現自己心臟的某個部位，在恍惚之間柔軟了起來。我像個飢餓的酒徒翻找冰箱、想找到蠶豆酥或牛肉乾下酒解饞般，尋找我的故事。

黑暗中，按開檯燈，攤開稿紙，一個句子像一道閃光般出現，它也找到我。

好好，就寫一個「公主徹夜未眠」的故事好了。黑夜中彷彿有仙女魔棒輕點，我對自己頷首。就是它了。

這六個字很美，但被太多人用過，我不想加入咬文嚼字重複朗誦的行列。

這是一個我在失眠的夜晚寫的……公主整夜不能睡的寓言故事。

☆☆☆☆☆

從前的從前有個公主，她整夜不能睡。從她發現自己不再是個孩子，她便開始失眠。

十六歲生日的時候，她的父王和母后告訴她，就像所有鄰國的公主一樣，她必須找到一個英勇的王子，用愛俘虜他，請他成為她的國王，為她消滅一條有三顆頭和六條帶刺尾巴的千年巨龍。

怎麼用愛俘虜一個王子？公主問。王后嘆口氣沒有回答，看看幾乎忘了怎樣說話的國王。

「我也不知道，我媽也沒有教我，我媽的媽也沒教她任何咒語或法術可以依循。

從前從前我也是個公主，也奉命去尋找一個可以降服千年巨龍的王子，於是我找到妳的父親，一個王子。」

「可是他呀，他說過他愛我，使我以為我已用愛俘虜他，他根本不肯為我去找那條龍。他太懶，不夠強壯，不夠精明，他會說他太忙，或者他沒有出征的心情，就跟我媽和我祖母的丈夫一樣，他們都沒有出征，所以那條巨龍，至少已經活了一千年，或者好幾千年。我們的希望在妳身上，妳要找到一個王子，為我們征服巨龍，為我們爭光，如果妳找不到，我們也可以幫妳找找看。」

為了大家著想，公主決定和其他公主們，一起參加舞會找找看，坐在小板凳上，等王子看見她嬌嫩的臉和華麗的衣裳。

公主很快的找到了舞伴，也找到約會對象。雖然馬甲束腰綁得她喘不過氣來，假睫毛刺得她的眼睛淚汪汪，太小的高跟鞋使她的腳跟和腳尖都遭了殃。

公主是個急性子的女孩，因此她第一個約會對象，就是第一個邀她跳舞的舞伴。聽說王子來自富裕的國家，公主因為太興奮而頭昏，跳了一支舞後馬上答應和他到後花園約會。王子在樹蔭下用力親吻了公主。噢，可憐的公主，她失去初吻的時候，還以為男女第一次見面的國際禮儀就是這個樣子，國王和母后都沒有教她。

王子對公主說：「妳認識我是妳的榮幸，因為我是每個公主夢寐以求的對象。

我的寶庫裡，有一支點石成金的魔棒。我的祖先傳了密咒給我：如果我找到一個真正的公主，魔棒就會開始發揮功能。」

第二次和王子出席舞會，王子指著別的公主對她說：「看，妳應該把腰再束緊一點，還要學她婀娜多姿的樣子，這樣才是個有女人味的公主。真正的公主在跳舞時應該輕得像隻燕子。」公主照做了。如果不是某一天她差點因為呼吸不順暢而休克，她可能會跟某些公主一樣讓自己變成十八腰。

公主看著鏡子裡瘀青的腹部喘了一口氣，對自己說：聽，我不知道愛是什麼，但我不愛那個王子，我見他一次痛苦一次。

再也沒有和王子一起出席舞會的公主，決定到不同的舞會獵取王子。

第二個王子對她非常溫柔，從他的眼睛裡公主第一次發現自己長得並不醜。一個夜晚，他們在玫瑰花園裡一起看月亮，當他的唇快碰到她雪白的頸項時，公主問他，願不願意為她殺掉三頭六尾的巨龍，王子忽然躲到椅子下發抖：「我從小最怕聽到龍的故事。」

公主嘆了口氣踩著高跟鞋離去，王子在她背後嚶嚶哭泣。所有草叢裡的紡織娘和青蛙馬上停止演奏浪漫曲。

一心為了未來努力的公主找到第三個王子。離開昏暗的舞會，她才發現英俊的王子其實穿了一雙比她的高跟鞋還高的高跟鞋，他扭了一跤還裝酷的臉顯得很滑稽。

公主笑得整夜不能睡。

第四個王子其實已經是有點年紀的小國國王，他利用燈光掩飾自己的魚尾紋，把自己的故事說成天方夜譚。在偶然的機會下，公主的侍女拜訪他的國度，打聽到他原來已經有一個妻子和一堆孩子。

第五個王子在第三次約會時就向公主調頭寸，公主一時慈悲把自己的小豬撲滿借給他，不久後發現王子買了一匹新的駿馬，駿馬後載著另一個公主。

第六個王子飽讀詩書，公主的耳朵陶醉於他的妙語如珠。他為公主朗誦了「王子屠龍記」的十四行詩，也爲她寫了「殺死龍的六十四種技術」，並且訓練公主如何做一個端莊賢淑的傳統公主。但當公主問他：「什麼時候你會爲我宰掉那條龍呢？」王子卻對她說，他從來沒有學過騎馬和用劍。正好一隻蟑螂從他們腳邊飛過，王子大叫：「喂，殺死它！我可以告訴妳，我媽是怎麼對付這些敗類的，快，脫下妳的鞋來……」

第七個王子看起來很能幹。他的父親聽說只是個流浪漢，但他自己一手建立了王國成爲國王。公主心想，這下子我找到的王子必然很勇敢。王子努力的帶公主去別的王國做「國民外交」，建立自己的聲望。公主好不容易才找到機會，問他將來會爲她殺掉三頭六尾的龍嗎？王子看了看自己密密麻麻的行程表說：「沒空，沒空，我自己還有二十條龍要應付，妳那條不在我的計畫之中，如果妳愛我的話，妳應該學點忍者的技術，替我放毒餌幹掉幾條，這樣我就會比較輕鬆。」

公主失望的掉頭就走，又是整夜不能睡。當月亮昇到中天的時候，王后忽然出現在她的床緣，對她說：「女兒，妳到底有沒有找到王子啊？人家隔壁的阿花公主

公主整夜不能睡

和小咪公主，老早就找到對象啦，媽可沒把妳生得比別人醜哪！妳別再挑啦！」

「可是⋯⋯沒有王子願意殺掉那條龍！」

「沒⋯⋯沒關係啦！隨便啦！本來我也以為妳爸爸會為我殺掉那條龍，沒想到，唉，他連一匹馬都養得不好，現在那匹馬已經不能跑，老早承受不了他的重量。」

「可是⋯⋯我如果找不到王子殺掉那條龍，該怎麼辦？」

「妳可以隨便找個王子，也許會生個公主，像我們所有的老祖宗一樣，等公主長大要她去找另一個王子殺掉那條龍，那就不關妳的事了。」

公主個性倔強，她沒有因此放棄努力。她開始學習騎馬和劍術，希望在舞會迷濛的燈光外找到真正的白馬王子。可惜第八個王子孔武有力，脾氣卻比暴龍還難駕馭，第九個王子在誇耀自己的騎術時被馬後空翻造成腦震盪，第十個王子敗在她的劍下時告訴她，沒有任何公主可以「真正」贏過一位王子。

再也不耐煩的公主氣得發瘋，蹬馬狂奔，跳過了王國所有標明「有龍出沒，危險」的圍欄，拿著她的劍尋找三頭六尾龍。

做個好命女

她越靠近那個龐大的身影，心臟跳得越厲害。然而，她離牠越近，牠變得越小。牠是一隻幻影龍。待她走到牠跟前時，牠已經像芭比娃娃一樣袖珍。龍用溫柔的眼光對她說：「請妳不要那麼……那麼凶……好……不好？如果……剛剛妳用……客氣一點的語氣……請我出去，我……會乖乖……迎接妳。」

公主和龍做成了好朋友。嚴格說來，牠只是條漂亮的小變色龍，只不過，牠會耍點法術，妳越害怕，和牠隔得越遠，牠就變得越大，難怪歷史上曾經記載，牠比喜馬拉雅山還高。

☆☆☆☆☆

每個故事都得有「完美」的結局交代，否則會使作者受到「不負責任」的責怪。雖然天已亮，而公主養了龍當寵物，獨自統治王國，不再參加有王子的舞會，然而，所有的王子公主都在背後叫她怪胎，有時她也發現，沒有愛情值得期待也使人寂寞難耐。公主還是整夜不能睡。

幾年後公主在野外騎馬時摔了跤，一個牧羊人伸出援手使公主免於昏迷，給她唯一一碗飯吃。於是……公主發現一個真正的王子，從他高貴而慷慨的眼神。

受歡迎的愛情故事總是免不了俗套。一個男人一個女人，不是分手，就是結婚。

與其寫分手，不如寫結婚。分手後還要面對他們結婚，因為我已睏。

那條龍在婚禮上免費製造煙火。

先讓他們享受這一刻吧！

接著，聰明的妳，可能會想到一個公主和牧羊人生活上的差距問題吧！沒錯，

如果還有一口氣在，人生中就會有種種變化……

公主枕著牧羊人的胸膛做了個好夢，我們祝福她，不再徹夜未眠。

我始終相信，故事是為了讓人心存希望而存在的，不是為了讓人絕望而存在的。晚安。

睡美人是漸漸睡著的

科技時代的睡美人，是慢慢睡著的。

她在決定託付終身後，

也不知不覺的將自身的決定權交給另一半。

瑞君在某個基金會擔任行政主管，負責企劃婦女成長營的系列課程，由於課程是免費的，而且邀請到了名師來主講，所以不到三天報名電話就額滿了，她只好婉拒那些較晚報名的人。沒想到開課那天卻遭遇了意想不到的困難。

竟然只有二分之一的報名者前來參加！她十萬火急的在開課前打電話給那些沒有來的學員，請她們及時趕來，卻得到許多讓她沮喪的答案，比如孩子要考試啦，家裡忙走不開啦，週休二日要陪家人啦。

「那也可以先打個電話來，把機會讓給別人啊！」也難怪她有點生氣。但最多人用的理由最令她懊惱：「很多人理直氣壯的說，是她老公不讓她來的。這是一個要求現代婦女追求個人成長空間的課程，這個理由簡直是當頭棒喝嘛！」

後來瑞君學聰明了，雖然是基金會出錢來辦講座，她都先收「保證金」，如果當事人都沒有缺席的話，就可以把保證金全數領回，這樣不但保護了真正想要上課者的權益，也讓她邀請來的講師覺得她真的用了力在辦講座。

女人的「睡美人」心態

瑞君在高中時就隨家人到美國，這位管理碩士覺得，在這裡辦女性成長營，最大的阻力就是「老公不讓她來」這句話，「難道到了現代，女人還要處處請求老公恩准嗎？」

我說，沒那麼糟。「老公不讓我來」這句話，不能從表面來看，內在可能蘊藏幾層意思。

做個好命女

妳連這個都要問我

第一種可能是：其實她老公根本不知道，這句話只是個藉口。報名後，她想了想，又因各種事由自己不想來上課，怕人家直接怪罪於她，所以讓不知情的老公當擋箭牌。

這就跟有人向男同事借錢，他說：「我回家跟老婆商量看看。」是同樣的道理。讓那個不必直接面對你的人來扮黑臉。

第二種可能是：老公真的很不講理，嚴格禁止她來。不過，現在本地婦女的權益其實多半都沒那麼低落。

第三種可能，是女人的「睡美人」心態。童話睡美人受了壞仙女的詛咒，在十六歲的時候被紡錘的針刺到了手指，從此一睡一百年。科技時代的睡美人，是慢慢睡著的。什麼詛咒使她入睡？應該說是古代「三從四德」裡的「從」字吧，她在決定託付終身後，也不知不覺的將自身的決定權交了出去。

睡美人是漸漸睡著的

「我很想來，但我先生不讓我來」──就算這個理由是真的，嚴重的溝通不良問題，也老早就存在於兩個人的溝通之間。如果一個女人已經習慣把任何做新鮮事的決定權丟給對方了，而另一半也會在心裡覺得：「妳連這個都要問我，實在不夠成熟，妳決定的事情都可能是愚蠢的。」

因而，對於她個人的意見，都保持著質疑或否定的態度。這種惡性循環不斷在日常生活中發生，使得她在詢問先生她是否能來時，心裡早就打了退堂鼓，直覺自己一定會得到負面答案：「我想去參加，你應該不會讓我去吧……沒關係，我只是問問看……沒關係，我還是不要問好了。」

慢慢睡著的睡美人，剛開始常會有一連串甜美的夢境。

「我先生不許我學游泳，他說我太笨了，一定會在水裡淹死。」游泳池畔，我會聽見一個穿戴整齊、坐在涼椅上等待池裡的朋友游完泳一起去買東西的女人，以甜蜜的語調這麼說著：「他呀，好討厭，什麼事都要管。」

從她臉上表情，我沒有看到一絲陰霾。至少，這個時候，還沒有。

別做鄉愿女

算命有時挺好玩，但請聊備一格，當做娛樂和閒聊的話題，就好，不要忽視；醫病要用對有效藥！

二十七歲的敏兒是個年輕優秀的中醫師。有一天，她姑媽打電話給她，問她，有沒有什麼藥方可以幫忙表妹生孩子。

表妹才二十五歲，結婚一年，應該還不必為不孕傷神，怎麼這麼著急呢？

敏兒也很想幫忙，但問清楚表妹的狀況後，她發現問題比她想像中還大，因為表妹問題根本不在於不孕症，而是嚴重的憂鬱症！

過去一年間，表妹已經鬧了三五次自殺了。

姑媽說：「唉呀，她現在這麼想不開，我也不知道該怎麼辦，我想，生了孩子以後，有點事忙，就會變好吧！我想先問問看妳有沒有好的方法讓她趕快懷孕，如果不行，我再帶她去看西醫婦產科。」

敏兒哭笑不得——明明該在精神科解決的問題，怎麼會求助於婦產科呢？這簡直是頭痛醫腳，敏兒痛切陳辭，說明這種狀況如果不尋求醫治，表妹的自殺遲早會成功的。苦口婆心的勸告之下，姑媽才同意帶表妹看精神科。

命比面子重要

此事發生過了個把月，敏兒打電話給姑媽，想問姑媽結果如何？姑媽在電話那頭嗚嗚咽咽說，表妹剛剛又被送入加護病房，因為她企圖想用娘家的晾衣繩上吊！

「妳到底有沒有帶她看精神科？」敏兒氣急敗壞的問。

「沒有啦……因為，我怕她婆家的人說她是瘋子。這樣不好聽……」

「妳女兒的命重要，還是好不好聽重要？要不，我帶她去！」

醫病要用對有效藥，也不要遺忘解決問題的真正方法，和妳在現實生活中的行動力。

所幸家人終於聽進了敏兒的話，讓表妹接受精神治療，情況稍有好轉。原來自小個性壓抑的表妹本來就有輕微憂鬱症，嫁入夫家後更因與婆婆同住屋簷下而產生種種問題，秉持著母親「一忍無難事」的家教，一直往心裡壓，終於到了她自己也無法控制情緒的地步。

不久前，敏兒看到了一則「有嚴重問題的年輕母親親手殺掉幼兒」的社會新聞，這母親的狀況跟她表妹差不多，只是在精神最不穩定時就依照家人或自己的期望生了一個孩子，回到娘家坐月子時，竟以利刃將孩子封喉，還不許別人救孩子，十分恐怖。敏兒對我說：「我想，如果當初表妹沒有就診，而光聽姑媽的話，先生個孩子，我怕今天那血淋淋的社會新聞主角，就是我表妹……」

醫病要用對有效藥

我們的教育程度，雖然已經提高到大學之門錄取率百分之百，但總還是不時可以聽到，有人言之鑿鑿的以怪力亂神或歪打正著的方式，解決人生中的大問

別 做 鄉 愿 女

35

題。該看精神科卻想以生孩子解決，只是一個小例子而已。碰上丈夫外遇找算命先生斬桃花、孩子難帶就找人驅鬼、讀書運戀愛運不順就花錢改名改運──大多數人還是篤信這樣的事情。

「算命先生說我有小老婆的命，我才跟一個有婦之夫在一起。」「我們的星座明明很合的，為什麼他會對我越來越冷漠？」每次接到這種問題，都不知該從何答起才好。

算命有時挺好玩，但請備一格，當做娛樂和閒聊話題就好，不要忽視……醫病要用對有效藥，也不要遺忘解決問題的真正方法，和妳在生活中的行動力。

壞命得想辦法除，好命得及時掌握。現代的好命女們，別做鄉愿女！

好睡的天鵝湖

兩人份的時間全投資在一個地方，當成一份使用，當然是浪費；同時也失去了接受自己成長的可能。

「這個月有個西班牙舞王來台公演，聽說他好帥哦，我好想去看看他怎麼跳，可惜……我老公不肯陪我去看。」一位身材曼妙的長髮女子，邊脫掉上衣邊說。

「為什麼？他不准妳看帥哥？」與她對話的短髮女孩，大約二十出頭吧，也有窈窕的好身段。

「不是。他呀，最沒藝術細胞了。他曾經陪我看過天鵝湖和卡門，妳猜他怎麼說？他說，以後看芭蕾舞劇可以找他，因為天鵝湖音樂聽了很舒服，可以在裡頭好好睡一覺；像卡門這種舞，拚命的踩地板，吵死了，哪裡睡得著？下次別想找他去看不能好好睡一覺的舞。

「他是開玩笑吧！」短髮女孩說。

「才不是，是真的！看天鵝湖時，他不但睡到打呼，而且打呼打得好大聲，讓我覺得尷尬極了，真想找個地洞鑽下去！」

「太誇張了！」兩人一起哈哈大笑。長髮女子顯然並沒有因此而不開心，只是把這件事當笑話講。

這位年輕太太是一位舞蹈教練，她的雅量讓我好生佩服。但我不知道，夫妻之間的南轅北轍，到底能當多久的「笑話」講？會不會有一天，她也像很多比她年長的太太一樣，埋怨著先生的不支持、不陪伴、不載她、不帶她去玩，使她失去許多可以好好發揮的機會，以及生命中的珍貴時光？

穿著三寸金蓮的女人心

我每一次聽到太太在怪先生不陪她、不鼓勵她，使她錯失什麼美好的機會時，我總會想：為什麼她一定要先生陪她，她才能做她想做的事呢？這個先進得不得了的現代，很多女人的心似乎還穿著三寸金蓮，要男人扶著走，她才能出門走點路。

生活中的事，並不像決定在哪裡買房子，需要夫妻開會、或同進同出才能做的事。男人跟女人在戀愛穩定後或婚後最大的不同常在於，男人常想單獨做自己要做的事，女人認為有男人陪才能做她想要做的事。

我們並不能怪罪這位覺得天鵝湖好睡，所以才肯陪太太來欣賞的先生。畢竟人各有志，也許他是個每天花好多時間工作的男人，需要好好休息。為什麼這位太太不能夠約舞蹈同好一起看表演，讓先生在家好好睡個不被干擾的覺？

好睡的天鵝湖

我看過好多走入婚姻的女人，從此再也沒有屬於個人的興趣與娛樂。未必出於被迫，只是怕被指責為「不負責任」，或依賴性太大，所以失去了自己的獨立行為能力。

何必浪費兩倍時間

現在仍有很多女人不敢踏入婚姻的理由，就是怕失去自由，怕從一個自由人，淪為一個凡事得請示上級核准的人。她們看多了上一代已婚女子的故事，就算想要有個美好的愛情結局，卻質疑自己是不是會失去原來享有的單身權益？

所幸我已經看到越來越多在結了婚之後相輔相成，一加一等於二或大於二的夫妻，而不是一加一只等於一的夫妻。

有時同進同出，有人相伴固然好，但沒人相伴時，何必自怨自艾？兩人份的時間全投資在一個地方，當成一份使用，當然是浪費，同時也失去了接受自己成長的可能。

讓他好好睡吧！妳，可以約朋友看天鵝湖，也許自己看，更能專心的看出其中精髓呢！

女人有自主的行動能力，男人也因此不再負擔過多的重量。

好 睡 的 天 鵝 湖

妳哪裡需要整型

妳想整型嗎？沒有人能阻止妳改變自己。

但是請先想想，那個讓妳不滿意的問題，

真的是改了外表就能改的嗎？

自從聽說韓劇的美女都是經過人工的大修整之後，整型風吹得都會女子的心好癢。

因為做節目的緣故，我認識許多優秀的整型醫師，所以總有人來問我：「妳可不可以幫我問問看，抽眼袋可不可以便宜一點？」或「我去把鼻子墊高好不好？」「我覺得我胸部太小，想要加到C就好……」

雖然我認為天生我材必有用──上天為我們安裝的種種材料，總有它的協調性，但我並不反對整型。

如果某個五官的長相確實影響了自信，也不妨在深思熟慮後動個小手術。

我就給過一位有塌塌的朝天鼻的女孩意見：「如果妳真的覺得不好看，就去整一整吧！」

她從小到大為其所苦，甚至連近視眼鏡都得經過特別加工才能戴上她的臉，

如果我再告訴她自然的比較好，未免太不了解她的痛苦。

技術比價格重要

美麗雖然像皮膚一樣薄，但沒有任何女人不希望自己看起來美麗一點，況且現代的整型術已經不像從前一樣，只要進過美容院，任何女人的臉都變成「歌仔戲明星臉」！豐頰尖下巴大大的雙眼皮，人人長得像表姐妹。

萬萬不要因為想變美麗，而美成了一個不自然的大眾臉，所以我總會提醒想美容的朋友，技術比價格重要。有時我也覺得女人的心理蠻荒謬的：割雙眼皮又

不是買豬肉，還討價還價？

有位朋友實在太可愛了，竟然因為價格便宜跑到北京墊下巴，回台後因為手術部位潰爛，只好又搭機到北京拿掉下巴，幾來幾往，花的錢足足可在台北墊兩個下巴了。

粗心的我竟然還沒發現，她從真下巴到假下巴又回復真下巴的過程中，長相有何不同，只覺得，那一陣子她好像把自己的臉累瘦了。

我不解的是，她本來就是個美女，為什麼還要整型？她的臉型沒有她自己說的那麼糟啊！

這個現象很奧妙：這些特別關心美容的女人，其實本來長得都很不錯。有的根本就已經是清秀佳人，絕對在中上之姿以上，卻最斤斤計較自己胸部不夠大，腰不夠細，下巴不夠尖。

是不是內心裡對自己並不滿意，才怪罪於自己的外表呢？

待整修的內心問題

美國有個研究機構曾經做過研究：女人靠整型增加自信，但整型後，自信心其實並沒有真正增加。原來自信不足的地方，還是潛藏在內心中，噬咬著她。有些「整型狂」，每天看自己不順眼，想去動刀的人，都有嚴重的心理問題。

也有一位整型醫師表示：一個女人，如果因為丈夫有外遇，才想要把胸部整大，以挽回丈夫的心，通常都無法真正挽回婚姻。後來再要求醫師把假胸部拿掉的人還不少呢！

前不久我曾在節目中訪問到一位全身都整過的人工美女，她說，最痛的是要把臉磨小的手術，術後好一段時間，臉跟豬頭一樣大，把骨頭磨掉之處簡直痛入骨髓，像被打入十八層地獄一樣，要四個月才能恢復。

我看著全身都整得很精緻的她，問：「那妳覺得自己還有什麼要整修的呢？」

她一派正經的說：「外表這樣就可以了，現在我要充實的是內心的問題。」

我提醒她：「內心的整修，可不只四個月哦！」

妳想整型嗎？沒有人能阻止妳改變自己。但是請先想想，那個讓妳不滿意的

問題，真的是改了外表就能改的嗎？

男人哭與女人哭

別用眼淚當武器。

在職場上，使用淚水超過三次，

就會像黔驢技窮寓言裡所說的一樣：

老虎看出驢子只會這一招，所以就把牠毫不客氣的吃掉了。

某一個公司的會議上，來自亞洲各地的地方主管齊聚報告，忽然間，有一位女性主管講起她開拓新業務上所受到的委屈，對同一地區的男性主管的袖手旁觀甚至橫加阻撓很是不滿。

說著說著，忽然哭了起來。當她的啜泣聲變成嚎啕大哭時，在座的男性都不知所措，像一群做錯事的孩子，只能呆呆看著她。

會場本來的火藥味，在女主管停止嗚咽後，看似平和了許多，好像一場春雨沖淡了燃起的火藥線一樣。

「對不起，我不該這麼衝動的，可能因為家裡的孩子疑似腸病毒，正在發高燒的緣故……」

這是好結果嗎？未必見得。吃午餐的時候，女主管仍孤零零的坐在角落。開完會後，男主管一提起這位女主管，用的代號都是：那個歇斯底里的女人！

另一人也哭了，下場卻完全不同。

有一位男性中年主管說起他工作上的障礙，竟然也失聲哭了出來。

大家都很驚訝，幾個女性主動走過去拍拍他的肩膀表示關心，他停止啜泣後，說：「對不起，我不該這麼激動，昨天我的孩子發燒，太太又出差，所以……」

吃午餐時，他的身邊坐滿了充滿關心的女人。

後來，所有女性都對這位本來兇巴巴的男主管改觀，說他是鐵漢柔情，以前真是錯看他了。

真情流露，也得公私分明。

不是每一滴眼淚，都可以獲得同情。

真情流露，也得公私分明

為什麼同樣的狀況，女人的眼淚在男人群中引起的是負面評價，而男人的眼淚顯得比較珍貴？

為什麼女性的眼淚被看成是示弱，男性的眼淚被看成是示好？

可能是因為傳統上，男兒有淚不輕彈，所以物以稀為貴。

女人該了解的是：哭給爸爸看，可能會得到妳想要的禮物；哭給男友看，他可能會認錯，被妳的淚水溶化；哭給老公看，床頭吵也許會床尾和；然而在工作上，這一招是行不通的，就算行得通，也不會通暢很久。

別用眼淚當武器。

在職場上，使用它超過三次，就會像黔驢技窮那個寓言裡所說的一樣：老虎看出驢子只會這一招，所以就把牠毫不客氣的吃掉了。

詢問男人對於女同事淚水的看法，有幾位男性主管也私下表示：「哭有什麼

男人哭與女人哭

49

用？我最討厭會用哭來搪塞職務上失誤的女人。」

跟男人比起來，女性是比較真情流露的。

女人願意分享心情，說出心事，多半的女性對於喜怒哀樂的反應，天生就比

較敏感。這對於心理健康，確實有正面幫助。

但真情流露，也得公私分明，不是每一滴眼淚，都可以獲得同情。

男人找出路，女人找退路

如果妳真的想要做個有出息的女人，還是得用正向的方式安慰自己。

找退路的心理會失去許多成長和挑戰的機會，

失去對壓力的免疫力。

如果妳進入了一個妳夢想中的公司，卻發現裡頭的老同事並不喜歡妳，而且會在暗中跟妳過不去，妳會有什麼作法？

1. 長期來說，我還是換個工作好了。

2. 反正我又不是領你的薪水，你不跟我合作，我也不跟你合作。

3. 你攻擊我，我也攻擊你，誰怕誰？

4. 沒關係，我會改變你們對我的觀感。

選1 的是羚羊——遇到事情就跑，永遠在倉皇逃命！

選2 的是鴕鳥——任由環境擺佈，小心積鬱成疾！

選3 的是蚊子——雖然別人也會受傷，但對方體積總比妳大，很可能一巴掌把妳打成重傷。

選4 的是鱷魚——總有一天證明給你看，我可不是會一直當木頭被你踩在腳下！（這只是個比喻，雖然鱷魚很醜，但請不要忽視牠的敏捷！）

這是一位企業家朋友自擬的小測驗，他問我，妳怎麼選擇？

老實說，剛出校門時，我是一隻羚羊，永遠想要避過難以面對的困難；後來我也曾經當過鴕鳥，下班和同事聚會時最津津樂道的是公司、上司的各種醜行陋規，以無可奈何的嘆氣做終結；有時被激到了，也會變成一隻憤怒的蚊子⋯⋯現在我雖然脫離了大機構，但身為自由業者，也一樣要面對各種複雜的人事環境，我想我已經變成了一隻「鱷魚」。

羚羊跑得快，但是跑不遠

其實，哪一個單位沒有鬥爭，沒有權力壓榨？在我們的成長過程中，我們總會面對無數類似的人際糾紛或升遷挑戰，只是在出校門後，我們碰到的人都不再那麼天真，所以解決困難的方式變得更複雜、更難操控而已。

我們都難免想當一隻羚羊，逃走算了，反正年輕有力跑得快，但跑久了，恐怕妳會發現，那個一直沒法解決的問題，在每個公司裡都會重複的發生。越想逃避，它會越想來黏妳。

羚羊跑得快，但是跑不遠。

「女性比男性在職場上更常有羚羊心理。」這位企業家說：「我當了好幾十年的主管，帶過無數新手，總是發現，同樣年齡、剛出社會的新鮮人，女性常比男性靈巧、勤勞又懂事，然而，再過了幾年，狀況就不一樣了。本來少不更事的小毛頭常變得不同凡響，一路往上爬，而本來聰明能幹的好女孩，常有各種理由在職場上失去了光芒。妳可不要很敏感的把它單純歸類於職場上重男輕女的問題而已。職場上大多數的男性一直在找出路，大多數的女性一直在找退路。

女性比較不必負擔「沒出息」的譴責

在傳統觀念上，女人也很「幸運」的有退路可找。男人如果失業，他可能會很自卑，女人失業卻沒有那麼大的壓力，一碰到傷腦筋的人事問題或工作瓶頸，她往往會想：「唉，我嫁人去算了。」「找到個好老公，我就不用工作，不用再受這種閒氣！」

女性比較不必負擔「沒出息」的譴責，所以不少年輕女子即使很有能力，對升遷並不積極，也比較計較「拿同樣的錢，為什麼我要多做那一件事？」

除非經濟壓力相當大，或自我期許很高，這種找退路的聲音還常常在一般女性的耳邊徘徊不去。

人生壓力處處都在，不管是在職場，還是在熱騰騰的愛情夢裡。就算妳不是鱷魚，也總得讓自己從「草莓族」變成皮堅肉硬的「百香果族」，要不，變成番茄也行，不要一碰就爛，爛得那麼難看。

如果妳真的想要做個有出息的女人，還是得用正向的方式安慰自己，比如：「度過了這一關，我會變得更好！」找退路的心理會失去許多成長和挑戰的機會，幾年下來，仍然不會增加對壓力的免疫力。

男人找出路，女人找退路

是監牢還是自己的房間

享受獨處，使我發現人生天空地闊，

世界並不只是個三度空間而已，有很多扇門等我開啓，

每一本書是一扇門，每一個想法也是一扇門。

獨處，在絕大多數的時候，對我來說，多半是一種享受。

如果拿食物來比喻時間的話，這麼比喻每個人都能懂。總是充塞著大事小事

的生活中，時間忽然空了出來，就好像眼前忽然擺上一桌美味的菜餚，你可以很

自由的選擇其中一樣或幾樣來品嚐，並不需要在意什麼麻煩的餐桌禮儀，也不必

等長輩先下筷子。也許時間還沒多到可以稱作滿漢全席，但如果我肯在有人來收

桌子前夾一兩道菜放進嘴裡，再餓壞了的靈魂也可以得到新的養分。

獨處的時間對許多女人而言，
並非想像中的滿漢大餐。

獨處是一件美妙的事情，也是一種緩衝劑，它巧妙的調和了所謂「現實與理想」的衝突，也是一種溫柔的安慰，讓我不再有「長恨此身非我有，何時忘卻營營？」的感嘆。

不過，想要把獨處看成是美味的食物，是一種習慣，桌前的食物每一盤都是你自由運用想像力上菜的，沒有培養上菜能力的人，很可能覺得獨處根本是在吃牢飯。

但我常常發現，獨處的時間對許多女人而言，並非想像中的滿漢大餐。

獨處時間是我眼中的美食

有一整個禮拜我忙得不可開交，好不容易在星期六下午回到家，打開電腦，想把我放在腦袋裡的種種想法寫成文章。

就在我打了一小段文字時，每星期負責來清掃一次的太太來了，她可能怕我無聊吧，非常殷勤的想陪我說話，談論清潔劑的用法和去哪個大賣場買比較便宜

是 監 牢 還 是 自 己 的 房 間

57

的話題。我只好告訴她，這一方面，她是專家，由她決定就好，請她不用管我，我還有些東西要寫呢！

不久，她用一種同情的眼神看著我說：「吳小姐，妳真的很可憐、很寂寞，妳沒有朋友可以陪陪妳打打麻將什麼的！」

我哭笑不得。

時間在這一刻，是我眼中的美食，而她卻覺得我像在吃牢飯！

拍廣告時也有類似的經驗發生在我身上。我習慣在化粧師為我化粧時看書，但那一位化粧師只要在我把視線放在書本上時，就開始連珠炮般對我說起東家長西家短的各種話題。她與我距離很近、聲音很大，而且每一句話的距離都「間不容髮」，又總是拿八卦雜誌才會問的問題來問我，使我頭痛欲裂，但礙於與她不熟，不好意思阻止她說話。

忍耐了四十分鐘後，她終於稍稍停止了，卻特意叫來我那位正在不遠處連絡各種公事的祕書：「喂，妳來陪吳小姐說說話，不然她無聊到要看書了！」

原來她是為了怕我無聊才這麼做的。在她的觀念裡，看書一定是「最後不得

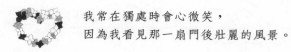
我常在獨處時會心微笑，
因為我看見那一扇門後壯麗的風景。

享受獨處是一種好習慣

享受獨處是一種習慣。讀書、寫作、唸英日文、繪畫等都是必須專心的活動，不像以前女人打毛線時可以一邊聊是非，如果有人不斷的來打斷，我不相信從事以上活動可以有什麼成就、有什麼樂趣。

英國女作家吳爾芙有一句廣被引用的經典名言：「一個女人如果要寫作的話，一定要有獨立的經濟能力和自己的房子。」其實，做任何需要心智參與的工作、從事任何精神上的活動都是一樣的。

也許有人會好客熱情或奉獻犧牲到連一點獨處時間也不願有，但對於我而言，如果失去了獨處的時間，不論我走到哪裡，這世界對我來說，不過是一座黑暗的大監牢。

已才會做的無聊事」，她並不知道對我來說，這是一種暫時脫離一下周遭環境的習慣，也是百忙之中「偷得浮生半日閒」的休息方式。

是 監 牢 還 是 自 己 的 房 間

59

獨處，使我發現人生天空地闊，世界並不只是個三度空間而已，有很多扇門

等我開啟，每一本書是一扇門，每一個想法也是一扇門；我常在獨處時會心微

笑，因為我看見那一扇門後壯麗的風景。

將獨處當成吃牢飯還是吃滿漢大餐？決定權只在妳自己。

好命女守則

就算靜靜的喝個下午茶，吃一塊巧克力，也是減壓的方法。

找出適合自己的小型逃走方式，別在夢中不斷的描畫大型

逃亡路線圖，才是真正的「活在當下」！

——摘自《做自己最快樂》

他急功近利，她注重表相

我認識的所有成功女子，都是能在處理任何事情時，懂得提醒自己「重點在哪裡」的女人，這是女性出類拔萃的小小利器。

有些主持節目的特殊經驗，想要和妳分享。

對於電視節目主持這個行業好奇的人，問我的問題，男女大大有別。

不分老少，女人最常問我的問題是：「妳上節目有化粧師嗎？衣服是妳自己的嗎？」

（衣服不是我自己的，化粧也是專業化粧師化的，以我粗枝大葉的個性來說，我很慶幸不必為找衣服上節目而奔忙。）

而男人最常問我的問題是：「做一集節目可以賺多少錢？收視率好不好？」

（以上問題，經紀人並不允許我在文章裡誠實作答。）

從這一點就可以約略看出來，對同一件事，男人和女人的反應很不相同。

女人更注重細節，這是一種體貼的表現，但推到極致很可能變成只看重表相；男人比較重視實際利益，這是一種積極的求知欲，但太過頭了未免急功近利。

我也仔細的觀察過自己——如果不留心觀察，我還沒有察覺呢！

我發現，我對自己主持的電視節目關心的焦點，常常和男主持人大不相同。

我觀看自己的節目時，會特別注意到整體造型好不好，化粧的效果是加分或減分，台風和音調適當嗎？而和我合作的男主持人，對收視率的高低總是比我敏感。沒有收視率就沒有廣告，沒有廣告就沒有節目，他們關心的是存亡問題，而我關心的是美不美麗，天哪！

什麼是最重要的

我也記得我參加過一次座談會，會中有一位相當傑出的女性，口才十分傑出，表現也很優異，會後群眾魚貫而出，好些男性聽眾還在原地群聚著探討講座內容，而好幾位女性聽眾竊竊私語的卻是：「喂，她的絲襪破了一個洞。」「她本人看起來比電視上矮……」類似的例子不勝枚舉。

我有一位朋友是位年輕的女教授，每次上電視時，都會特別要求自己的爸媽觀賞一下節目。電視播出後，她打電話問爸媽，他們覺得她怎樣？爸爸總會對她的意見發表評論，會告訴她怎麼說更恰當，媽媽則根本不在乎她說什麼，只是一再的提醒她：「妳太胖了，該減肥了！」

急功近利，沒有不好，但不要變成短視近利、緊張焦慮；重視表相也是一種好習慣，但可不要忽視內裡更珍貴的東西。

我認識的所有成功女子，都是能在處理任何事情時，懂得提醒自己「重點在哪裡」的女人，這是女性出類拔萃的小小利器。

他急功近利，她注重表相

不做火山孝女

有些金錢上的忙，不幫好像有點過意不去，

但身為女人確實得好好想想：不要幫了忙，卻增加自己的財務壓力，

可能還有沈重的副作用侵蝕你們之間的愛意。

以前有人把一擲千金，不惜一切尋求歡場女人真心的男人，叫火山孝子。

床頭金盡，佳人再也不肯對他展歡顏，是火山孝子的宿命，這種愛情投資當然很危險。

妳一定不相信，錢能夠買到一個人的真心吧？

可是天底下卻常有這樣的女人。

社會新聞上有個奇女子，她是學校的會計，愛上了學校裡已婚的男老師，不

用溫柔與愛幫忙，比用錢來幫忙一個男人會令他感激。

惜挪用公款購買雙B豪華轎車來贏得男老師的芳心。

愛車的男老師並不知道那錢是女會計挪用的，被她重金買下的愛情禮物感動了。但感動的時間當然有限。後來女會計悔悟了，向學校自首，並歸還了兩千五百萬元。

她侵占的公款達三千萬，無力還給學校的五百萬，就是拿去買車用的。

「太傻了。」妳會說。

女人常為愛負債

愛情和佔有欲常令一個女人盲目，但當火山孝女確實不值得。她也許可以很速成的以金錢求得一點歡愛，但在那男人心裡，她必定比不上她送的車可愛。

她傻，但是她並不孤單。天底下還有很多女人，在不知不覺間成為和她一樣的火山孝女。

「明天沒拿出二十萬來，我的股票就會被斷頭，如果連妳都不幫我，我真不知道會有誰幫我？」被錢弄得焦頭爛額的男友說。

「如果明天拿不出三百萬來，地下錢莊就要我斷手斷腳！」欠下賭債的丈夫說。

「我哥哥要買房子，少五十萬，妳如果有的話，可不可以調一下？」「我想換一部新車，這樣妳也可以坐得舒服點，妳覺得好不好？可是我的錢還不夠付頭期款……」

以上這些說詞都是很常見的，有用心的男人常拿這些話來煎熬有愛心的女人，使她們付出所有積蓄。

這些都是我認識的女人們為此負債的原因。

有些人上一次當學一次乖，有些人因為愛，一而再、再而三一貧如洗，只因她們沒張揚出來，所以沒上社會新聞。

這種忙該幫嗎

還有個女友急著讓失業已久的男友有工作做，幫他買了一台拖車頭呢！結果

還來不及保險，車子簽收不到一個禮拜，車子竟然被偷了，兩人也因此翻臉。

有些金錢上的忙，不幫好像有點過意不去，但身為女人確實得好好想想：不

要幫了忙，卻讓自己的財務增加侉大壓力，卻還有沈重的副作用來侵蝕你們之間

的愛意。

有的忙幫了之後，讓妳愛的男人自尊受傷，那就更划不來，儘管他在妳拿出

存款簿的那一刻，都用充滿感激的眼神看妳。

用溫柔與愛幫忙，比用錢來幫忙一個男人會令他感激；只不過前者還需要耐

心，後者只需咬一咬牙，不耗時間而已。

好命女守則

說愛的時候百般真心，但面對未來可得千般小心。
女性主義不會敗在愛情和買衣服上，
但會敗在借錢給男人這件事上。

——摘自《非常誠實有點毒》

不做火山孝女

剝開收禮之女的內心世界

硬要，是吃相難看，正常女人很難做到；

然而，如果沒說妳要，又常是一輩子要不到，

男人會以為妳真的不要。

曾有一個稱得上漂亮的女主播，和一個外國有錢男人第一次單獨相約，就要了價值約新台幣兩百萬的禮物。引來好多人搖頭、唱嘆、叫罵，但女人內心裡除了品頭論足、評斷是非之外，硬要剝開來看的話，裡頭到底還有一些疑惑、一點酸味，心想⋯⋯

啊，她是怎麼辦到的？

為什麼我為那個男人做牛做馬，連個兩萬塊的禮物都不曾收過？

男人不要小看女人的細膩心思，
其實女人對於她收過的好禮物，都記得好牢。

哪個女人不喜歡漂亮又高貴的禮物

我的姿色不算差，爲什麼我找不到稍微慷慨點的男人？

我還在三溫暖裡頭聽到兩位光溜溜的歐巴桑爲此雞同鴨講呢！一個說：

「哇，原來世界上有那麼貴的手錶？要是我，拿現金多好？」

另一個應和：「對嘛，這個查某囝仔不夠聰明，一次不要拿那麼多嘛，多跟他交往幾年，可以削得更多啊！如果離婚的話，哇，那就賺歪了！」

我聽見好多衛道人士批評年輕世代的拜金問題。依我看來，不要亂怪E世代，要論「價值觀扭曲」的話，從老到少都很扭曲，男人也不會比女人在愛情上不勢利。要找「有嫁粧」「顧家」「幫夫」的男生，說穿了還不是爲了自己過得好，和拜金主義殊途同歸。可不是只有六年級女生才現實勢利。

硬要，是吃相難看，正常女人很難做到；然而，如果沒說妳要，又常是一輩子要不到，男人會以爲妳眞的不要。

男人應該要明白，哪個女人不喜歡既漂亮又高貴的禮物？除非故作清高，否則很難不被手工精製的名牌皮包、號稱「一顆永流傳」的鑽石打動自己的心。

如果那是情人為了討自己歡心而送的。

如果她要你不必浪費錢，如果她說她不要，只要你的心意到，那只是為了表示，她是個體貼的女人：看你收入不過如此，她因為想跟你過一輩子，不想竭澤而漁，不想讓你為送她禮物而餓肚子──不代表她真的不要，或永遠不要。

男人不要小看女人的細膩心思，其實女人對於她收過的好禮物，都記得好牢。對於爛禮物，也真是刻骨銘心。

我算是個有點粗枝大葉的人，平日打扮不太淑女，也不愛戴珠寶，但那可不代表，送我珠寶名錶我會不開心。

檢視自己愛情史上的收禮流水帳

回首我記憶中收禮的流水帳，唉唉唉唉唉！竟然沒有一個讓我開心的好禮物不能責怪女人喜歡價值高昂的禮物。
女人無法相信承諾時，只好相信禮物。

是情人送的。我根本沒有百分之一的資格可以自稱愛情專家！在看到「削凱子」的新聞的那一瞬間，我覺得自己在愛情史上真是「太不名譽」的遜斃了。

我也沒有資格感嘆命苦，當然也收過名牌珠寶、名錶、名牌皮包及精緻水晶、名家陶藝、豪華郵輪旅程、健身俱樂部會員卡、超過每夜五百美元的飯店住宿……為了怕大家亂猜，所以我要詳加解釋一下：以上種種戰利品不是走秀走來的啦，就是節目製作人、經紀人、廣告廠商、所代言的商家的心意，讓人銘感五內。

以上，竟然，竟然沒有一樣是情人送的！

我收過的超爛禮物倒都是本來可能會成為情人的人或過往情人送的！

比如生日時收到一束由爛報紙包著的白玫瑰。（因為由花市直接採買便宜許多，才會長成那個樣子。）

比如情人節時收到一朵朵顏色不一、插在我們家郵筒的塑膠花。（上面還有一張卡片，代表他對我的愛是永遠不謝的……）

比如一幅他在中學時代上美術課的畫。（這對他可能很有意義，但要我供在

剝 開 收 禮 之 女 的 內 心 世 界

我家牆上實在很令人嘔氣。

比如一個應該是買給三歲小孩玩的積木玩具。（他可以花三萬元買一件西裝

外套，卻只肯天真爛漫的花三百元給女友當生日禮物！）

比如想挽回漸行漸遠的感情的男人，卻可以一邊哀哀切切，一邊忘了我的生

日……

比如一個錶面比我手腕粗的運動錶……

寫著寫著，我竟然有點想哭。當然這些禮物老早被我丟棄在視線之外，但還

真是很難忘記啊！

我怕我越想越多越覺命運多舛、獨立蒼茫、孤苦無依，就此打住。

往好處想吧，還好我還沒像很多主婦一樣，在生日或情人節時收到「她想要

的」拖把、炒菜鍋、吸塵器，哭笑不得。甚至男人還把分明是自己喜歡的東西買

回來，當做女人的生日禮物，其實是送給自己。

不能責怪女人喜歡價值高昂的禮物。

女人無法相信承諾時，只好相信禮物。

做個好命女

72

如果有些男人口口聲聲說「我有錢了妳就可以享福了」，現在卻只對自己大方，對女人那麼小氣，那麼，女人最好還是別聽他癡人說夢了吧！

好命女守則

女人可以自發性的對自己小氣，因自覺是個「賢慧的查某人」而沾沾自喜；但不會認為，對她小氣的男人是值得她付出的好男人。這一點，到底還是比萬有引力更有引力的不滅定律。

——摘自《給愛一條活路》

剝 開 收 禮 之 女 的 內 心 世 界

媒人看不出來的事情

好媒人，要懂得分際：

推銷不要過火、干涉不要過多、

電燈泡不要當太久、愛情中也不需公道主，

所以切莫反客為主啊！

我們來談「媒人」。

這個在網路戀愛世界裡快要變成恐龍的名詞，其實還是左右了好多女人的婚姻，只不過媒人從長輩變成朋友而已。

在男女授受不親的過去，所謂的「姻緣天注定」其實是「姻緣由媒人注定」。媒人如果偏心祖護一方，另一方可能會在男婚女嫁之後發現自己上了大當，認命的人便是一輩

媒人是交通警察，
在姻緣路壅塞不通時，讓大家的路好走一點。

子完蛋。在以父母之命為重、男女不太容易個別交往的時代，媒人美言幾句，往往能夠左右父母的意見，和傳統女人一生的命運。

我聽過好多因媒妁之言結婚的上一代女性，把自己的不幸歸罪到媒人身上。為什麼不告訴我他是花名在外呢？為什麼不說明這家子的公婆既無理又苛刻呢？為什麼不坦白說他們家看起來有錢，其實只是個空殼子呢？有時這個媒人還是自己最可靠的親人。這下更糟了，萬一婚姻破裂，連親屬關係都一起搞砸。

媒人不好當。以前的媒人，責任實在重大。現代的媒人，雖然已經失去了舊時代的重要性，但也還是常常會變成「在如膠似漆時被遺忘，在不共戴天時被埋怨」的角色。在我看來，很多憑三寸不爛之舌推波助瀾、以為自己在「做好事」的媒人，實在單純到愚蠢的地步。

「唉，要我做媒人還要包生兒子，我上一輩子欠他啊？」當怨偶找上媒人協調時，媒人常這麼嗟嘆。

而被介紹人再怎麼無辜，到底也還是自己點過頭輕易承諾了婚事，也是糊塗到危險的地步。

媒人看不出來的事情

「因為我信任他，相信他的眼光啊！」怨對著媒人的曠男怨女，往往會找出合理化的藉口，抹除自己的責任。怪別人總比怪自己好過些囉！

當各式各樣的媒人都要小心。人們在急著尋覓姻緣時最盲目，所以為朋友當月下老人的人，得有「功成身退、功不成身也退」的心態，不要太相信自己的眼光和第六感一定是正確的。被你牽線的人不是種豬，他們有權利看不對眼。你也不是全能的上帝，不要替其中一方拍胸脯保證、不要催促、不要「以配對成功為己任，置別人幸福於度外」。

願意結婚不代表愛情永保安康。

媒人不保愛情險

其實，要媒人為我們深入觀察理想對象是不可能的。就像「職業介紹所」不可能完全了解被介紹人的可用程度和真實的工作態度一樣。

我看過好幾個離譜又經典的例子。在鄉下長大的小米，最聽大哥的話，大哥很欣賞自己做生意認識的阿杜，說好說歹把年輕漂亮又涉世未深的妹妹介紹給阿杜，自己和阿

當月下老人，得有「功成身退、功不成身也退」的心態，
不要太相信自己的眼光和第六感一定是正確的。

杜之間的生意往來，親上加親，順暢無比。小米與阿杜同居，在懷孕五個月時，才發現

阿杜怪怪的，怎麼他越來越常出差呢？有天跟蹤阿杜，才發現阿杜已是有婦之夫，也是

兩個幼兒的爸爸。離開後的小米很怨恨哥哥出賣她，哥哥也很無辜，他確定阿杜的身分

證配偶欄是空白的（在台灣，很多已婚的人配偶欄是空白的）。殘局很難收拾，兄妹之情

至今很難回復。

親密關係中更有許多媒人看不出來的事情。

談過戀愛的人必然承認，萍水相逢時，我們會把自己最美麗的一面端出來；深入交

往之後，往往會一一發現對方的祕密；一起生活過，才能了解他是不是真的能夠長久相

處。每個人都有很多私密情事：酒肉朋友不會知道、爸媽不太清楚、長輩不可能了解、

就算是知己也無由窺見、也許連他本人都無法對自己坦白的私事。

媒人只能看出「他應該是個好人」，看不出他愛人的能力，也看不出他的「性能

力」！

媒人看不出來的事情

有些事，媒人不會知道

最近，我的朋友愛莎和交往一年的Ａ醫師分了手。分手後，Ａ以淚洗面百般挽回：「妳好歹也告訴我，我哪裡做得不好？」愛莎避不見面，也不給原因。原本視Ａ為乘龍快婿的父母和將Ａ先生的體貼看在眼裡的朋友都大感不解，父母還把愛莎罵個狗血淋頭。

愛莎始終保持沈默。

身為朋友，我的習慣是，不主動問朋友分手的理由，除非他自己想說。

有一回愛莎與我共品上好威士忌，她吐了真言：「唉，分手的理由，叫我怎麼說出口呢？老實告訴妳，我是在和他上床之後才想分手的，因為他實在——（以下省略，總之是先天性的問題，不是技術性的問題）唉，不提也罷！婚姻可是一輩子的事，我可不能忽視這個問題啊！我不是不想說清楚分手的理由，而是說出來更傷他，也會讓人家誤解，以為我是個『慾女』呢！」

媒人是交通警察，在姻緣路壅塞不通時，讓大家的路好走一點，但可不能一直引領

做個好命女

78

妳向左轉向右轉、護送妳一路平安到家。當然更不能幫妳開車回家。

好媒人，要懂得分際：推銷不要過火、干涉不要過多、電燈泡不要當太久、愛情中也不需公道主，所以切莫反客為主啊！

好命女守則

妳願意抱憾以終，或拿終身大事讓別人賭博嗎？

不，當然自己來比較好，

如果失敗，那也是屬於妳的失敗，雖敗猶榮！

——摘自《校園戀愛學分》

媒人看不出來的事情

妳是個「賢慧的查某人」嗎

剛認識時，還是挑一點吧！

總比偽裝自己是個「賢慧的查某人」好！

我們來做個寫實的忍耐度測驗。

如果妳跟交往不久的男友一起去逛量販店，妳發現家裡常用的牙膏正在特價中，於是妳一口氣拿了半打，結果妳的男友覺得妳太不理性了，很不客氣的把妳已經放在推車中的五條牙膏丟回售貨架上，妳會生氣嗎？會生氣到什麼程度呢？

1. 他實在太沒禮貌了，我當場就會發火。

2. 我當場會不高興，雖然沒有表現出來，但心裡已經決意跟這種人分手。

3. 我會跟他好好溝通，希望他改掉這種蠻橫的習慣。

做個好命女

4. 我想他是對的。我真的要好好改一改。

我們來看看自己的「溫順」指數吧！選4的人，是最溫順的，為了愛情，妳可以犧牲自己的面子問題；選3的人，也具有傳統賢妻良母的溫良恭儉讓性格；選2的人，打從心裡酷得很，只能忍一時氣，但長久來說可萬萬得罪不得；選1的人，根本不吃眼前虧，是直爽乾脆的類型。

這些選擇無關對錯與好壞，只與妳的忍耐度有關。

該挑的地方還是得挑

我想，如果是個「剛交往不久的男友」，多數現代女子會選1或2，才剛認識他就這樣管我，將來還得了？

如果換成是「已經有親密關係的男友」、「同居男友」、「老公」和「孩子的爸」呢？相信這個無理蠻橫的人與妳關係越密切，妳選擇溝通和服從的可能性越大，也許妳還會安慰自己說：「唉，他就是這個脾氣，沒辦法，還是想想他的好處吧！」

女人的忍耐力常會隨著年齡和親密關係的程度加大，這是人之常情。

長一輩的女人常常怕年輕的女孩找不到對象，往往對適婚年齡卻還沒有男友、或暫時沒有男友的女孩說：「眼光不要太挑，太挑小心沒人要！」其實我是很不以為然的，年輕女孩，挑，沒什麼不對。只要不要把挑和刁難畫上等號。

該挑的地方還是得挑，因為，如果在關係尚未穩定前不挑，我們必然會越來越不能挑，如果在初識之初，女人沒有讓對方了解自己的原則、底限何在，隨著關係日深，可能會從「慈悲寬容」變成「忍辱偷生」，從「無言以對」轉化為「含冤莫白」。男人何嘗不是如此呢？

我們的寬容度必然會越來越大，我們與日俱增的「成熟」中，必含有一些妥協的因子。因為心理上的顧忌和依賴會越來越深，交往時，妳一定得挑他的性格、他的人品，得考慮這樣的人可以承擔妳的厚愛嗎？又能陪妳走多久的路？

一個野蠻老公的悔過書

上述測驗是我在網路上看到一篇「老公的悔過書」後擬的。

這個老公寫悔過書的原因，就是如上所述，很激動的把老婆多拿的牙膏自作主張丟回架子上，他真的沒想到這個「小小的舉動」使老婆跟他打冷戰到要離家出走的地步，結果只好寫悔過書，一併為以前的小氣和野蠻處道歉，並且每個月還要多給老婆五千元零用金做為永久懲罰。也許還應老婆要求，把悔過書貼在網路上示眾，以示悔改。

小夫妻吵架，算是有了溫馨結局。

這封悔過書讓我這個旁觀者看得哈哈大笑，但我想，有這種小氣又莽撞的老公，雖然他沒有什麼大不赦的瑕疵，也必然是各種滋味點滴在心頭，一定有好多氣要受。

兩性之間的互動很有趣，如果妳在初識時隱藏自己的個性，對他一點也不挑，後來越來越挑，對方反而會有上當的感覺。

剛認識時，還是挑一點吧！總比偽裝自己是個「賢慧的查某人」好，除非妳打算一輩子不為自己主張什麼！

好命女守則

真正的愛情，要用真正的自我來談。

自我的缺點要靠時間與自覺逐步修正，不是遮蓋起來就沒事。

不管愛得如何轟轟烈烈，在戀愛階段，觀察及等待是必須的。

——摘自《真愛非常頑強》

做個好命女

84

幸福不是現實條件的總和

幸福需要一顆能夠體會的心，能夠消化的胃，能夠付出的手……

也需要小小的不足、小小的飢渴，

才會讓我們覺得，連白開水也好喝！

儘管外表總是亮麗光鮮，人生簿上一點敗筆也沒有——純蕙卻很知道，自己

有多麼的寂寞。

她從小就很順遂。家境相當的優渥，身為成功企業家的父母送她唸最貴的私

立小學、管教嚴格的私立中學。

為了怕她無法適應升學壓力，唸完高中後她就被送到加拿大讀語文學校，接

著又順利的唸了當地最好的大學。

未畢業前，她已與同樣在當地唸書，也是和自己家裡有世交之好、家境也相當富裕的伯群談了戀愛，大三那年就在長輩的祝福下嫁給了伯群。

英俊又有爲的伯群娶了貌美又沈靜的純蕙，舉行了浩大的婚禮。純蕙婚後很快的就懷孕了，包括純蕙自己，大家都不認爲她還要回學校拿到文憑。未來純蕙的少奶奶之路，並不需要任何保證書，所以她也就在家相夫教子，等伯群拿到碩士之後，兩人一起回到台灣，伯群爲家族企業打拚，她仍像個城堡裡的公主一樣，在傭人的簇擁下，過著好些年雍容華貴的生活。

不快樂的少奶奶

她也曾享受名媛的生活。只要哪個名牌辦派對，她總會收到貴賓邀請卡。有一段時間，生活中最大的娛樂就是和一群貴婦人爲了派對，特意購買數十萬的名牌衣飾出席，故意優雅的走到時尚記者的眼前，希望他們能夠欣賞她的好品味。

這應該是很多女人夢想中的生活吧，可是純蕙已經厭倦了。只有純蕙知道自

幸運並不等於幸福

己內心有多麼的寂寞。

好一陣子，她在夢中驚醒，坐在自己親手佈置的豪華客廳裡，失魂落魄的感覺到，彷彿有好多無聲無息的蟲子，躲在她看不見的地方，大口大口啃咬著她的五臟六腑。她變得不愛出門，處處打不起勁來，連擠出微笑都變得很困難，內心裡常有喋喋不休的聲音，問自己活著到底為什麼。

跟幾個老同學聊起自己的反常狀況，大家都只會笑她人在福中不知福。

在另一位貴婦的介紹下，她去找心理諮詢師，幾個心理諮詢師的說法都差不多，要她小心自己的憂鬱傾向。「不只是我，我那幾個人見人羨的貴婦朋友，都是心理諮詢師的常客！」純蕙苦笑道。我遇到純蕙時，她已經好多了，她自己開了一家咖啡廳，不只當老闆娘而已，還親自在裡頭端盤子，平時也很熱中參加慈善團體的義工活動。

碰到純蕙，是因緣巧合，我發現了她小巧精緻的咖啡館，她發現了我，笑語盈盈的來與我打招呼。

「前不久，我看到妳的書中引用了一句話：幸福不是所有現實條件的總和。

我覺得很有道理。我，是很好的現身說法。我以前是個心理上兼物質上的購物狂，常告訴自己，如果有什麼，我就快樂了。比如說，能夠嫁給我老公，能夠生一個孩子，擁有那部千萬跑車，我就會真的快樂了。但我總發現，在我擁有了那個東西之後，那一瞬間確實有滿足感，但不多久我又陷入同樣的不快樂中……」

「我也不能保證，我現在『總是』感覺很幸福，但目前為止，我蠻享受這種付出心力的感覺。我承認我一直很幸運，但我也一直在找幸福。幸運並不等於幸福。」

走出咖啡館，她的話和著咖啡香，仍留在我的脣齒之間。

幸福是什麼，每個人的定義不一樣，但是，確實不是你擁有的條件越多，你就越幸福。幸福需要一顆能夠體會的心，能夠消化的胃，能夠付出的手……也需要小小的不足、小小的飢渴，才會讓我們覺得，連白開水也好喝！

【寫給妳的第二個故事】
冬之女王

冬之女王

你問我為什麼成為冬之女王？我身不由己，我只是一個來自赤道的女孩子。本來我沒打算成為女王，我只是一個嫁到冬之王國的新娘。

命運的變化總是讓你想不到。我，被命運找到，它自動為我編織了皇冠。

我是夏日國度裡的富商之女，我叫小葵花。

年輕的我發誓要找一個不一樣的男人，因爲我聽說，愛情來臨時必然要有山崩地裂、驚心動魄的感覺，那樣的愛情才眞的值得收藏。

我不知道自己是怎麼愛上他的，也許就是因爲他給我不一樣的感覺，他和平常追求我的男孩完全兩樣。我生長在靠近赤道的國度，皮膚黝黑的男孩們總是懶洋洋的對妳微笑，他們愛唱歌，像陽光一樣的散播著熾熱的溫度；他不一樣，他是冬之王子，他表情緊繃且膚色蒼白到幾乎可以看見藍色的血液在血管中緩緩流動，抿成一線的嘴唇似乎從未因笑意而開啓。

他像一隻站在熱帶雨林中的國王企鵝，很快的吸引了我全部的注意力。他到我國留學，我在學校舉辦的「超自然研習營」認識了他。

當所有的男孩都以專注的眼神讚美我由鮮花織成的衣裳時，只有他不偏不倚的坐著，聽著講師解讀深奧的宇宙原理。

聽說他是冬之國度來的貴族，他的身上穿著雪白色的貂鼠大衣。他不會流汗，下課時從不肯走出冷氣強勁的教室，除了精確的回答老師的問題之外，他從不主動對任何同學交談。

我的父親管理花草之國所有的花園與紡織廠，因而我有豐富的花朵以及花奴可以為我編織所有流行的服飾。為了吸引他，我勤於裝扮，為自己設計了由紫色非洲菫織就的及膝裙、由橘色九重葛為質料的襯衫，秋天剛抽出嫩芽的芒草編的靴子⋯⋯然而，當所有的男孩圍繞著我，希望邀我共進晚餐的時候，他只是匆促的丟過來一個冷漠而絕望的眼神，挑逗我的自尊。

研習營結束的那一天早上，奇妙的轉變發生。我穿著一件由牽牛花織成的背心上課，他悄悄的走到我身邊，近到我的皮膚可以感受到他呼出的冷空氣，他笑也不笑的對我說：「小葵花，可以讓我摸妳一下嗎？」

我臉紅心跳，好一會兒我才發現，他的眼睛盯著朝開夕死的牽牛花直瞧，我對他點點頭，他纖長的手指慢慢接近我。當他觸到柔弱的牽牛花花心時，花心竟結成薄薄的冰，像被撕碎的紙片一樣灑落地上。

做個好命女

「對……不起……」他如死灰，全身發抖，好像他剛剛殺了人似的。

「一點也沒關係。」我說，牽牛花沒幾個時辰就謝了，這樣的衣服到下午也會縮成一團，得丟進垃圾桶裡。我不在意，他對我好奇，已經使我的心跳加速到無法承受的地步。那天黃昏，他靠近我，送我一個白色的小盒子：「在我的國家，沒有這麼多顏色的花朵，我只能送妳冬之國唯一的一種花，來彌補我對妳造成的損失。」

盒子裡有一片小小白白透著亮光的東西，即使是在父親的實驗室裡，我也沒有看過這麼美麗的小東西。

「這是花嗎？」

「是的，它是雪花，我們冬之王國唯一的花，我的母親，女王陛下用家傳咒語，讓它在火中也不會熔化。」

冬之王國是什麼地方啊？我以為，除了我們這個終年受陽光眷顧的國度之外，這個世界上再也沒有其他國家。

那個晚上在惜別晚會之後，我帶他到爸爸所管理的溫帶花園參觀。這時的溫室

裡滿是燦爛的罌粟花與薔薇，還有一百種顏色的天竺葵。我只是想要捉弄他，在他

低頭嗅一朵血色薔薇時吻了他的臉頰。

他嚇得全身酥軟，像堅硬的冰塊化成一灘水，好一晌才回過神來，用他冷冷的

唇堵住我的嘴，這時候我一生中最美妙的經驗發生了。彷彿原本在我體內躁動的那

股熱氣，自然的藉由我的舌頭湧進他的身體，我體會到一種美妙的平靜，像熱帶雨

林中的蘭花在我心中徐徐開放。

那是前所未有的感覺。一種絕妙的溫柔在我的身體中竄流，使我像海平面上的

小水母一般不由自主的晃動。

圓圓的月亮隔著透明的水晶玻璃俯瞰著我們，他臉上僵硬的線條溶解了，我看

到一抹微笑像漣漪一般漾了開來，縱然短暫，卻是我所見過最漂亮的微笑。

然後他告訴我，我必須嫁給他，冬之王國的律法規定，他必須娶第一個吻他的

女孩子。

這一切來得太突然，我從沒想到要當一個王子的新娘。他以雙臂緊緊箍住我的

腰，我的全身好像浸泡在酸麻入骨的檸檬汁裡。他說：「我知道，只有妳能拯救我，讓我不要再置身於荒涼曠野的無盡冰涼，只有妳可以改變我的命運。」

在那一刻，我是多麼相信，我可以用一身的熱流，使他溫暖，使他的手指不再那麼僵硬，使他的氣息像春風一樣馴良。

誰能告訴我那不是愛情。只有愛才有這麼大的力量。

☆☆☆☆☆

「小葵花呀，女大不中留囉！如果妳堅持，我們也只好同意。」我的父親說。

「我們家從來沒有人嫁給一個王子，跟一個王子聯姻，畢竟是一件風光的事情。」我的母親說：「可是妳要知道，我們這麼尊貴的家族也有傳統，嫁出去的女兒和謝掉的花一樣，不可以再回到花園裡來，妳可明白？」

雖然不願意讓我嫁到一個陌生的國度，父親還是送我一整個溫室的花朵當成嫁粧。我的丈夫率領了一整隊穿著白衣騎著白馬的雪國武士來迎娶，他們明亮的盾牌把飄下的細雨反射成千千萬萬道的彩虹光。

姊妹們以豔羨的眼神目送坐在透明花轎中的我離去。唸著家族傳統的祝福：

棉花兒飛絮，棉花兒飛絮，不管飛到哪裡去，落地生根有志氣。

越靠近雪的國度，我的心跳得越快。走過了楓紅山莊和落葉山頭，眼看著就到了冬之王國。我以為自己忽然得了色盲。冬之王國的山是白的，水是白的，大地全是雪白的，天空飄著棉絮一樣的花朵，舉目望去只有白色，如果沒仔細看，連迎親隊伍都像消失在雪地中一樣。我明白了，難怪冬之王國永遠屹立不搖，沒有人敢來攻打他們，因為沒有人能到白色覆蓋的土地，和一支隱形的精銳隊伍作戰。

一切對我來說如此新奇，我還來不及恐慌。王子將我安頓在「雪之花」的新宮殿裡，擁抱我之後，他的臉色不再冷若冰霜。我們度過了寂靜而綺麗的夜晚，看著雪景與極光。他的身體使我平靜，消滅了我心中如滾燙岩漿般的思念；我使他溫暖，他的臉龐染上了紅暈，直到天亮，嘹亮的鐘聲把我從他的臂窩中喚醒。

做個好命女

急促的敲門聲通知我們：「女王要接見你們，快點！」

「你是王子啊，」我說：「一個僕人的叫喚聲竟然如此不敬！」

他聳聳肩，無奈的把嘴閉閉成一直線。

「在我的國家，即使囚犯也沒受到這樣的無禮對待。」我抱怨。

「不久妳就會習慣了，我就是這樣長大的，雖然是王子，好像身在牢房。在妳的國家留學的時光，是我最快樂的時光。」

我有些擔心。

「沒關係，從此我和妳站在同一陣線上，只有妳能改變我，妳要堅強。」他說。

越靠近女王的宮殿，他的表情越冰冷，好像他與方才擁抱我的那個人完全無關。女王的寢宮有七重門，每一重門上，都有像鐘乳石般的冰刺。

最後一道門被衛兵們推開時，我的心也差點凝成了冰。我看見高高坐在雪貂椅上的女王，王子像死刑犯一樣噗通跪下來：「母親陛下早安！」

「今天你慢了五分鐘！即使是新婚之夜，也不能通融！」女王說。「因為將來你

97

冬之女王

要和我一樣，統治冬之王國！」

女王的下巴指向我：「妳！剛來的女人，我的媳婦！要向我行跪拜禮，直到妳的膝蓋因虛弱而發抖，否則不能起來，這是規矩！」

「我們國家沒有……這樣的法規。」王子囁囁嚅嚅的說。據說這是他此生唯一的反抗。

「我所說的話，就是規矩！每一條都會馬上被司法部隊抄錄下來！」女王繼續說：「由於妳可能成為未來的皇后，因此妳必須努力學會入境隨俗，別怕，我們會教妳怎樣變成冬之王國的人！」

女王下令檢視我的嫁粧。宮女們把溫室裡頭的花卉送了上來，所有珍貴的蘭花都凍成了冰花，女王皺了皺眉頭說：「看，多醜陋的顏色！除了白色，沒有任何顏色適合皇族高貴的血統。你們說，是嗎？」

「是的，除了白色。」文武百官很有默契的複誦這句話。

我匍匐在地上，冰涼的感覺漸漸滲進我的身體。似乎連牆壁都不斷釋放著冷空氣，我的腳趾開始不聽使喚，然後是手指、頸項，寒意慢慢入侵到心臟，我的眼睛一花，完全失去了知覺。

☆☆☆☆☆

「別理她，」他說。「從我一出生，她就沒有笑過，她也沒有擁抱過我。妳是第一個擁抱我的女人，我的愛，我相信有愛，就可以克服一切困難。」

冬之女王，他的母親，在我們甜蜜的小家庭中，不斷伸出她的魔掌，她命令衛兵們拔掉我溫室裡新開的玫瑰花，不許她的人民在我的花室外聚集和探望。有時候我會在半夜裡驚醒，彷彿感到有人在我們床畔徘徊。

聽說冬之女王會一種隱身術，她可以自由進入所有的門窗，王子在擁抱我時顯得十分驚惶。她不許我燃火來煮食芬芳的菜餚，只許我們食用冰冷的食物。三個月內我的溫室裡所有的花都枯乾死亡，她派來宮女們送一大批受了詛咒的雪花，用那些永不凋謝的結晶體來點綴完全荒廢的花房，那個時節正是大雪紛飛，我躲在稍有溫度的地窖裡，以顫抖的手寫了一封家書：

「這裡美極了，我的婚姻非常幸福，我們已經有了愛情的結晶，我相信，他一定是個全世界最美麗的孩子。」

每一封信都要經過女王的郵局，蓋上雪的印戳。

我很想掉眼淚，或許我的父親可以從模糊的字跡中讀出我的憂鬱，請人來救我，然而，天氣太冷了，我的淚水一離開眼眶，就結成了冰。

我的丈夫在她母親的命令下不眠不休的學習著冬之王國繼承人的高級法術。慢慢的我發現，只要他的手指接觸過的地方，都結上一層薄薄的霜，他呼出來的氣息越來越冷，他脆弱的皮膚下流動的血液越來越藍，瞳仁的顏色也逐漸改變，然後他開始用一種陌生人的眼睛看我。只要我一碰到他，他的表情就扭曲而痛苦，他總是喊著：「好燙！」

有一天，他說，他再也忍不下去了，他要像他的父親一樣，逃離這個鬼地方。

做個好命女

他的父親，是個從沙漠來的酋長，他的部落在某年冬天，被冬之國度的軍隊一舉攻佔，年輕的女王俘虜了他，他用愛情俘虜了女王，冬之王國在那時候曾經停止下雪，地面上長出美麗的青苔，人民第一次發現一隻被南風吹來的蝴蝶，然而，女王的丈夫卻在生下王子後和一個從溫帶被俘虜來的女奴私奔了，只留下一封信說：愛老早結成冰了，他永遠不會再回來！

冬之女王再也沒有笑過，把自己關閉在密室中，苦苦修練著家族傳下的冰封魔法與雪的兵法。在她的法力下，冬之王國除了白色之外沒有別的顏色，符合她的潔癖。

冬之王國的貴族應該有藍色的眼睛，因而我必須在她的監督下修習魔法，讓眼睛變藍。這樣的修練，我再也忍不住了。我們逃走吧！

「我的母親從來沒有擁抱我，她說我的眼睛是棕色的，像極我來自沙漠的父親，我們決定逃亡。那個夜裡，我的丈夫運用催眠術使所有的宮女和侍衛入睡，我和他躲過了雪梟的攻擊，穿越了碎冰之河，逃到了落葉山。我的叔叔在那兒有一座莊園，可以讓我們暫時居住。

我再一次看到會冒著煙的食物時，情不自禁的大吃大喝。忘了我所受的一切痛苦。然後我寫信回家，希望能夠得到父親的幫忙，和冬之王子回國居住時，卻收到這樣的回信：

妳，卻不能把傳統拋棄。

棉花兒飛絮，棉花兒飛絮，不管飛到哪裡去，落地生根有志氣。我們雖然寵愛

信是我母親的筆跡。

我忽然明白，即使我不願回到冬之王國裡，我哪兒都不能去。我的丈夫雖然在落葉山莊鬆了口氣，但他的腸胃卻禁不起冒著熱氣的食物，他飽受腸胃炎之苦，每天望著山背後的冬之王國嘆氣。

在我們的新生兒哇哇大哭的夜晚，他帶著孩子失蹤了，我知道，他悄悄回到冬

之國度，他自小生長的地方。他恨那裡，卻不能離開那裡。

☆☆☆☆☆

我變成一個流浪的女人，再一次踏進冬之國度，用皚皚白雪為外衣，尋找孩子的蹤跡。就在我快要餓死的那一剎那，腦袋突然變得很清楚：如果我沒有積極一點，我永遠找不到自己的孩子，為了對付冬之女王，我只有比她更冷酷。

我懇求冬之女王讓我回到王子身邊，低聲下氣的把自己的身分降為乳母。我恪遵女王的命令，不去擁抱我自己的孩子，也不去安慰他。女王說，這樣他才會變得像千年冰一樣的堅強。我在暗中窺看王子所學的每一種法術，且牢牢記住。我為自己的孩子伴讀，進入圖書館，認真學習每一種詛咒，在孩子十歲的那天，我的法力已經所向無敵，只消一句咒語，就將女王送給王子的所有冰肌雪膚的年輕女孩，全部送到不見天日的冰雪魔獄裡去。

我要奪回我的地位和我的孩子。女王震怒，但她已經老了，敵不過我的法術，

我將她變成冰的雕像，讓她永遠站在全城都會看到的地方。

我的丈夫竟然哀求我，請我對他母親放手。可是我的心已經比任何冬之王國的冰更堅硬，那是修習魔法的代價，我沒有辦法讓女王不記取教訓。這是王子最後的反抗。在我的丈夫逃亡後，我成為唯一的女王，統治冬之王國。這時候，我已經忘了怎樣擁抱我的孩子。

現在，我的肌膚，比初下的雪還白；我的眼睛，比最清澈的天空還藍；我的心，比千年的冰還硬。

這就是我的故事，你一定不相信，我曾是來自花草王國，熱情得像一鍋沸水的女孩子……

※※※

現在，我是冬之女王。

這是一個真實的故事，只是我把它改寫成一則童話而已。

做個好命女

一覺醒來希望自己未婚

我們在熱烈追求愛情「結局」的當口，
不會想到自己在未來的某一天一覺醒來，
竟希望自己未婚。

一覺醒來，收音機裡正在探討一個統計數字：有人做了一個婚姻調查，雖然大多數台灣人對自己的婚姻表示滿意，但有百分之二十八的人，希望自己早上一覺醒來，還是個無婚一身輕的單身貴族。

百分之二十八，其實不算高，不值得大驚小怪。

不過，跟美國和澳洲的已婚者比起來，有這種「奢望」的人算是比率挺高的，美國夫妻只有百分之十六，澳洲是百分之十八。在台灣，「跳進去的想跳出來」的人比率是比較高了些。

香港學者分析，認為這象徵著三地對婚姻的態度不同。言下之意，似乎是台灣人對婚姻態度比較不認真。我不這麼認為，事實上可能正好相反。

美國式婚姻離離散散乃兵家常事。跳出去也容易些，所以如果有了婚姻問題，不是離，就是找婚姻專家懇談，不必只在夢醒時分，意識朦朧之際，懊惱自己過去嚮往的婚姻夢原來沈重。本地婚姻的傳統約束力還是比較高，大多數人還是相信婚姻是一輩子的決定，而進入婚姻的男女壓力也自然沈重，多數婚姻之所以能夠維持，壓抑忍讓重於溝通。

一進入婚姻，即失去部分或全部的自己，走入婚姻越久，「自己」這個生命體往往變得氣若游絲，而「大家」都認為這樣才是理所當然的美德，仍是本地婚姻的大問題。

過去嚮往的婚姻夢原來沈重

做個好命女

106

相關的數據還顯示，有六成的丈夫希望妻子更熱情。（我想，妻子們也不是不想熱情，只是每天身心俱疲忙到晚，已經沒有力氣熱情。）另外四成呢？是已滿意於太太的熱情相待，還是不再奢望？

相對的，有六成的妻子希望丈夫更尊重自己。七成夫妻希望討論一下婚姻生活為何缺乏了情趣。（以上兩者，據我觀察，一要求討論下來，往往變成了指陳對方錯誤的吵架。）

無論如何，這些數據有助於我們反省，到底我們要的是什麼樣的婚姻？兩個喜字湊在一起，等於愛情成功，是我們代代相傳的信條。

大家都覺得，能夠趕緊尋覓到終身歸宿總是好的，乃至於好多人在很年輕的時候，把婚姻想得太簡單。我們在熱烈追求愛情「結局」的當口，不會想到自己在未來的某一天，一覺醒來，竟希望自己未婚。

夢醒時分不再騙自己

婚姻不是結局，是過程。美滿婚姻，更必然是一個冗長的過程。走入婚姻前，確實不能只憑俗話說的「要靠一股傻勁」。這一代對婚姻的要求高多了——不只要有人相扶攜，還要能圓夢；不只要做愛，還要能做自己。

對渴望早日進入婚姻者，這個數據雖然潑了冷水，但也還是有它的人性趣味。——有近三分之一的已婚者在做白日夢，希望他們還沒結婚，至少，我已經了些。一位剛離婚的朋友看到這個數據後，打電話給我，開玩笑道：「我稍微好過不必在夢醒時分騙自己了！」

我笑了——她還真有幽默感呢！我相信，曾因破碎婚姻傷神買醉的她會慢慢好的，我相信。因為自嘲本身就是一種療傷的能力。

不過，我也相信，那些希望自己一覺醒來是單身的人，即使夢想成真，百分之九十的人也會在幾年後又被愛情之火燃燒，又想重新投入婚姻。

認為「姻緣圓滿人生才圓滿」的價值觀，對我們來說實在是根深柢固，很難逃脫。特別是在寂寞得萬蟲鑽心的時候，總會覺得走上姻緣路才能覓得解藥。

其實，老是感覺寂寞或混亂的人，如果不去尋找病因，婚姻只會讓他更寂寞、更混亂。對婚姻的渴求，對於現代男女的空虛心病，只有麻醉作用，沒有治療效果。

這一層道理，希望一覺醒來發現自己還是未婚的人，應該都懂得。

一覺醒來希望自己未婚

愛情爲什麼會變成這樣

我相信愛情，

但婚姻中所需要的愛情，

並不只是當初決定結婚時沖昏了頭的快感而已。

我在報上讀到一個很荒謬的新聞，眞使人哭笑不得：

有一個太太發現丈夫有了外遇，找了徵信社去查。知道丈夫正與情人在某個賓館投宿，於是帶著弟妹及親友共六人，浩浩蕩蕩去捉姦，把門踢開後，發現丈夫跟情人和衣睡在一張床上。由於她知道現在光是同宿一室的話，不太能夠構成妨害家庭，所以她與親人就強力撕破丈夫和第三者的衣服，企圖要拍下他們的通

做個好命女

110

如果小小恨意在生活中不斷累積，滴水穿石，
再厚的愛情根基也會毀損。

姦照片。

丈夫惱羞成怒，為了保護第三者，和太太互毆起來，所有親友都加入戰局，結果後來變成八個人互控傷害，法官將八個人各依妨害自由及傷害罪起訴，變成大鬧劇。

我想，這一椿婚姻，大概也很難維繫了。

讓愛情變質的病毒

類似的婚姻鬧劇不少，當然還有更慘的例子，枕邊人成為仇人的例子時有所聞。最令人唏噓的是，這些翻臉翻得很難看的夫妻，當初多半都曾經是濃情蜜意的愛侶，結婚時誰不想天長地久呢？

曾經相愛，發願相守，愛情怎麼會變成這麼不堪呢？

讓愛情變質的病毒，在每對情人之間不太一樣。在華人的婚姻排行榜上，有幾個大項，比如：雙方家人的介入、對金錢使用方式的歧異、某一方的暴力傾向

或粗魯言語、外遇、生活習慣無法妥協、婚前的期望與婚後生活落差太大……只要有任何一點變成一個難解的結，都會使情人變成仇人。

現實生活中的試煉太多了，難怪有很多人都會感嘆：「唉，得不到的才是最美好的。」

想像中總是比較美好，其實，如果妳還是原來的妳，妳和那個得不到的情人結婚後，狀況可能不會比現在好太多。明白這一點，我們才察覺自己原來是人在福中不知福。

感情穩定不可以缺乏的應變能力

據我的觀察，抽象一點來看，原因大概是幾個：

感情穩定後，我們的態度變得太快，卻又缺乏應變的能力。

在走入婚姻前，我們有足夠的衝動，卻對兩人是否能夠相處缺乏了解的耐心。

我也曾經在《早知道早幸福》中寫過，年輕女子只想到要當風風光光的「一日新娘」，比較少想到往後是平平實實的一輩子。

一般男子也常只想到「娶個老婆好過年」，想成家之後就可以好好打拚工作了，卻忘記老婆不只是想要嫁給你而已，還需要你一輩子的愛情。

在某一次餐會裡，有位三十而立的男性朋友宣布了婚訊，開玩笑說：「結婚後我就不必追她追得那麼累了。」結果在座所有男性竟異口同聲發出：「別傻了，你只會更累！」再加上「唉」的嘆息聲。

這男人的想法好天真。我對婚姻好壞的判斷，並不是來自那一對佳偶是否還維繫著如膠似漆的婚姻關係。我覺得，好夫妻，就是多年後也還是好朋友的夫妻，壞夫妻，就是變成仇人的夫妻。

外遇當然是洪水，一夕間可能衝垮愛之橋，也別小看那些被我們隱忍不發，或我們覺得對方理所當然應該忍耐的小事情。如果小小恨意在生活中不斷累積，滴水穿石，再厚的愛情根基也會毀損。

我相信愛情，但婚姻中所需要的愛情，並不只是當初決定結婚時沖昏了頭的快感而已。

關心愛情的考績

固然想要愛得長久，就不可能期待愛情每天都像燦爛煙火，

但好歹也得關心一下：愛情的溫度計，溫度是不是已經降得太低？

這一年，你的愛情考績及格了嗎？

「換另一句好嗎？我已經結婚了，所以不要寫這一句，我寧願妳幫我寫財源廣進！」

演講後，有位年輕的上班族女性拿書來給我簽名。我為她寫上愛情順利（很沒創意，對吧？卻是我的誠摯祝福），她很有禮貌的堅持我換上另一句話。

「結了婚後就不要愛情順利了嗎？」我向她開玩笑。

「嗯，也對哦！只是我現在好像更關心別的東西。」她也笑了。

想要提高愛情考績，
就不能忘記曾經學會過的溫柔與甜蜜。

她說得好，她說出了好多現代女子的心情。我看過一則關於台灣職業婦女的

調查報告，上頭說，現代的職業婦女（多半指已婚者）有百分之三十三最關心的

是金錢，百分之三十最關心工作，只有百分之五不到的人最關心愛情。

好現象是，現代的女人不一樣了，她們知道，人生不能只有愛情，也不再文

謅謅的說：「愛情是男人的一部分，但卻是我們女人的全部。」

她們不只怕嫁錯郎，也怕選錯行；關心前途也關心「錢」途。

然而從這樣的調查中也可以看出一個危機：婚後，女人就不再關心愛情，有

些人對愛情的態度好像在應付聯考一樣，考過就算了。態度的轉變好明顯卻不自

知——一旦找到對象，對愛情的關注程度，簡直是從「無時無刻想著他」，到「拜

託你少煩我行不行？」

定時測量愛情的溫度

有位很有幽默感的太太說得好：「我常怪先生變了，婚前他會剝蝦子給我

關 心 愛 情 的 考 績

115

吃，婚後卻叫我不要買蝦子，免得他又被我唸。我們只要一抬槓，我都會把矛頭對向：他變了，不再對我那麼好。有一次他氣不過，對我說，難道妳沒變嗎？我以為他想要批評我的身材，正像一隻刺蝟等著要攻擊他微禿的腦袋和脾酒肚時，他卻說：『喂，妳記不記得，我們剛結婚時，我回家，妳都會給我一個吻，含情脈脈說：你回來了，累不累？現在，妳總是頭也不抬，連我走到妳身邊，妳都沒問候一聲？以前，妳想要我時，都會溫柔的說：嗯──親愛的，我們要不要浪漫一下？現在，妳說的是：喂，要不要？一副在餵餓狗的樣子。難道妳就沒有變嗎？』以為感情穩定了，結婚了，就不再關心愛情了，常就把愛情凍死了，是多半的人都有的惰性。

固然想要愛得長久，就不可能期待愛情每天都像燦爛煙火，但也得好歹關心一下：愛情的溫度計，溫度是不是已經降得太低？這一年，妳的愛情考績及格了嗎？

只有愛情，人生會很無聊；沒有愛情，人生會很空虛。

想要提高愛情考績，就不能忘記溫習曾經學會過的溫柔與甜蜜。

下輩子不讓他欠你

容我提醒：就算是上輩子欠他的，這輩子也不要過度的還。

還太多了，

豈不是害了他下輩子欠你？

「妳相信相欠債嗎？」她問我。

我靜靜的等她把自己的故事說完。

「他對我實在不好，我也知道他一定不是個可以託付終生的人，可是我總下不了決心離開他。」她的視線始終低垂。

「有多麼不好？」

「很容易發脾氣，一發脾氣就砸東西，讓我活得像隻驚弓之鳥。好幾次，我被他扔過來的東西打傷，還得騙家裡的人，說是自己不小心跌倒的……

他的工作也不穩定，應該說是時運不濟吧！他又沒辦法當人家的手下，只想做老闆，幾次生意失敗下來，目前，所有的親戚都是他的債權人——我嫁給他，一定很辛苦……」

她越說聲音越沙啞，眼眶也紅了，唯一讓她雙眸映射出一抹亮光的，是她手上的那張喜帖：「來參加我的婚禮吧！」

她嘆了口氣，說：「我和他是上輩子相欠債，所以這輩子要來還他……」

不能濫用相欠債理論

類似的歡喜冤家，常常出現在我的周遭。相守，不安穩，離開，又割心肝。

看著她遠去的纖細背影，我不免感慨。

老一輩的人喜歡說夫妻是相欠債，這句俗語挺有意思的。

兩個人為著一個共同的家，或為了愛情長相廝守，必然各有犧牲與付出。

但「相欠債」這個詞，也常被濫用、誤用。如果不是「互相」欠債，而是單方面一直賴債，那麼，關係就會失去平衡，久而久之，總有人不甘連連虧損，雖然捨不得離開，卻也不能無怨。

「就算是我上輩子欠他的吧！」有人會這麼自我解嘲。

容我提醒：就算是上輩子欠他的，這輩子也不要過度的還。還太多了，豈不是害了他下輩子欠你？如果妳真的是個宿命論者，就得斟酌一下，別讓他在今生欠下還不了妳的債務，下輩子換他慘兮兮，這是冤冤相報何時了。

「相欠債」是「有借有還、再借不難」，愛情帳本才不會有被虧空的危機。

下輩子不讓他欠你

119

女人的邏輯

男人看見自己，常因事業失敗；

而很多女人第一次看見自己，

竟是因為男人終於狼心狗肺的拋棄，

或者歷經變故，讓她清楚，只有自己能夠砌瓦築牆、擋掉風雨。

「妳的人生還有什麼計畫？」第一杯咖啡喝完時，她問我這個問題。

窗外的天灰濛濛一片，溼氣寒涼，還好咖啡廳裡有著咖啡香和暖意。多年不見的老同學約我喝下午茶，她曾是我的手帕交，無話不談，只可惜上了大學後，學校隔得遠，漸漸失去了連繫。

這個問題好大，我偏著頭問她：「哪一方面的計畫？」

做個好命女

120

「比如說，生孩子啦……」

「我可不可以說老實話──目前還沒有計畫。」我苦笑：「我們可不可以不要討論這個問題？這種問題一討論下來，很容易變成沒有人會被真正說服的辯論賽。」

我深知她的立場。剛剛喝那杯咖啡時，我已經知道她這些年來都在為同一個問題困擾，那就是：她已有一男一女，正在為該不該聽婆婆的話再生一個男孩而傷透腦筋。婆婆的理由是，再生一個男孩比較「保險」，而丈夫的薪水在供應全家四口的開支和給公婆的月費上，已經捉襟見肘。

我盡量不要發表意見，因為我不是她，即使同是五年級的女人，她所處的環境，我畢竟陌生。

「妳真不像女人，可是如果妳沒有小孩，那……」

「那我老的時候會很孤單，對不對？這個理由，我聽了一百次以上，可不可以換一個新鮮的？」

「人家……某女主持人那麼忙，都生了小孩，還是雙胞胎。」

「人家要，我就一定要嗎？」這個邏輯使我一頭霧水。

「咖啡喝這麼多不好。」她說。

「我知道。」

「不過，我本來也很愛喝咖啡的……咖啡確實很好喝，可是我為了懷第一個孩子戒掉了。」

「妳很偉大。」我說。我知道討好者心中最需別人討好。

她安心的笑了。雖然沒有找到共同的話題，她終於得到了認同，我的討好也順利成功，這一剎那間我們彷彿恢復了友誼。「那麼談談別的計畫吧？聽說妳常去旅行，最近還要去什麼地方？」

「吳哥窟吧！」我隨口說。

「什麼窟？那是什麼地方？跟妳老公去二度蜜月啊？」

「噢不，我常想自己去旅行。」我據實說。

「真的？告訴我，」她的眼睛開始放射出光芒，身子往前傾，壓低了聲音：「妳的婚姻是不是有了問題？不然為什麼要一個人去？跟我說沒關係，我不會告

做個好命女

122

女人不是邏輯不好，是太想對人家好。
反而沒聽到別人的聲音。

訴別人……」

我像一隻愚蠢的小蜘蛛，不斷被隔壁蜘蛛結的網絆住。這些我解不開的蜘蛛絲，不經意就會出現在我的生活裡。

這時，我總好想衝到外頭，淋淋剛剛降下的冷雨。

女人習慣用非黑即白的思考

美國女作家艾瑞卡·江曾說：「如果做個女人就要經常抱怨、或向人嘮叨生孩子的喜悅，那我寧願不當女人，當個聰明的修女算了。」

她看了我一眼，應該察覺了我企圖終止這個話題的決心，馬上轉了個大彎：

「其實沒小孩也好，我大學一畢業就結婚，一結婚就懷孕，一懷孕就沒有機會工作，有時我也覺得小孩是惡魔。沒小孩也好，我就看過有一對夫妻，像那個王建煊夫婦，沒小孩他們也過得挺好的，可以做慈善事業。妳還是不要生的好。」

我知道她犧牲立場，不過是希望能表達一點她的善意，可是這並不是我的心

女 人 的 邏 輯

123

意：「可是，沒有計畫，並不代表我永遠不要小孩啊！」

類似的狀況，我碰過好多次了。未婚時跟一群已婚女人碰頭，大家只會問妳什麼時候結婚。當妳很肯定的說還沒有計畫時，過了一會兒就會有人回頭安慰妳，其實婚姻並不美好，若給她有機會重選一次，她會選擇不要結婚。那時，我也通常會說：「可是，目前不想結婚，不代表我永遠不結婚啊！」總會換來她的一陣愕然，好像我是故意在語言上惡作劇來捉弄她似的。然後，她會全然釋懷的重問：「那妳到底什麼時候才要結婚哪？」

我總發現，女人，喜歡用一分鐘思考或評斷屬於一輩子的問題。所以比較上來說，女人最喜歡算命，喜歡被算命仙簡簡單單用一語定終身，對於人生意義，卻可以一輩子不搭理。

大部分女人思考現實問題的方式，也很有趣，常是非漆黑即慘白。不是「我一定要」，就是「我永遠不要」，不太能夠明白，人家只是「現在不要」。

比如說，到熟人家中做客，妳一定常遇到這種情況：明明是剛吃飽才來，女主人端來一盤蛋糕，妳搖頭說吃不下，她會很沮喪，再三強調那塊蛋糕好吃。妳若不接受，她會再端來一盤水果。妳若說，抱歉我現在很飽真的吃不下，她會說吃水果有益健康，不吃水果不是好習慣。

如果上述的角色調轉爲關係親密的男人和女人，女人屢屢勸食，而男人現在無福消受，女人多半會大大生氣——年紀大的生悶氣，年輕點的發脾氣。

蛋糕好吃、水果有益健康，我知道，我只是「現在」吃不下而已。然而，這卻是殷勤的女人無法接受的邏輯。

美好天性卻遮蔽了自己

不是邏輯不好，是太想對人家好，反而沒聽到別人的聲音。

想要對人家好，是想要在人際關係中獲得肯定。討好，才不會跟大家不一樣，被孤零零的遺失。

這是女人幾乎都有的美好天性，想讓自己發揮一種像「無色透明黏膠」的特質，讓旁人因爲她而感覺溫暖。這種人格特質十分良善、可以消弭爭戰，但是如果一味熱呼呼的拿一輩子去討好，只能跟著大多數人，走著所謂大家認同的路，自己內心深處的聲音，常會變成年久失修的斷井殘垣。

風來雨來，仍然躲在不能夠遮蔽的斷井殘垣中，繼續聽聽大家怎麼說，或叨叨絮絮的抱怨著命運辜負，始終沒想要花點力氣把它修整得完整堅實。

這樣的斷井殘垣，拆掉重建竟比慢慢修復容易。總是要等到平地一聲雷，摧毀所有，才不得不重整四壁、搭起新屋宇。

男人看見自己，常因事業失敗，而很多女人第一次看見自己，竟是因為男人終於狼心狗肺的拋棄，或者歷經夠大的變故讓她清楚，千呼萬喚也不會有人應，只有她自己能夠砌瓦築牆、擋掉風雨。

舊世界瓦解後，新世界建立，歷經辛苦，忽然看到自己，是很多上一代、這一代傑出女性走過的路。

當妳登上婚姻船

我們得用有智慧的天真，而不是愚蠢的天真來面對婚姻和愛情。

就像一艘要航向遠洋的船一樣，打造得越堅固，準備得越充足，就不怕可能發生的暴風雨。

有位相當年輕貌美、在媒體工作的女性朋友，正與某個企業家之子熱戀時，曾經對我說：「我覺得你們這些常寫有關愛情文章的作家都很討厭，總是要寫出人性中不太美好的一面，要叫人家提防些什麼。我覺得你們的想法都很小人，談戀愛結婚都是很美好的事情啊，只要信任愛情就好了，雙方相愛，怎麼會有問題呢？我現在就什麼問題都沒有。」

「那很好啊！」我沒有為自己辯論些什麼。我想，她才大學畢業不久，這也許是她第一次談戀愛。每個人的路都得自己走，儘管我們再怎麼想讓別人少受點傷，還是別在別人開心的時候敲警鐘吧！

不多久，報上出現她傷心落淚的消息。因為她大方承認了自己的戀情，但對方卻是一味否認，整個新聞看來像她自作多情。對方的父母也表示，根本不知道這件事情，又說，兒子認識的人很多，這種自己放消息想當豪門少奶奶的女人並不是第一個。她當然是又氣又急，但這件事是有苦說不出的，越辯越糟。

戀情見光死，風險多三分

知名人士談戀愛十之八九會落入見光死的下場，壓力太大、有太多人推波助瀾，比一般人談戀愛更是風險多三分。後來這一段戀情當然是見光死了，所幸在我看來，她的個性變得成熟許多，學會如何在談戀愛時保護自己、保護還未紮好根的愛情，現在已經尋得她所要的美好歸宿。

我認識一位美國牧師朋友，十年來曾經為兩千多對新人證過婚，他說：「我我們可以天真，但得用有智慧的天真，而不是愚蠢的天真來面對婚姻和愛情。

總是企圖在結婚禮樂響起前，先點醒新人：『你們已經有面對婚姻難題的準備了嗎？你們遇到雙方難以溝通時都怎麼處理？對彼此處理金錢的方式是否能夠接受？有沒有想過，萬一遇到了重大爭執或對方有外遇該怎麼處理？』可是，竟然所有的新人都會相視而笑，以不可思議的表情看著我：『牧師，你所擔心的一切，在我們之間都不會發生！』這位牧師說，我們離婚率這麼高，原因就在此。很多該在婚前想到的事情，我們都認為，這些事都不會發生。

離婚率越來越高了，它就像籠罩在女人心頭上一塊越來越龐大的烏雲。這當然不是個好現象，但也不值得太悲觀。為什麼呢？套用一位大陸研究婚姻學者的說法：因為以前中國人的婚姻，其實常是「高穩定，低品質」，看來沒事，但裡頭其實有很多事。婚姻穩定只是沒打算離婚，但品質常是「不足為外人道」。

離婚率升高的啟示

以前的人只追求穩定，現代人顯然更重視婚姻的品質。以前的人結婚是希望多個人賺錢、有人做家事、傳宗接代、可以享受性關係。現在的人要求的不只這些，我還希望找到可以溝通的「靈魂知己」，希望我們在結婚多年後還願意跟另一半相約去喝下午茶，我們也希望另一半願意跟我們終老，是為了愛，而不是不得已。現代人在婚姻中要的東西，其實比自己想像多得多。

離婚率的升高在提醒我們：我們從離婚率高升的警示中，應該多學會一些事情。我們可以天真，但得用有智慧的天真，而不是愚蠢的天真來面對婚姻和愛情，就像一艘要航向遠洋的船一樣，打造得越堅固，準備得越充足，把未來可能發生的暴風雨算進航程的風險裡，又不要畏懼起航。

妳還得有救生艇。雖然沒人喜歡用救生艇，但如有萬一，它還是安全保障。

只要有風浪，船身總會有點搖晃，就算不能一帆風順，也可以不要因為驚嚇而不知如何掌舵！說到船，我又想起上個世紀初鐵達尼號的故事。船開航前，一位船員得意洋洋的對記者說的話，還在一部紀錄片裡被完好的保存下來呢！他說：

「像鐵達尼號這麼堅固的大船，什麼東西都撞不沈它！」

啊——

婚姻搖頭族的心聲

在這樣的時代裡，逼人結婚是不道德的。

請尊重現代不婚族的選擇，

因為，只有時光能改變她們的答案。

五年級（一九六〇年）以前的女人，如果在三十歲還嫁不出去，所面臨的壓力一定很龐大。因為那個年代，男大當婚，女大當嫁，就是同志也會被迫娶個老婆傳宗接代，女人幾乎沒有辦法理直氣壯的說：「我不結婚！」

現代的適婚年齡女子，理直氣壯說自己不想結婚的，已經很多了，而且還有越來越多的趨勢。雖然，這些不婚族，未必是真的發誓不想結婚，有的只是現在還不打算結婚，或現在還沒找到可以結婚的對象而已。她們可不是以前廣東一帶的「自梳女」——把頭髮梳起來，表示矢志不加入婚姻的行列。

現代不婚族，充其量只是覺得「結不結婚沒那麼急」的不婚族。

有的是被上一代破裂的婚姻影響，不想像上一代的女人一樣，長久陷於感情的困境走不出來。有的是被這個社會的離婚率和朋友的婚姻悲劇嚇到，慶幸著自己因為不曾擁有，所以也不會失去。有的是被逼婚逼怕了，不想再談這一類話題。

有的不想和男友的家人共住同一屋簷下，所以拿不婚來延宕一下。有的是覺得現在談的戀愛挺好的，卻還沒把握這一輩子是否能跟他在一起。男女朋友聚散較容易，婚要離比較難。有的害怕結婚生子會阻礙她們人生事業的發展。

理由大概是上述幾個，每個人理由不一，但聲稱自己不婚的女子多半很有主見，共通點在於：她不想因為未婚，而受到異樣眼光的質疑。

「不管我結婚或不結婚，我想，每個人都可以有他自己的答案。我也有我的答案，你願意為我祝福嗎？」有一次我在報上看到一位號稱自己是「婚姻搖頭族」的年輕女孩投書，寫出了現代不婚族的心聲。

做個好命女

132

至少不會找癩蛤蟆當夫婿

不把結婚當成必要大事的女人，也許不會太容易找到要娶她的人，但也不會草率找錯人。上一代大可不必為她著急，為此辯論更是不必。

至少，她不再有「沒魚蝦也好」的心態，會找來一隻癩蛤蟆當夫婿。她也比較知道自己要什麼，也應該不會談戀愛談到沒了自己。

但是天下事真的是很難預測的。很多人在舊時的同學會中都會發現：當初那個斬釘截鐵不婚的同學，偏偏成為兒女成群的賢妻良母；唸初中就十分熱中戀愛的愛漂亮女性，卻搖身一變成為單身女強人；立志當女總統的，成天和柴米油鹽打交道；而立志當家庭主婦的，往往變成走在時代最尖端的新女性……每個人的路徑，都在不知不覺間悄悄的改變。

我認為，在這樣的時代裡，不管誰逼誰結婚，都是不道德的。請尊重現代不婚族的選擇，因為，只有時光能改變她們的答案。

全世界都是妳

就算我們會從非洲、美國、印度……變成阿富汗，我們生命史上的經歷過程，也都各有它的優點，一片荒蕪地也可能翻身成為最有潛力的土地，全世界都是妳。

朋友傳了一篇很有創意又很毒辣的短文給我。

這篇文章，一定是男人寫的，用國家來形容不同年齡的女人：

十八歲到二十歲的女人是非洲，半開發半蠻荒，物產豐饒；二十到三十歲是美國，已開發，極度資本主義，吸引你去消費；三十到三十五像印度，熱情而慵懶，有說不出的魅力；三十五到四十是法國，經過歷史的淬鍊，優雅而冷漠，四十到五十像南斯拉夫，總為過去的錯誤付出代價，五十到六十的女人像西伯利

如果一種關係像亂麻一樣纏住我們，
也得趁妳還有活力時好好清除它。

對女人的最大諷刺

以前剛上大學的女生都聽過「大一嬌，大二俏，大三拉警報，大四沒人要」，如果妳真要聽信這樣的話，那妳就會以為自己的價值感一上大學就急遽變少，憂心忡忡的女生大有人在。

後來的男生更更毒了，網路上曾經有好長一段時間，為大一到大四找盡各種比喻來形容，也有更刻薄的呢！比如：「大一大二是籃球，大家搶來搶去；大三是躲避球，大家閃來閃去；大四是足球，人人踢來踢去。」

亞，荒涼而令人卻步，六十到七十像內蒙古，只有過去的輝煌歷史，七十以上的女人是阿富汗，沒有人想去觀光。

看到這裡，一定有好多女性在抗議了。

這當然是男人對女人年齡的刻板印象：女人只要沒了青春，好像什麼都沒了一樣，一定會色衰愛弛，一定會乏人問津……

全 世 界 都 是 妳

135

大學畢業後進入社會，有很多女生都覺得鬆一口氣，因為她們又變成了最年輕的社會新鮮人，感覺自己又重新嬌俏了起來。

好像變老以及沒有人要，對女人來說是生命中最大的悲劇和諷刺。

前不久一位女性立委在立法院罵一位未婚的女性政府高官「老處女」，根據的就是這樣的心理吧！她自己也一樣「老」，只因曾結過婚，可證明自己不是「處女」，所以感覺自己是「技高一籌」吧！

雖然擔心著青春易逝，是每個女人的心事，然而我們也都明白，擔心是沒有用的，不如運用我們的有限時間，我們容光煥發的青春年華，去做妳想做的事：擁有青春時，如果我們的環境不容許我們夢想，那就得毅然決然到容許我們作夢的環境去。

如果一段愛情只能以破壞力腐蝕青春，在妳手腳健全時就要遷移到安全的所在。

如果一種關係像亂麻一樣纏住我們，也得趁妳還有活力時好好清除它。

那麼我們老了，絕不會活成西伯利亞或阿富汗，我們仍是一塊豐饒的沃土，

做個好命女

136

如果我們的環境不容許我們夢想，
那就得毅然決然到容許我們作夢的環境去。

男人又是哪個國家

雖然失去思春期的求偶激情，但有更多深刻的生命經驗，成為我們的養分和歷史。

就算我們會從非洲、美國、印度……變成阿富汗，我們生命史上的經歷過程，也都各有它的優點，一片荒蕪地也可能翻身成為最有潛力的土地，全世界都是妳。

如果妳不喜歡網路上的這篇刺眼短文，那我也可以運用幽默感將它回敬給男人：

二十歲以前的男人像剛果，潛力無窮，但騷動連綿；

二十歲到三十歲的男人像南美洲，物產應該很豐饒，但還未完全開發；

三十到四十歲的男人像南非，已經很開發，但無法克服內部種種衝突；

四十歲到五十歲的男人像英國，很有歷史，很世故，但必須面臨經濟衰退問題：

五十歲到六十歲像北歐，生命騷動止息，但也有大半進入冰凍期……

「頑固的老男人像伊朗，專制的男人像伊拉克！如果妳不想一輩子罩著頭紗不見天日，那麼就請為自己好好打算吧！」有一位剛走出不愉快婚姻悲劇的女性朋友，一定要我這麼補充說明！

好命女守則

身為現代女子，不必撿石頭來換現金，
不受只能撿一顆的規定，可以拿起了又放下來，
妳大可以掂掂掌心中石頭的分量，換一顆又何妨。

——摘自《做自己最快樂》

妳需要的不是烏鴉，而是天使

這個時代，大環境已不再那麼壓抑女人，

到底是什麼東西讓我們看不見自己？

女人的心中到底有多少潛藏的恐懼或恐嚇，

使她不敢努力實行自己的夢想？

有一部電影，很悶，叫做時時刻刻（THE HOURS）。

我說它悶，不是說它拍得不好，而是其中三位演技精湛的女演員，都努力的

呈現了女性的壓抑面，三個處於不同時代的女人，一樣都花了無數時間和自己的

困境暗暗的周旋。

儘管豐衣足食，心靈卻像黏在蜘蛛網上的垂死蝴蝶一般，被茫然與無奈侵蝕

了光陰，直到青春不再卻也找不到出路。

它是一部手法精緻的電影，卻不是一部思考深入，依原作推演的電影，導演默默的把女性的無奈跟女同性戀劃上天真的等號，這是好萊塢式的簡易推理。

撇開這一點不談，這部電影的沈悶情節卻也能讓人聽出一點絃外之音。那就是，女性在不能夠獨立自主的年代，心情確實苦悶，即使有人愛她，有個幸福的家庭，甚至已經成了一個母親，她內心的掙扎並未因為現實環境的舒適而削減；歲月流失而一事無成對她而言仍是深沈的恐懼，她還是沒有辦法拿別人眼中的幸福來說服自己。

我也可以依劇情做個簡單的歸納：十九世紀的女性才華被時代壓抑，二十世紀的女性被傳統壓抑，二十一世紀的女人擁有了自由，卻茫茫然看不見自己，恐懼未曾稍減，自我在精神上的壓抑還是很沈重。

這個時代，大環境已不再那麼壓抑女人。

到底是什麼東西讓我們看不見自己？

女人的心中到底有多少潛藏的恐懼或恐嚇，使她不敢努力實行自己的夢想？

勉勵妳自己的遊戲

我們不妨來玩一個造句遊戲。

在成長過程中，打從長輩或妳自己嘴裡，妳曾經聽過多少「如果XX的話，妳就完了」或「如果妳XX，妳就會嫁不出去」的恐嚇呢？（以上這兩句話其實是一樣的，因為在上一代女人的眼中，嫁不出去也等於完了。）

青春期的時候，上一代媽媽會有意無意的實施性教育：「如果妳還沒結婚就跟男人怎麼樣，妳就完了。」

「吃那麼多，誰敢娶妳？」

「不會做家事，妳就會嫁不出去。」

「書讀得好有什麼用，誰敢娶妳？」

「女人太聰明，哪個男人敢娶妳？」

在重要的場合或公開談話時，也可能有人告訴妳，或妳會告訴自己：「如果妳說錯話、表現得不好，妳就完了。」

所以，女人的人生路上常有許多擋住她前路的銅牆鐵壁，像處女情結（妳要潔身自愛當然很好，但是因為薄薄一片膜而陷入許多年的痛苦實在沒必要）、有害怕成功的心結、有永遠不敢說出自己真實意見的傾向（怕說錯話、說出真實意見，別人就不再喜歡我）、有歇斯底里的情結（心思敏感的人長久處於壓抑狀況，想不歇斯底里也難！）只能永遠留在沒有自信的泥淖裡。

精神上越壓抑自己的人，內心深處這種恐嚇式造句出現得越頻繁。嚴重者已經不需要他人恐嚇，自己的內心深處就有一個晚娘面孔，耳提面命的訓導：「如果XX的話，我就完了！」

心裡有提醒自己的聲音固然很好，但可不可以換個方式呢？

妳需要的是：「如果XX，妳就會成功。」建立一套勉勵自己的機制，是建立自信的開始。在妳心中，妳需要的不是烏鴉，而是天使。

妳就是自己的天使。

不做網中之魚

妳不可能討好所有人，被百分之百的人永遠讚許。

妳當然可以創造一些話來讓自己不那麼耿耿於懷，

生龍活虎的證明自己的能力！

妳一定聽過一句話：「一個女人在一群男人中維護貞潔，比在一群女人中容易。」為什麼呢？因為一群女人，閒來無事的話，可以嚼舌根嚼得妳體無完膚。

當然，這是百年前的老話了。現在的女人，不像百年前的女人有時間閒嚼舌根，道人長短。

然而，深為流言困擾的女人卻不曾少過。在我們的成長過程中、求職生涯裡、親屬關係中，我們都或多或少的因為一些流言或謠言困擾過。

流言的困擾

因為主持節目的緣故，我聽了許多三、四年級女人的婚姻個案。其中，最令他們惱火的閒話排行榜，大致有幾句話。

最嚴重的是婆婆看媳婦不滿意，偷偷告訴兒子：「注意，你老婆跟某某人有說有笑，小心她偷人。」至少有三、四個案例為表明自己清白，聽了這話後竟然「以死明志」，還好並沒有造成什麼大礙。疑神疑鬼的老公如果一直懷疑老婆有外遇，被氣到沒話講的女人，也常會採取激烈手法抗議。

其次就是姻親的閒話，說她的男人娶了老婆後就成了「妻管嚴」，變得自私自利。很多人都有一種成見，好像結了婚的男人不會自己變「壞」，都是被老婆帶壞的。這樣的話也使很多女人受不了。

我不是個天生好脾氣的人，我真的很能體會那種聽了莫須有的編派後，像一只燒開了的水壺，氣咻咻的感覺。事關名譽的話，可能還不只是沸水在心中燒而已，也許更像被丟個手榴彈一樣，感覺自己被炸個體無完膚。

做個好命女

144

找出怒氣的源頭

生氣當然可以，請容許她們生氣，容許自己生氣。不要急著用浮浮泛泛的空

解我，當事人當然難過。

連在學的學生也不例外，我常常收到初中、小學女生的mail，說她們為班上某些人的謠言氣到想自殺。因為在這個年齡，我們最在乎的就是同輩的看法，朋友誤

現代的家庭主婦受到同等困擾的還很多，上班族婦女，更還有另外的氣受。

位置，她當然會生氣，也值得她生氣。

在喉。設身處地著想，我如果是她的話，家族的看法在她人生中佔有多麼重要的

她會更生氣。有些話傳到我耳裡時，已經讓這位太太氣了幾十年了，仍如梗

這時萬萬不能安慰她說：「別生氣，就讓別人去說好了。」

中說出來的，引得婆婆或夫家誤會她。這也很讓女人百口莫辯。

還有，她明明克勤克儉，卻說她奢華享受。或把莫名其妙的話編派成從她口

話，如「因為懂得，所以慈悲」「退一步海闊天空」「不要那麼小心眼嘛」「生氣會變老，所以別生氣」來當滅火器，想要馬上消掉她們的氣。這些話是好話，可惜被濫用了，常會讓我們找不出憤怒的根源，也常被用來含糊抹平一個人的個性。壓抑情緒對人毫無好處。

我們都是人，有個性的人，有原則的人，所以有生氣的權利。生氣跟發燒一樣，本身是一種症狀，不是病，它讓人很難受，卻在提醒我們，內在有某個部分出問題了，必須好好把它找出來。可以生氣，可以辯白，但問題在於，要氣多久呢？

氣得太久了，確實只會破壞免疫力、失去往陽光多處走的能力。

在生氣的時候，我會想辦法提醒自己：不要生太久的氣，不要做網中之魚。

那張網如果是別人故意編來羅織你的，別讓「有心人士」稱心如意。

同為女人，但被女人排擠是很多成功女性都有的經驗。寫過相當精采的旅遊書如《推開文學家的門》和《瀑布上的房子》，幾乎環遊了世界的傑出女作家成寒就曾經說，她為了夢想活得很帶勁、很努力，但在追求夢想的過程中，曾幾度

做個好命女

146

遭女生的排擠、打壓，心裡很難過。直到一位長輩對她說：「妳要同情她們，因為她們沒有別的路可走！」

她說這句話點醒了她，至少使她不那麼難過，繼續積極行動下去。

妳不可能討好所有人，被百分之百的人永遠讚許。妳當然可以創造一些話來讓自己不那麼耿耿於懷，生龍活虎的證明自己的能力！

不做網中之魚

尊重別人的恐懼

一個懂得尊重妳的恐懼的情人，一定是好情人。

他的愛一定比他的要求多。

著名導演阿莫多瓦在他的奧斯卡得獎之作「悄悄告訴她」這部電影裡，有個片段很有深意：

男記者送一位勇於接受任何危險挑戰的女鬥牛士回家，女鬥牛士發現廚房裡有蛇，嚇得涕淚縱橫，歇斯底里的衝出家門，回到男記者的車上，要求他幫忙。

男記者看盡了女鬥牛士對付蠻牛時的英勇神態，雖然不太理解為什麼她會怕一隻小小的蛇，卻也很誠懇的對她說：「我尊重別人的恐懼。」

這一幕戲十分體貼，讓我很感動。

接受他的小恐懼，別強迫他，生活更有情趣。

它也讓我想起一位男性友人的分手故事。

他說，他天不怕地不怕，最怕坐雲霄飛車。有一次和女朋友參加公司的旅行團，相偕到東京去玩，到了迪士尼樂園，女友卻堅持要搭雲霄飛車，而且還一定要他相陪。

「如果你連這個都不肯陪我，就是不愛我。」說什麼女友就是不肯讓他一個人留在地面上。

女友的脾氣硬得很，簡直是不能忤逆。他在眾目睽睽下，心不甘情不願的接受了這樣的指令。結果一下來就吐了滿地，心裡更是怨上加怨，回國後兩人就分手了。

被強迫的，都有副作用

「你愛我，所以你一定要ＸＸ」很多人對情人都有這樣的要求。ＸＸ可能是「孝敬父母」，也可能是「借我錢」，也可能只是「打蟑螂」或「跑跑腿」……

尊 重 別 人 的 恐 懼

149

我曾經看過一個大老闆的太太笑著說：「他呀，碰到什麼大事都從容不迫，就只有在看到蟑螂的時候慌了手腳，像個可憐的小男孩，我覺得他那樣子好可愛！」接受他的小恐懼，別強迫他，生活更有情趣。

情人間彼此總有要求。有要求，不是不對，只是常常把話說得太尖硬，處理得不夠細膩，忽略了對方聽這話時的心理感受和當時狀況。

相信妳也必然贊同：最高妙的要求，不是脅迫，而是讓他自願。在任何感情關係中，被強迫的，都是假的，都有副作用。

如果妳對他要求十件事，他統統都辦不到，他一定不是好情人。

但如果他就有那一兩件事辦不到，就尊重他吧！

我看過女人要求木訥的男友去做汽車銷售員，賺更多的錢；也看過男人要求在工作上很有企圖心的女人辭掉工作當家庭主婦，下場——不說也罷。

一個懂得尊重妳的恐懼的情人，一定是好情人。

他的愛一定比他的要求多。

自古才子難相處

如果真能從戀情中學得一些東西，沒成功也未必要有遺憾吧！

因為和才子在一起的女人，總是真情付出。

真心，就對得起自己。

敬媛的前男友，是她唸大學的同學，同時也是個公認的才子。

他寫得一手意興遄飛的好文章，也是校內的學生意見領袖，雖然態度總是很高傲，人也不算好相處，但師長和同學提起他來，都還是翹起大拇指，說他是學校裡的風雲人物。

當敬媛和他的戀愛由傳說變成事實之後，不知有多少人稱他們為金童玉女、才子佳人。清秀的敬媛不是絕色美女，但她的人緣之好、聰明能幹也是人人稱

道，自從變成了校園才子的女友，也就一手包辦了照顧男友生活起居的工作。由

於兩人的家境並不算好，為了籌措男友當國際交換學生的旅費，敬媛還利用晚上

時間到處兼家教，甚至到夜市擺攤，希望男友達成他的夢想。

男友很會在公開場合感激敬媛，但感激是一回事，體貼又是另外一回事。在

男友追求夢想的路途上，鞠躬盡瘁的敬媛越來越瘦。

男友也沒有辜負敬媛的「栽培」，唸完研究所後考上公費留學，這時敬媛早

出了社會，把所有積蓄自動拿給男友換成了美金，希望他能夠在國外過好日子。

由於家裡負擔很重，敬媛只能癡癡的在國內等他回來。

金童身邊的憔悴玉女

妳一定很想知道，這一對金童玉女有沒有長相廝守？答案是：男友果然唸完

了博士，也回國了，但他身邊老早有了老婆，是國內企業家之女。敬媛還接到了

喜帖。

按照我的觀察，和才子在一起的女人，
多半是苦水滿腹。

沒有人敢安慰敬媛，因爲她一定很傷心。

過了好些年，敬媛也結了婚，婚後與我約好喝下午茶，自己提起往事，搖了搖頭說：「其實他娶別人也好，我實在太累了。」

太累了？

「雖然，愛情路走了那麼多年，沒有終成眷屬，好像很虧。但大家只看到他彬彬有禮、意氣風發的時候，完全沒辦法想像，當他退出別人的目光焦點時，只是一個連自己生活也沒辦法照顧的孩子，不時會發脾氣，沒靈感也會發脾氣，在別人面前不敢發的脾氣也都拿來在我面前發。我不像他的情人，反而像他的傭人。女人自古愛才子，他以前認識的女人，和交過的女朋友們，都跟我一樣欣賞他的才華，老早把他寵壞了，他把我對他做的一切都當作理所當然。現在，我過著有人疼惜的生活，反而輕鬆很多。」

「……而且，我在和他交往時，還要應付許多同樣愛才不惜獻身的女人，那種辛苦，眞是……很難對外人說。」

自古以來，有兩種男人一定受女人歡迎，那就是「財主」和「才子」。（通

自古才子難相處

153

常一般定義上的才子，指的多是有文藝上的創意，而且口才伶俐的人。有趣的

是，男人未必會太歡迎「財女」或「才女」。）

重視現實的女人愛財主，重視精神的女人，愛才子。這兩種人，前者在諂媚

聲中長大，後者在掌聲中長大，在成長的過程中，都被寵壞了。（如果他是財主

加才子，就會被寵得更壞，但我好像還沒看過這種兩全其美的傢伙。）

真心，就對得起自己

就以我認識的才子來說吧，我發現這些才子們，果然都風流倜儻，即使已有

固定女友，都還不難找到飛蛾般的女子投懷送抱。並不需要長得太英俊太瀟灑，

只要能語驚四座，能舞文弄墨，都可以過著曼妙的生活。

他們真正安定下來，願意固定伴侶時，都早早過了四十歲，多半娶的是個比

他們年輕很多且務實的女子，忽然搖身一變變成好爸爸。

也許是玩夠了，浪子回頭了，願意和一個女人組成家庭，過尋常生活，真是

重視現實的女人愛財主，重視精神的女人，愛才子。

「橫眉冷對千夫指，俯首甘爲孺子牛」的最佳寫照。

看在那些「前女友」眼中，眞是不可思議。

這世界需要才子——我寫這篇文章，不是來批評才子，也絕對不是要女人別跟才子談戀愛，才子自有迷人之處。只是按照我的觀察，和才子在一起的女人，多半是苦水滿腹。

但「才」字的奧妙就在於，有些才子旁邊的女人雖然苦水滿腹，回憶當時戀情，不管才子當時多麼花心，多麼讓她傷心，她還是會不悔的說：「啊！他還是教了我許多東西。」

才子很像「鍋巴」那樣的東西，不能天天當飯吃，但是，它的味道確實比白飯來得好吃。

我想，如果眞能從戀情中學得一些東西，沒成功也未必要有遺憾吧，因爲和才子在一起的女人，總是眞情付出。眞心，就對得起自己，儘管，本來她並不想把青春孤注一擲。

他感受得到妳的愛意嗎

妳那麼愛他，

他感受到妳的愛意了嗎？

請問問他，問問自己。

我的朋友麗娟從小模樣可愛，乖巧懂事，成績又很優異，所有的師長都很喜歡她，很多同學的爸媽都想要認她當乾女兒。唯一讓麗娟感覺，她永遠沒有辦法討好的大人，就是她媽媽了。

麗娟早熟懂事，是因為她總是看著媽媽的臉色長大。她的爸爸任職林務局，常常在山林間奔走，並不能天天回家，也許就是因為這個緣故吧，當公務員的媽媽把這個長女當成了出氣筒。儘管麗娟那麼聰明，她總是沒有辦法了解，這天媽刀子嘴太殘忍，讓別人無由體會他的豆腐心。

媽又為了什麼事罵她或打她，她總是活得很恐懼。

「我拿了全班第一名，我會說，那有什麼用，以後進社會誰管妳唸書第幾名。我考了第二名，我媽也會說，哦，妳看人外有人天外有天，別以為人家都不如妳；弟弟妹妹頑皮了點，她也會對我說，妳還真會做榜樣。」

也不只是麗娟的耳朵每天在受罪而已，偶爾回家的爸爸也常聽見自己的太太說：「為了賺那幾個錢，值得那麼賣命嗎？」或「我的命就是沒鄰居楊太太好，人家的老公那麼會做家事，不知道是哪輩子修來的福？」

媽媽唸過書，所以罵人從不帶一個髒字。

沒有一樣不挑剔

長大之後，麗娟當了牙醫。媽媽常說：「妳如果再聰明一點，妳就是真的醫生了。」她決定要嫁給一位工程師，媽媽也說：「當醫生不如嫁醫生。自己累個半死做什麼？」麗娟生了女兒，媽媽的第一個賀詞竟是：「沒生男孩，婆家會看

他 感 受 得 到 妳 的 愛 意 嗎

157

不起妳。」雖然媽媽會問她，要不要回娘家做月子，她一想到自己要躺在床上接

受媽媽的疲勞轟炸，抵死也要住在坐月子中心裡。

雖然麗娟總是很努力，但麗娟的運氣並不算好。麗娟的先生有了外遇，兩人

協議離婚，媽媽當然又找到了冷嘲熱諷的機會。

幾年來，媽媽似乎從來不放棄為麗娟的婚姻失敗找原因。有一次竟然一定要

麗娟抄下某整型醫院的電話：「一定是妳的胸部太小，所以人家不要妳。」有時

還會打電話來說：「唸那麼多書沒有用，連一個老公也留不住。」「妳如果當初

生個男孩，他就捨不得跟妳離婚了。」

媽媽當然不知道，此時麗娟已經得了憂鬱症，靠著精神醫生的藥物，正在與

心裡頭的惡魔奮戰呢！

直到有一天，精神有點恍惚的麗娟發生了車禍，她才第一次發現媽媽的愛。

昏迷的時候，彷彿聽見媽媽頭髮散亂的坐在一旁失控大哭：「妳是我的心肝寶

貝，妳不可以走！老天爺，請救救她，拿我的命來換都沒關係……」

她醒來的第一句話，就是鼓起勇氣來問一直守候在身邊的媽媽……「媽，妳真

把愛藏在冷言冷語中的人，就像一隻刺蝟，
尖銳的外表使人不敢去想像，原來它也是隻溫血動物啊！

的有愛過我嗎？」

媽媽愣住了……「除了你們，我還有什麼親人？難道妳不知道，我一直很愛你們？」

是的，在此之前，麗娟完全不知道。這時她也明白，每一句冷嘲熱諷，曾經都是反話，都是關愛，只是她、父親和弟妹，從未感受到愛的溫暖，只感受到母親的「口業」。

讓他聽見愛的聲音

訥於表達的人，我們可以從他的行為中感受到愛意；但把愛藏在冷言冷語中的人，就像一隻刺蝟，尖銳的外表使人不敢去想像，啊！原來它也是隻溫血動物啊！麗娟從冷嘲熱諷中傾聽到一點愛的聲音，竟然花了三十多年。

麗娟的母親，可不是特例。很多對子女要求過度嚴苛的父母親，都是一樣的。刀子嘴太殘忍，讓別人無由體會他的豆腐心。

他 感 受 得 到 妳 的 愛 意 嗎

159

每一次我到大學演講時，都會做個調查：你是在充滿愛的家庭長大的嗎？還是在冷嘲熱諷、備受打擊的家庭中成長？還好這些大學生的父母都不在場，否則一定難以置信：在備受打擊的家庭中長大的，至少占三分之二。很多同學會說，我知道他們愛我，只是從表面上看來，好像不是那麼一回事。

這算是有進步了。五年前，大約有十分之九；十年前，三百個只有一兩個認為自己的家庭充滿愛了吧！

你那麼愛他，他感受到你的愛意了嗎？請問問他，問問自己。

【寫給妳的第三個故事】
番茄

番茄

Pomme d'amour

（番茄，法文，意謂愛的蘋果）。

我知道，我一直是個不起眼的人，好像菜
市場裡的番茄，在任何季節，任何攤位，
你都可以找到它，它不是不可口，但是因
為太容易找到，沒什麼特別，所以永遠沒
有人覺得它值得珍重的咀嚼，在很多的菜
色之中，都缺不了它的滋味，雖然它總是
配角。

推開門的時候，她背對著我站著，安靜的攪拌沙拉，穿著泛黃蓬蓬裙的她，身材膨脹了一倍似的，地上的影子像一團濃濃的墨魚汁。

拉開椅子坐下來之後，她緩緩的轉過身，我看到一張圓嘟嘟的臉，泛著不太自然的粉紅色油光。

那是一張我看了一百遍也不會記得的臉，像你走在鬧區街上，隨時會迎面而來的臉龐一般，你不會對它皺眉頭，也沒有對它微笑的慾望。

對我的眼睛來說，這樣的臉龐會像一陣吹過的風，不會留下任何印象。

我只會知道，她有一個鼻子，兩個眼睛，一個嘴巴，只能說出這樣貧瘠的形容詞。

「要吃什麼？請看桌上菜單。」她的聲音既不剛硬也不柔軟，既不是客氣，也不是不客氣，既不動聽，但也還不至於不悅耳。對我的耳朵來說，這樣的聲音，即使再努力捕捉，也找不到它的特徵，很難在記憶中留下任何檔案資料。

菜單上都是番茄，價格嘛都是在這樣平凡的小餐廳裡會有的正常價格。番茄鑲牛肉、番茄蛋炒飯、番茄咖哩雞飯、番茄豆腐湯，還有番茄乳酪披薩、番茄燴羊肉、番茄燉血腸、番茄雞尾酒、番茄蛋糕。我想，最簡單常見的口味總不會錯，我點了一客番茄義大利麵。

這時我才注意到，光線昏暗得像個洞穴，佈置得毫無特色，不外乎是桌子和椅子以及吧台的餐廳裡流動著微細低沉而單調的輕音樂，彷彿是薩克斯風的聲音，沒有任何個性的曲調。她不疾不徐的把麵端到我面前。我默默吃了一大口除了新鮮番茄渣和番茄醬外，什麼也沒有的義大利麵。

「好吃嗎？」由於沒有別的客人可忙，她拉開我面前的椅子坐了下來，認真的看著我。

「嗯……」我盡力在番茄的濃厚滋味裡尋找除了番茄之外的其他味覺，但我的舌尖彷彿也失去了判斷力似的。「嗯……嗯……」我努力的點頭，把和一般義大利麵沒什麼不同的麵條呼嚕呼嚕捲進嘴裡，像日本人用力吸著涼麵似的。「我認得你，你是個寫東西的人吧，因為……你右手的中指第一個指節，有不太正常的彎曲，你至少非常勤奮的寫了十年以上。即使改用電腦，那樣的彎曲也不可能改變……」

沒有想到她會有這麼敏銳的觀察力。

「沒有人會注意到我，我只好努力的注意別人。」她搓搓白白圓圓的手指，對我擠出一個微笑，我發現她有兩顆潔白的門牙，其他的牙齒以差強人意的方式排在像番茄嫩肉一樣柔軟的牙齦上。這個想法使我感覺眼前的番茄麵越來越難下嚥。「除了這個，我沒有什麼好跟別人講的，我的故事非常無聊，非常無聊……」在昏暗的燈光中，彷彿有一隻手，像打沙拉醬一樣，把我清醒的意識快速的攪碎。她並沒有停止訴說她的故事。

「我從小就是一個無聊的小孩，連我在內，我爸媽有五個孩子，生活還過得去；我是中間的那一個，不曾被重視也不能說被忽視。我從小就長這個樣子，不美，嗯，也不太難看，我爸爸為我取了個綽號叫做番茄。我在學校的成績，也很普通，如果大多數人及格，我也會及格，大多數人不及格，我也會不及格，總之，我就是那個大多數人，我也平平安安的接受了大多數人應該受完的教育，永遠保持在中間。我從來沒有什麼好運氣，也從來沒有任何壞運氣。

「老師從來沒有誇獎過我，只有在一次作文課寫『我的志願』的時候，我說我沒有什麼志願，我只希望成為一個平凡的人。因為平凡中可以看見偉大嘛，不需要每個人都立志當總統的。我想要當個平凡的女人，嫁個平凡的老公，生平凡的孩子，像個平凡女人，每天上菜市場時，為一把蔬菜少幾塊錢和老闆抬槓半天，為了臉上一個青春痘傷傷腦筋，有小小的高興和悲傷就夠了。老師把我的作文當眾唸出來，他說，這篇文章很有「個人特色」，平凡就是福，不要好高騖遠，從此我更認為當個普通人就是我的生活目標。

「我的人緣還算不錯，因為我沒有討厭過任何人，也沒有被任何人討厭過。在我十八歲以前，從來沒有人追過我。倒是替我的姐姐和妹妹和同學傳過許多次情書，我從來沒有質疑過，為什麼沒有男人要寫信給我呢？好像本來就該這個樣子，人家不注意我，是應該的。如果有人注意我，一定是因為我的裙子破了個洞，或者褲子的拉鏈忘了拉上來。」

我停止進食的動作，不由自主的乾笑了一聲，她的眼睛閃動著一絲光芒，好像有人拿了顆小石子丟進她心中的一潭死水裡。

「那妳為什麼會開和番茄有關的專賣店呢？這……並不是……尋常的餐廳啊！」

「我畢了業，跟大多數人一樣，不知道自己有什麼專長，可以做什麼，只知道，自己是活著，要吃飯睡覺就是了，反正這是我的志願嘛！我到阿姨的餐廳幫忙，打算混口飯吃，這樣不知不覺過了五年多。二十四歲那年，認識了第一個男人，他是在我正想拉下鐵門的時候踏進來的。他喝了很多酒，一進門就喊餓，我說，打烊了，廚師走了，沒有東西吃。他問我，妳可不可以幫我煮個麵？我看他可憐，把剩下的麵條加上僅有的番茄和鹽，煮了一碗奇怪的麵給他吃，他吃得津津有味，好像那是世界上最美味的食物似的，轉眼盤底就要空了。

「我驚訝的看著他。他滿是淚水的眼睛像剛送到魚市場紅澄澄的新鮮鮭魚子，顫抖的嘴巴小聲的說：這是我媽媽煮的麵的味道啊！

「打從我出生以來，心裡第一次充滿了感動，以為自己煮得很好吃。我開始研究番茄料理，等著他第二次上門來。大約又過了一個月，他再次失魂落魄的在打烊前推開了店門，開口叫我，番茄小姐！

「你怎麼會知道我的綽號呢？」我問他，他說：「因為我永遠記得妳的番茄麵啊！」沒有答腔的我，那時正在看一本有關前世今生的書，還以為番茄是我們前世約定今生來相認的密碼呢！

「那天我正學著如何用番茄汁調出像『血腥瑪麗』般的粉紅色雞尾酒，他多喝了幾杯，醉了，我陪他在店裡坐到天亮，他醒來時吻了我，說，妳真是個好女人。非常非常好的女人。

「從那一天開始，我期待著他會在打烊後，推開我的店門，叫我，番茄小姐！

……喂，你渴了嗎？要不要嚐一嚐我剛剛做的法國式番茄血腸，免費招待哦！

不知不覺，我已經把番茄義大利麵吃得精光，並不是因為它太好吃，只是她一直說話，而我沒有別的事做的緣故。

「我不喜歡吃太腥的東西。」我說。

「不會，我保證，番茄會把所有的滋味遮蓋掉，雖然它是很普通的東西，卻有很大的威力喲！」

她把一小盤血腸送到我的面前。

我先試吃了一小口，果然，我還是吃到了濃濃的番茄味，血腸好像只是在提供一種口感而已。

我不斷蠕動著嘴巴，只是為了要把故事聽完。

☆　☆　☆　☆　☆

『妳嫁給我吧。』後來他常常在晚上來試吃我的新產品，有一天我正在煮菜的時候，他看著我的背影說。因為喉嚨塞滿了食物，所以他的聲音含糊不清，但我的耳朵可是異常靈敏，我期待著他這句話好一段時間，只是沒想到他會說得這麼快。

「我轉過身子，對他說：『你為什麼要娶我呢？』

「他遲疑了一會兒說：『因為妳是我生命中對我最好的女人。』那天他的表情一點也不沮喪，從口袋裡掏出一疊厚厚的鈔票對我說：「嗯，給妳，妳想要什麼樣的戒指，就自己去買吧，遇到妳之後，我的運氣變好了。」

「就這樣，我辭掉了餐館的工作，先讓他搬到我住的地方，以後我只要專心的為他煮番茄料理就好了。我知道，我一直是個不起眼的人，好像菜市場裡的番茄，在任何季節，任何攤位，你都可以找到它，它不是不可口，但是因為太容易找到，沒什麼特別，所以永遠沒有人覺得它值得珍重的咀嚼，在很多的菜色之中，都缺不了它的滋味，雖然它總是配角。

「在我的愛情中，我終於變成主角了。如果妳和我一樣，從小就是個不起眼的女人，妳會了解，這樣的夢想實現對我來說有多重要。我們住在一起沒有多久，我就知道，賭徒是他的職業。賭徒的脾氣只有兩種極端，一種是非常沮喪，一種是異常興奮，沒有中間值。我們的婚禮還來得及舉行，漸漸的，他開始討厭我的番茄料理。一開始，我會想，忍耐一下，忍耐到他賭贏錢的那天，我就有好日子過了。很不幸的，他的手氣背了好久，後來他對我說：

「我忍耐妳難吃的番茄菜已經很久了，現在一看到妳的番茄臉就想吐！」像一個投手，把我的番茄當成棒球，向我丟了過來。

「你以前不是這樣說的⋯⋯」我也生氣了，你知道，我不是個聰明的人，我分不清楚是什麼原因使他過去的感覺和現在這麼不一樣？

「我終於知道，他從小沒有爸爸，媽媽只顧著打牌賭錢，根本不會做菜，只把家裡當旅館，常常忘了小孩有沒有飯吃。什麼都沒得吃的時候，還好後院有一棵野生的番茄。他的媽媽常要他去摘番茄，用菜刀隨便剁了幾下，加上白煮麵和鹽巴，就送到他面前。

☆ ☆ ☆ ☆ ☆

「我忽然了解，他完全不欣賞我的菜，他也不會真正喜歡我的，我再也不想看到他了，哭著要他走，他不肯走。於是⋯⋯喂，你要再喝一杯番茄雞尾酒嗎？」她的眼眶紅了，我基於同情點了點頭，其實，她的料理還不賴。「後來呢？」

「後來，」她臉上的笑容忽然變得很神秘⋯⋯「既然我為他花了那麼多心血做料我不太喜歡她的番茄雞尾酒，黏黏稠稠，好像有一條長長的鼻涕滑進咽喉。

理，他也應該為我的料理做一些回饋。我趁著他睡著的時候，脫光了他的衣服，拖著他到廚房，把他五花大綁了起來……

「喂，我的血腸和番茄雞尾酒好吃嗎？」她忽然從故事中抽離出來，關心起她的新產品。

不會吧。

一股噁心的感覺俘虜了我，我的胃像個乾衣機一般開始旋轉，腥紅色的液體從我的嘴巴裡湧出來，潑濺到桌面上。胃還在翻轉著，直到方才吃掉的東西全部吐清為止。

「怎麼了？」她的臉上沒有太激烈的表情，毫不知情的看著我。

「妳……妳殺了他？」

「我？怎麼可能，」她笑了，把一個櫻桃小番茄塞進嘴裡，「我不過是個普通的女人，連監獄都不收我這種普通的女人。我只是……我強迫他吃下我每一種新產品，並且告訴我，好吃，太好吃了，你現在吃的料理，都是他說好吃的哦！為什麼你把它們都吐出來呢？我只是說故事給你聽，你不也是一個說故事的人嗎？故事不都是想像的嗎？和夢一樣，與現實相反。和夢不一樣的是，我們可以編派結局，滿足我們不能完成的各種慾望……」

我不敢看她既慈悲又猙獰的笑臉，撇過頭，我在一面哈哈鏡前看到自己的臉龐，就像逐漸膨脹的紅番茄。

☆　☆☆☆　☆

番茄是個虛擬故事。

一個作者不該為虛擬的故事解釋太多，除非那個故事無聊透頂、味同嚼蠟、沒人看懂。

就跟很多被文評家長篇大論探討和解說的，都是正常人很難看下去的東西一樣。

如果要在這裡畫蛇添足的寫一些「創作動機」的話，我要說，這個虛擬故事是兩個可能的我在對話。

番茄很營養，可是很多，很容易長，很平凡，多到你記不得哪一顆番茄的滋味曾令你難忘。

我想我至今所有的努力，只是不想成為一顆精神上酸酸澀澀的番茄而已。

寫給二十歲的自己

為了怕再過幾年後，我像悼念二十歲太會浪費人生美好時光那樣，悼念自己曾有的美好青壯年歲月，我越活越充實，對夢想也越來越有行動力！

變老是一件壞事嗎？從體力和皮膚的光澤度來說，是的。但是，如果妳已經到了開始想念學生時代的時候，不妨認真、仔細的回想，妳真想回到二十歲那個「美好的年代」裡去嗎？

我想，不見得。只是妳忘記那個年紀所有的憂愁。妳記住的是青春無敵的那一部分而已。

某一個夜裡，為了仔細細細懷那個年代，我寫了一份情書給自己……

給自己的情書

我認識妳，但妳永遠不會認識我。雖然我也是妳，而妳也是我。

經過了這麼些年，我重新召喚妳，妳的樣子已難拼湊。妳留著長髮、瘦弱到不相信自己的人生中會有積極減肥的一天。妳唸大三，在台大法律系，常常蹺課，反正一上課也老是不知不覺就睡著了。妳說妳對唸法律沒有興趣，但卻不知道該對什麼感興趣。妳總是以緊緊抿著的嘴角掩飾自己的徬徨和恐懼，妳害怕自己離開家鄉求學，好不容易唸了第一志願之後還是沒出息，又不知該朝哪兒用力。

妳總覺得自己不該一生平凡，但卻不知專長在哪裡？

寫作嗎？是有點興趣，但沒有什麼信心，總是興致勃勃的投稿，總是沒幾天就收到厚厚的一疊退件。大家都說，寫作是不能當飯吃的。

妳太缺乏愛，一談起戀愛來卻昏天暗地，完全沒有自己。熱戀期過後，才暗

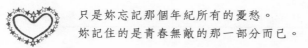
暗感覺身邊的男人並不恰當，卻又不知道哪樣的男人適合自己。

妳很計較愛與被愛哪邊少哪邊多，總是為了小事在生氣，很像一個抱著柴薪的人，對著火爐大喊：「給我溫暖，不然我就不給你木柴。」

妳逃避著，不敢說出自己的意見，怕失去友誼和別人眼光中的和氣，卻還是覺得自己一直被孤立。

妳當然不怎麼愛自己。妳討厭自己的單眼皮。

妳的心情常常很低迴，感嘆人生好沒意義，卻只好繼續把日子混下去。

現在的我想起妳，總想到那一張被種種恐懼和猶豫退票的青春，沒有用力的活，也沒有用力的玩，總還有些惋惜與悵然。

但我還是要說，我愛妳。感謝妳在日後的路途中，主動或被動的做了許多正確或錯誤的選擇；感謝妳在跌倒後再無奈也依然爬起來；感謝妳懂得漸漸長大，即使是那麼渾渾噩噩活了下來，還是沒有放棄寫作，沒有放棄尋找自己，於是才能活成了今天的我，讓我能夠過著我要的生活。

讓我還有機會證明，其實所謂未來沒有什麼好怕的，怕，也沒用。

寫給二十歲的自己

177

不回頭也不悼念

其實，就算我想恢復二十歲的皮膚和吃不胖的身材（別傻了，打一公噸的胎盤素都不可能），我並不想回去那麼青澀的年代。

為了怕再過幾年後，我像悼念二十歲太會浪費人生美好時光那樣，悼念自己曾有的美好青壯年歲月，我越活越充實，對夢想也越來越有行動力！

好命女守則

沒有任何一代的女人比妳更幸福，所以妳有權利也有義務讓自己幸福。

妳是歷史上過得最好的一代了，相信我，妳擁有最美好的自由。

——摘自《早知道早幸福》

做 個 好 命 女

懶其所懶，愛其所愛

像我這樣一個女人，生在古代，動不動就干犯「七出」之條，更別提什麼婦德婦功。想到我可以安然活著，真得感謝這個時代。

哈雷路亞！光想到這是一個懶人可以光明正大好好活著，我就不能不深感幸福。

我很喜歡一個人發呆，異想天開時還會旁若無人的笑起來。奇妙的是，懶洋洋發愣時，藏在我腦海裡的念頭，總是比颱風圈旁的雲層飄動得勤快。

發呆時我曾經想過，如果我早生個幾十年，我想，我一定很難好好活下來。

為什麼呢？因為我實在沒有一點當時女性的美德。而早些時候，我們的社會對女性的要求太單一、太嚴苛，很多冰雪聰明的女人，像一個「家用機器人」

般，過了一輩子。

我絕不是個很好的家用機器人。

對於做家事，做那些小時候台灣母親輩認為「女孩子一定要會做」的事，我都不感興趣，也沒有天分。

我是家政老師最頭痛的學生。記得學打毛線時，我從來沒有搞得清楚，什麼是上針是下針，又粗心大意，老是忘了把上課所需要的東西帶來，常被老師罰站。老師說，妳這樣長大了怎麼得了？我還會頂嘴，說有錢何必自己織毛衣、繡衣裳！

不但不感興趣，沒有天分，而且也沒有意願想學。

我唸中學時的學科成績，以數學課最差，但還至少摶得上中上水準，家政課一向比數學課更讓我頭疼。

安然過關，是因為我有個曾經當過裁縫的祖母，她總是無怨無尤的把一切家事，包括我的作業攬在身上。我還有很棒的鄰座同學，就算是考試時間有限，她也可以一次做兩個，幫我交差。

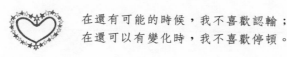

懶理由實話實說

不只不會應付家政課。即使高中離了家，到台北來唸北一女，得一個人租屋在外，照顧自己，我並沒有學會任何生活美德。

記得當時宿舍設備清簡，外地生都得自己用手洗衣服，這差事比叫我把長恨歌、祭妹文都背起來還難過十倍。有好幾回，我竟然將衣服泡進水裡，過了一星期還忘了洗，結果，發出了可怕的酸腐味外，有一次還出現蟑螂的浮屍。這真是一個回憶起來就令人作嘔的畫面，偏偏我在懶惰之餘還很愛乾淨，當然不再洗了，只好以快刀斬亂麻的方式偷偷丟掉。

我不但懶得做家事，還有理直氣壯的懶理由，而且還是真的呢！我的手只要一碰肥皂水就會爛得跟受了滿清十大酷刑一般，我的皮膚尚且還對黃金以外的所

我知道，能幹的女人都很願意幫忙笨拙的女人做這些事，而且會煥發著母性光輝，而博取能幹女子的同情，示弱總沒錯。沒實力何必逞強呢？

懶其所懶，愛其所愛

有金屬過敏，屢試不爽。所以，沒辦法，我就說嘛，我注定不能做牛做馬。

當然囉，懶人一定是很愛為自己找藉口的，因為，動點嘴皮子找個理由，總

比「一生懸命」的去做事來得容易許多。我至今還不明白，這種極度的過敏反

應，是先天遺傳，還是後天心理作用。

我也討厭擦地板，雖然專家說擦地板和有氧運動消耗掉一樣的卡洛里，但我

還是寧願氣喘吁吁的跳有氧去，不願與地板共享韶光。

我還不愛整理東西。如果沒有電腦，要出書時，我大概沒辦法找全原稿。還

好，天佑我也，科技越來越進步，懶人越來越有保障。只可惜還沒有人發明一種

比較科技的方式來管理衣櫥，這樣我每天可以省去二十分鐘找衣服的時間。

煮食上，我是個「王語嫣」。看盡天下食譜，說了一口好菜，但只有心血來

潮才做菜。這心血來潮的機率，近年來，一年應該只有一兩次吧！

這只是一時間暫時想到的。我在現實生活中瑣瑣碎碎的無能和懶散，再寫下

去就是族繁不及備載了。

像我這樣一個女人，生在古代，動不動就干犯「七出」之條，更別提什麼婦

德婦功。

想到我可以安然活著，真得感謝這個時代。哈雷路亞！光想到這是一個懶人可以光明正大好好活著，我就不能不深感幸福。

能活在分工如此精緻的時代，我應該燒了好幾輩子的香了吧！

我已經把我的祕密告訴你了。在這一瞬間，我彷彿聽到我的曾曾祖母、祖母、母親、各直系女性尊親屬們，發出了沈重的嘆息聲，不約而同的說：唉，這種丟臉的事妳也敢講！

我敢講，其實是因為不覺丟臉。

實話實說有什麼好丟臉呢？

愛其所愛，不能太懶

「我看妳做好多事，可是每次看到妳，妳都很從容不迫的樣子，甚至有些懶洋洋的！告訴我們，怎麼做時間管理？」

懶其所懶，愛其所愛

這樣的話，我不知聽過多少遍了。竟然有很多朋友都想問問，我是怎麼做時間管理的。他們說：「每天在電視機前面看到妳，在廣播中聽到妳，到書店還是得看到妳，聽說妳還在旅行、潛水、還有學舞、作陶、上攝影課？妳有幾個分身呀？」

這樣的恭維讓我備感虛榮，我心裡頭那根不爭氣的狗尾巴會開心的搖晃個不停。不過，說實話，嗯，我沒有那麼忙，如果我硬說我忙，那一定是我不想做那件事。

我向來堅持每天睡足七小時。睡不飽時，怨天尤人，靈感全無，深感不幸，且EQ盡失。

在我從來不肯按牌理出牌的腦袋裡，是沒有所謂時間管理的。如果你真覺得我的時間哪裡夠用，只有如下「祕訣」可提供：

一是，目前我只做我想做的、喜歡做的事。

二是，我做的事透過四通八達的大眾媒體，你剛好都看得到。

三嘛，我因為太懶，不太常應酬，從不打麻將，不做任何殺時間的事情，也常懶到忘了開電視打發時間。

我知道我現在很幸運，可以只做我喜歡的事。衛道人士可能會害怕，我散播這樣的想法之後，人人都只做他想做的事，天下就會大亂。

我的時間管理方式，在他們看來，其實就是某方面的「不負責任」而已。

懶人並不勉強自己。我也不。可是我還喜歡某些挑戰所帶來的新鮮感，我不太喜歡大家都覺得太容易的事情、人人都應該會的事情、人家說我一定學不會的事情。當我遇到真正有興趣的事情，我的活力就戰勝了我的懶惰。

像我，不可能懶於寫作，因為我太、太、太喜歡。像喜歡自己的紅血球白血球一樣喜歡。不做就不對勁的事，我不懶。

幸好我縱然有許多惰性，但還有一些匹夫之勇。我討厭生命像一潭死水，到了某種年齡，就始終不肯前進。

在還有可能的時候，我不喜歡認輸；在還可以有變化時，我不喜歡停頓；在生活還有無限可能時，我不願故步自封。

吸引我的永遠是眾絃齊奏中最獨特的聲音，讓我感動的永遠是願意拚命一搏

懶 其 所 懶 ， 愛 其 所 愛

卻又能瀟灑放下的真性情。

愛其所愛，我知道，不能太懶。懶於愛其所愛、只願固守安全地區的人生，

必然空留遺恨。

懶散的最高境界

懶其實有好多層次。每個人的層次不同。

有人勤於瑣事，卻懶於為自己的生命找出路。

有人勤於邁向過勞死，卻懶於找出更有效率的做事方式。

有人勤於掙錢，卻懶得為生活的美感投資。

有人勤於尋覓愛情，卻懶得為每一個愛人付出。

有人勤於外在裝飾，卻懶得讓自己免於無知。

有人勤於在政壇商界鑽營，卻懶於修整名譽。

有人勤於回憶，卻懶於創造未來。

不做就不對勁的事，我不懶。

有人勤於讀萬卷書，卻懶於走萬里路。

我懶，但我貪心，所以不想失去更美好的東西，我為自己的懶找到最高指導原則。

其實每個人都不可能面面勤快。每一個人要的東西不同，所以懶散的地方不一樣。懶散的最高境界，是建立了自己的價值觀，所以不必管他人怎麼想；儘管世人汲汲營營，他還在那兒安安心心。

我好想和你分享一首少數可以算進「古典懶散文學」的一首詞，朱敦儒的

〔鷓鴣天〕：

我是清都山水郎，

天教懶慢帶疏狂，

曾批給露支風敕，

累奏留雲借月章。

詩萬首，酒千觴，

幾曾著眼看侯王？

懶 其 所 懶 ， 愛 其 所 愛

187

玉樓金闕慵歸去，

且插梅花醉洛陽。

朱敦儒是南宋時的人，皇帝要他做官，要他到京師去，他卻說自己的個性是

「麋鹿之性，自樂閒曠，爵祿非所願也。」寧可回到洛陽過他閒散的日子。這樣

的懶人，有誰奈何得了他？

又有誰能看不起他？誰能說他浪費生命，誰能說他沒出息？

懶其所懶，愛其所愛，人生所以多光彩！

做 個 好 命 女

妳不是賣火柴的小女孩

在自憐之後，我們還得有些重見天日的行動力。

可別把人生最精華的時間，

都花在和賣火柴的小女孩一起哭泣。

其實，安徒生童話裡頭有很多殘忍的故事。其中之一，是賣火柴的小女孩。

我第一次讀完賣火柴的小女孩的故事時，應該不到十歲吧，被這個故事嚇得

好多天睡不著。

賣火柴的小女孩，爹不疼娘不愛，天寒地凍的時候只能蜷縮在街角賣火柴，

希望能夠得到一點錢貼補家用。她從窗戶外看到好多人家裡都在歡度聖誕節，準

備吃火雞大餐，而她所擁有的只是賣不出去的火柴，於是她一根一根的點燃了火

妳 不 是 賣 火 柴 的 小 女 孩

189

柴，每點燃一根，她就看到一個虛擬實境……

這世上，唯有已經離去的祖母是疼愛她的，最後一根火柴，她看到最疼愛她的祖母來接她，歡喜的投入祖母的懷抱。

第二天，有人在街角發現一個凍僵了的小女孩，她已經沒有了呼吸，在夢中安詳離去。

多愁善感的女人都擅長自憐

這個故事，真的太悲哀了。

賣火柴的小女孩在故事中死去，然而她的靈魂彷彿附身在我身上。在成長過程中，我常常看到賣火柴的小女孩，那是我——一個曾經不時自憐的自己。

看到別人的爸媽對她那麼照顧，家庭那麼溫馨和氣，我覺得自己身世堪憐。

看到別人表現傑出，就覺得自己懷才不遇。

看到別人戀愛談得好，就覺得自己是天下最可憐的女人，為什麼就是我找不

做 個 好 命 女

190

到好男人……

「我看她們都那麼幸福，不像我……」其實家家有本難唸的經，不能只看表面。過得再順遂的人都有不是那麼一帆風順的一面。

所有多愁善感的女人都擅長自憐。我不算最嚴重的，有人在人生路上一遇到小挫折就說是因為自己家世不好、長相不佳、命盤帶衰、生為女人太倒楣……自憐的情緒像一缸陳年的醋，把她泡得一身酸腐味。

那樣的酸腐味根本沒法招來好運道，有人想親近，也會被嚇跑。

找個暖和的地方保護自己

自憐是不錯的精神鎮定劑，但劑量用多了，人就很難清醒。除了自憐，應該還要附加其他藥方。一味自憐，內心必然脆弱，不管外表是多麼堅不可摧。

我曾在影劇版上看到得了奧斯卡獎的影后妮可基嫚剖析自己，她說：「我是個內心脆弱的人，每一次要嘗試新角色時，我總是有點歇斯底里，很想逃走……」

因為她沒有逃走，每一次還是都接演了「實在不像她可以演得好」的角色，她才擺脫了花瓶的陰影，繼續在銀幕前發熱發光。

自憐是個陰暗的洞穴，在裡頭，我們會覺得很安全。但在自憐之後，我們還得有些重見天日的行動力。可別把人生最精華的時間，都花在和賣火柴的小女孩一起哭泣。

在現代，賣火柴的小女孩，除了點燃小小火柴取暖（她應該知道，火柴是不能取暖的！），應該找個暖和的地方保護自己，也許，就去敲那些幸福之家的門吧，說不定會有人歡迎她一起過聖誕節，請她吃火雞大餐！

試探可能性，比坐著自憐好！

好命女守則

早一點發現，早一點看見，
早一點聽到幸福的敲門聲，
早一點舞動人生，妳一定會遇見讓妳幸福的人。

——摘自《早知道早幸福》

夢想是會生利息的

我努力實現我的作家夢，它自動生了很多利息給我！

沒錯，夢想是會生利息的，

只要感興趣，不要輕易打退堂鼓。

這些年來，每一年我都要求自己，去做一件新鮮事。

原因無他。我不喜歡生命如停滯的死水漸漸腐臭的感覺，也不希望哪天「老狗學不了新把戲」這句名言不知不覺落在我身上。

我也還記得少年時代做讀書筆記時，曾經抄錄過一句很毒卻也一針見血的話：「很多人過了二十歲就死了！」我不想加入「很多人」當行屍走肉。

有好些年，寫作是我的唯一，我把自己寫成蒼白虛弱、腰痠背痛，還寫歪了頸椎，飽受夏天雨欲來時全身都當警報器之苦。有一天痛得受不了，我忽然悟到，如果我只重視寫作，卻輕忽眞正的生活，那麼，我不過像一個在服食迷幻藥以脫離眞實生活的傢伙，擁有的人生不過是一株枝葉繁茂的假樹。

於是我一邊做復健治療，一邊爲自己找新把戲以脫離失去了平衡的生活。9
6年，我莫名其妙的主持起電視節目；97年，我成爲帶狀節目的廣播主持人；
98年，我開始學陶藝；千禧年，我發現海底世界的美麗；接著，我演了舞台劇，以上都跌破我自己的眼鏡。

這可從不在我的少年夢想之一。

我從來沒有表演的欲望或天才。

幾年前，我上過綠光劇團的表演班，只不過想去玩玩，看看能不能去除我在電視螢幕前的羞澀感。

天知道，我其實是個內向的人，我習於獨處，卻要花許多時間，才能在大衆面前去除我的不自在。

上完三個月一期的表演班，發現自己也還可以跟原本陌生的一大群人彼此混

做 個 好 命 女

每一次在掙扎取捨的時刻，
我的心裡就會浮出另一種頑固的聲音。

得很開心，也學會怎麼樣用丹田之氣說話才不致嗓子啞掉，是我最大的收穫。沒想到過了幾年，我的表演班老師劉長灝當了劇團經理，忽然打了電話給我：

「喂，吳念眞導演要爲我們導新戲，來演一個角色好嗎？」

只要聽起來很好玩就輕易答應別人，是我至今未改的毛病。我當下說：「好啊，一句話，沒問題！我們再聊！」

第一次參加排戲時，離演出不到兩個月，我才知道自己的角色是演「中學美少女」黃韻玲的媽；而且還是一個精神不太正常的歐巴桑。

對不起，我還是要強調小玲比我老。這這這，簡直是太爲難我的挑戰！我想，一開始就退出有失面子，那就排戲排排看，如果覺得無法勝任，再找個理由推掉吧！

果然一排戲就遇到很大的困難。我心裡頭那隻叫做「閉塞內向」的蟲子又鑽出來肆虐了。眼看著演路人甲和路人乙的年輕團員，都十分放得開，排什麼就像什麼，我簡直受不了自己的拙與笨。

夢 想 是 會 生 利 息 的

試過才知道可不可以

和他們對戲時，我慢半拍。

演「武打戲」時，我打得不痛不癢，其中有一幕戲，我得像個瘋婆子一樣打女兒，又被眾人拉住——不管排了幾次，不管我自己覺得多費力，旁觀者看來一點也沒有逼真感。

導演後來忍無可忍，又不敢對我發火，只好對團員訓話：「你們不要因為她是吳淡如，就不敢大力拉她！」

劇團裡頭的老鳥也忍不住了，挺身而出拿著保特瓶敲自己的頭，使著苦肉計對我說：「看！用力打下去沒關係，會痛不會死！」

不是我不敬業，而是我……我從沒打過人，深怕假戲真做，把自己打傷。

不管我如何對自己「心戰喊話」，就是豁不出去。排戲期間，如果有朋友看到我在哀聲嘆氣，必然是等一會兒得去排戲。

我不喜歡生命如停滯的死水漸漸腐臭的感覺，
也不希望哪天「老狗學不了新把戲」
這句話不知不覺落在我身上。

眼看黃韻玲和綠光團長李永豐演技都很出色，排戲時也能讓旁觀者爆笑連連，戲一到我開始說話就冷了，別人心急，我更急。

劇團為了怕萬一，同一個角色總有「代理人」，我的代理人大學還沒畢業吧，但揣摩角色總是微妙微肖，以青春年華演瘋歐巴桑，沒人懷疑她是否勝任的問題。

掙扎了好久，我沮喪的安慰自己：「我真的不是演戲的料，我只能做自己。

反正我以後又不打算做這一行，還是趁早退出，以絕後患！」終於鼓起勇氣找到劇團經理，表明退出的意願；他能吃到一百多公斤不是沒道理的，因為體胖，所以心廣，一點也不怕我砸他的招牌，只是拍拍我的肩膀說：「傳單都發出去了，妳不演，很奇怪的，放心啦，船到橋頭自然直！」

我沒那麼樂觀，深怕自己是一粒老鼠屎，搞壞人家一鍋好粥。

每一次在掙扎取捨的時刻，我的心裡就會浮出另一種堅定的聲音。即使被「演出失敗、觀眾砸雞蛋」的噩夢嚇醒，在半夜忽然從床上跳起來，那個聲音就會在驚魂甫定後告訴我：「妳可以因為表現不好而失敗，但不能因為孬種而失

夢 想 是 會 生 利 息 的

敗！妳得真正試過，才知道自己行不行。」

心戰喊話催眠潛意識

演出的日期越來越逼近，死馬只有當活馬醫。我和自己約好，就算現實生活中，我清明到怎麼瘋也瘋不了，一上台，我必須忘記自己，讓瘋子像乩童附在我身上才行。

我甚至利用職務之便，動不動就找人請益：瘋子要怎麼演啊？許傑輝、趙自強、郎祖筠都曾在我面前演過「瘋子看電視」和「瘋子打人」的劇碼。

我連走路都在背台詞。

直到最後一次排練，我都不認為自己的演出是及格的，但我繼續向自己心戰喊話：「上了台，跟排練時一定不一樣，妳……應該會更自然！」

「過了這個挑戰，妳一定會覺得自己又跨過了一個大門檻！」

心戰喊話是潛意識的催眠。記得我在廣播節目中也曾訪問世界排名第一的撞球王趙豐邦，他在每一次得打「不太可能打進」的球時，總會對自己說：「因為你是趙豐邦，所以你打得進這個球！」說也奇怪，只要他能鎮定的對自己說這句話，十之八九，球都會乖乖入袋。

考驗總是要來臨。雖然我已熟悉大場面的主持工作，但當舞台劇演員是頭一遭。開演前，我強顏歡笑，以掩飾自己心跳加速到呼吸困難的事實。

戲一開始，連緊張的時間都沒有。我只記得，我是個外表看來很正常的瘋歐巴桑，說我該說的話，做我該做的事。

發現自己的無限潛力

「人間條件」的第一場演出，我的處女秀，我聽見了觀眾熱烈的笑聲與掌聲，知道場子沒有被我炒成冷飯。五場演出，比我想像中更輕易的結束了。

熟能生巧，我試圖在每一場演出中加料，在戲一開鑼時，它彷彿變成我自己的真實生活，我唯一的任務變成使它生動且深刻！

夢 想 是 會 生 利 息 的

舞台劇最大的好處是：觀眾的反應絕不虛偽，他們覺得戲好不好，台上的演員馬上就會知道。我知道，我沒有搞砸它，相反的，我竟然也覺得我自己演的瘋婆可愛極了。

最後幾場的演出，全部滿座。在慶功宴時，劇團經理才告訴我實話：「其實導演最擔心的人是妳，沒想到妳一場比一場老到，還會適時的掌控舞台的節奏！」

我也先後遇到一些看過戲的朋友對我說：「天哪，我看到最後謝幕時，才知道那個人是妳，差太多了！」

我爸爸也來看了戲，最好笑的是他在開演後半個小時，問我媽：「她怎麼還沒出來？」才知道台上的瘋歐巴桑就是我！這至少表示，我不是個演什麼都像自己的爛演員。

「我根本不知道妳會演戲！」這是演出後，我所聽過最自然的讚美了。我一方面樂得飄飄然，一方面也老實回答：「其實，我也不知道我會演戲！」

後來有一位記者來訪問我，她揶揄我說：「為什麼妳總是有這麼多機會，可以表現自己，我們想做的事，都被妳做光了！妳該不會這下又立志當職業演員吧！」

「我只是想玩玩，我也不認為，除了寫作之外，我還有其他的天分，但是——」我的腦中靈光閃動：「應該這麼說吧！有時候，夢想是會生利息的：我努力實現我的作家夢，它自動生了很多利息給我！」

沒錯，夢想是會生利息的，只要感興趣，不要輕易打退堂鼓。

好命女守則

美豔女星桃莉巴頓曾說：
在我看來，你喜歡彩虹，就得忍受雨。
頗有哲理。不過，雨也不難忍，
它使晴空不令人厭煩，變得那麼值得盼望。

——摘自《學會過生活》

夢 想 是 會 生 利 息 的

201

享受孤獨中的小小快樂

妳要不要試試看？

這是一個很安穩的階梯，培養小小的獨立性，

讓自己看見自己的心靈還能接受多大的活動空間！

每個星期三，我在做完現場的廣播節目後多半會有幾個小時的空檔，我的電影日就是這樣來的。

我習慣到某個購物商場附設的電影院看十一點左右的早場電影。早場有優惠，而且人很少，電影院小貓兩三隻，我可以一個人坐一整排，感覺到整部電影是專為我一個人放的。

多麼奢華的享受啊！

買完票之後，我會先買一杯咖啡，如果有陽光就更好了，我可以坐在購物中心廣場邊，想像自己又回到了巴黎的露天咖啡座。

「嗨，我看過妳的節目。」這天我走進購物中心時，有幾個女士和我打招呼。「妳也來逛街？」

「不是，來看電影。」

「哦，好好哦！我好久沒有看電影了。從結婚以後都沒有了。我老公根本忙得沒空陪我看電影。」其中一位說。

我笑著回答：「可是，我是一個人來看電影的啊！」

「妳老公呢？」當形單影隻時，我已經習於接受這樣的疑問。

「他要上班啊！我有空時，他未必有空。」

「哦，一個人看電影，不會很寂寞嗎？」她喃喃自言的說。

一個人看電影，當然很可能很寂寞，如果我們的心裡習慣對自己說：「看，那我們一定會連喜劇都看成悲劇。

我好孤單，我好可憐，別人都是儷影成雙，只有我是苦海女神龍……」

做個能夠享受個人娛樂的女人

我本來也不是一個能夠享受屬於個人娛樂的女人。五年前，也許我也會咕噥著「好討厭，都沒人陪我看電影」吧！二十歲左右時的我，腦袋裡更認定「只有約會時才看電影」，男友第一，連女友陪我看我都覺得自己好孤單。現在想來，這種想法真是有趣。

一個人看電影有很多好處：你可以暫時脫離熟人的視線來大哭大笑，盡情融入劇情，可以更專心的欣賞導演說故事的能力和畫面的美感，可以不要為了看文藝片或動作片而鬧彆扭，可以在小小的孤獨中得到一些深深的啟發。當電影院裡周遭的燈暗下來時，我的某一層思緒就活了，在現實世界中很多沒法安靜思考的

把這樣的孤獨當成享受，當成一種「調節性的靜坐」活動，就會怡然自得。

這也是一種利用時間享樂的方式，我喜歡超大銀幕，即使再忙，我想看的電影很少錯過。

事情，也會隨著劇情來我心中叩門。

據我的調查，能夠把一個人看電影或喝下午茶，當成享受快樂而不是咀嚼孤獨的人還不是那麼多。

妳要不要試試看？這是一個很安穩的一小步，培養小小的獨立性，讓自己看見自己的心靈還能接受多大的活動空間！

好命女守則

孤獨也是愛的一部分。當他說「我得好好靜一靜」時，並不意味，妳得誠惶誠恐，怕失去他的愛，成熟的愛人尊重愛人的孤獨。

——摘自《自戀總比自卑好》

享受孤獨中的小小快樂

不虛榮也不虛偽

我並不認為，女人應該屏除一切虛榮心，找個最窮的男人嫁。

我的意思是：

經濟並不應該是被放在第一位的考慮重點。

我的朋友蘭兒從小就是美人胚子，曾經參加過選美比賽，二十出頭時有好多人追求她，她在眾多追逐者中選擇了最窮的一個。

她對當時狀況還很津津樂道：

「某一天，我在片場拍片拍到深夜，就在快要收工的時候，有人跑來告訴我，門外總共有三個男人在等我。一個開賓士，一個開ＢＭＷ，一個騎機車，我呀，二話不說，就走向那個騎機車的，接過他遞過來的雨衣，消失在那兩個富裕

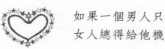
的追求者眼中……」沒多久，她嫁給那個騎機車的。

她和那個騎機車的傢伙度過了一段儉樸的歲月，生了三個孩子，等孩子都上了幼稚園，再度踏入演藝圈演戲，雖然不過三十出頭，演出的已經是「上一代」的角色了。

「所有的人，包括我媽，都笑我傻，選一個最窮的，注定要吃苦。」她笑著說：「我是吃了些苦頭，到現在算是苦盡甘來，夫妻間感情也還不錯。放眼那些當年和我一起參加選美的女性朋友，我還算是找對了男人、最有福氣的一個。」

與丈夫度過「貧窮夫妻百事哀」（現代沒有什麼「賤」字可言）階段的蘭兒，是個很有智慧也很實在的女人。但請不要誤會我舉這個例子的意思。我並不認為，女人應該屏除一切虛榮心，找個最窮的男人嫁。我的意思是：經濟並不應該是被放在第一位的考慮重點。蘭兒放棄雙B，選擇機車，是因為她老早愛上騎機車的男人，有把握和他同甘共苦。她選的是人，不是車子所代表的經濟條件。

選到最窮的男人，不保證一定會苦盡甘來。

不虛榮也不虛偽

207

有潛力肯努力一定有機會

我也剛好有另一位朋友，她在大學時代四個追求她的男人中選擇一個最窮的，結果那個男人後來還真的發了，開了雙B轎車後，就冷面冷心的拋妻棄子，爲了怕她分財產，還不惜誣賴她罪名，兩人告上法庭呢！

選人最重要，而且要選一個妳真正愛的人。愛過，就算不愛，至少也算忠於自己、對得起愛情。

仍然有很多女人會碰到「愛情與麵包」的選擇題。常有人會問我，她到底是要選擇「對我好但是比較窮」，還是經濟狀況比較富裕的？其實這個問題很難解答，因爲我不是她，不能單憑這麼簡單的陳述給她意見。但我總會說，如果妳不想在將來恨自己，就該看重愛情、看重那人人品，不要以經濟條件斷高低。

選男人萬萬不要虛榮，雖然婆婆媽媽輩吃苦吃怕了，最怕女兒又選上個窮小子吃苦，常有很多勸女兒「擇富棄貧」的理由，但那只能當成參考，選男人絕對不能只選錢。這個時代和過去三、五十年都不一樣，這已經是個「有錢的未必會一直有錢，有潛力肯努力一定有機會」的時代，妳現在看上他的家業華廈，哪知道明天是否就會「眼見他樓塌了」呢？

清醒看清楚愛情

我手邊還有案例，一位從小也是美女的友人，選了企業家第二代嫁了。新婚一個月後，該公司竟然宣告破產！她願望落空，黯淡無光的婚姻因為面子問題拖了十五年才閉了幕。

如果一個男人只是二十出頭，潛力無窮，女人總得給他機會。

但我們也不必虛偽到要「棄富就貧」。如果一個男人已經蹉跎了好多歲月，到了中年，卻還是一窮二白，那麼，現代女人在選擇要不要嫁給他時，恐怕得清醒一點。

國內有位知名的企業家曾說：賺錢在現代不只是賺錢，還有幾層意思。賺錢表示你做對了事情，如果不賺錢，表示沒做對事情。錢也是個資源，可以讓你做你要做的事情。

如果他到中年還無特長、也沒個固定工作，又一窮二白，甚至得靠妳資助才能過活，表示他還沒有做對過事情。妳又何必急著慷慨就義？何妨等他稍有自信？

不虛榮也不虛偽，才能看清楚愛情，看清楚人品。

感情左右性情

常被性格乖戾的情人或親人惡整的人，自己的性格往往也會變得很難搞；

和樂觀豁達的人在一起久了，也會有向光性。

我們會被情人影響的程度，總是出乎自己的意料！

有一句名言說：女人談不好戀愛時，做不好工作；男人做不好工作時，談不好戀愛。

拿它來驗證我身邊的男男女女，它「多半」是準的。當然現代的性別角色沒那麼刻板了，我也看到不少例外。有些女人，因為想忘卻不愉快的感情經驗，寄情於工作，不知不覺變成女強人；也有一些現代男子，雖然沒法子在職場得意，卻在人生低潮期有了覺悟，反而讓他更珍惜現有的感情關係。

服務業最容易看出工作與個性的關連。不管男女，工作與個性必然相互影響，有好個性的人，比較容易捧穩好工作；有好工作的人，也比較容易保持好個性。而不管一個人在什麼行業，感情和個性的互動總是牽連密切，感覺自己幸福的人，比較不會勾心鬥角、隨便發動攻擊。

麗惠就是一個很明顯的例子。她表面對人很熱絡，但背地裡卻常在網路上散播媒體同行的黑函或謠言；有一陣子我避免和她做任何言語上的溝通，因為不管我跟她說什麼話，在她嘴裡一反芻，傳出去的時候總是走了音、變了調，為我惹來很多麻煩。多年來，她只有不知情的新朋友，沒有老朋友——老朋友早都翻臉了。

雖然她愛以鬥爭方式力爭上游，然而她的運氣卻也好不到哪裡去，聽說她談戀愛的運氣更是背透了！美麗而精明的她，竟經歷了好幾段騙財騙色、以淚洗面的戀情。

原來一個人只要感到幸福，
就會呈現出不一樣的個性與風度！

壞情人讓妳變小人

原以為她不會改變的，但有一回遇到她，竟然發現她變了好多，氣色紅潤、聲音表情都不再那麼尖銳而虛偽。本來打算對她敬而遠之的我，忍不住開口對她說：「最近妳看來很不錯啊！」

她回答的語氣天真得令我意外。她說：「我最近可出運了，最近認識一個教書的男友，對我真的好好，從沒有人對我這麼好！我想我的好運終於來了！」

在她溫柔的表情中，我再也看不到從前那隻會在背地裡攻擊別人的刺蝟。

我為她的轉變感到無比訝異，心想，原來一個人只要感到幸福，就會呈現出不一樣的個性與風度！

我總發現，常被性格乖戾的情人或親人惡整的人，自己的性格往往也會變得很難搞；和樂觀豁達的人在一起久了，也會有向光性。我們會被情人（有感情成

感情左右性情

213

分的人）影響的程度，總是出乎自己的意料！

好情人未必能讓我們變聖人，但壞情人常讓我們不知不覺變小人，大家同流合污。還是找到一個願意給自己帶來好的影響力的情人吧！好情人不必讓妳事事順心、美夢成真，卻可以讓我們過得心情舒坦、溫柔待人。

好命女守則

太多女人，不肯思索人生的問題，不肯謀求有效率的解決，只把自己被辜負的一生推到那個「不負責任、沒出息」的男人身上……如果連妳越長越難看，都要怪男人，那麼，男人的責任真的是宇宙無敵超級無限大呀！

——摘自《新快樂主義》

女人有錢有尊嚴

現代女子都明白，

錢雖然不能買來一切，

但常可以買來尊嚴和自由。

「我富有過，我窮過，有錢比較好過！」

(I've been rich. I've been poor. Rich is better.)

這是一本暢銷書的書名，中文譯爲：《女人要有錢》。作者是美國一家投資

銀行及證券管理公司的董事長，名叫茱蒂‧瑞斯尼克。

她的人生歷史實在太曲折了。

生爲富家女，有個很會做生意的父親，茱蒂根本不知道理財爲何物，也不知

道錢有什麼重要的，因為在她成長的過程中，她從來沒有缺過錢。就跟身體一直

很健康的人，並不知道健康的重要一樣，茉蒂也以「我不會理財」為榮，跟很多

年輕女孩一樣，畏懼著理財，也覺得人生最重要的事，就是找一個好歸宿，那麼

她就永遠不必擔心錢的問題了。

她果然嫁給了另一個有錢人家的孩子，結婚後雖然覺得自己很無聊，想出去

找事做，但總被先生一句「幹嘛做事，我養妳」搪塞掉。

生了孩子之後，她對日漸兇暴的丈夫和沒有品質的婚姻越來越不滿，直到有

一天，她發現自己滿腦子都是怎樣殺死老公的念頭之後，她決定做她家族中第一

個離婚者。

茉蒂帶著兩個年幼的女兒離開第一任丈夫，回到還算富裕的娘家，媽媽一直

勸告她，趁著孩子還小，還有男人喜歡、願意接受她可愛的小小孩時，趕快結

婚，媽媽才會心安。所以茉蒂的當務之急還是找個男人。

倒楣的她在此時又發現自己得了子宮頸癌，還好手術還算成功，但深覺無聊

的她只好以酗酒和嗑藥來打發時間，又一再的掉入與有婦之夫的戀愛中，把自己

做 個 好 命 女

216

沒有獨立的經濟能力，
「做妳自己」其實都是個口號而已。

搞得很慘，還好心理分析師和戒毒中心，以及向來對她寬容的父親救了她。

靠男人不如靠自己

她的人生真正改變是在父親猝死於拉斯維加斯之後。

父親死後，她竟然發現父親是個賭鬼，家中早已一文不剩，債主還不斷找上門，父親的公司營業狀況雖然還算良好，但公司股東看準茱蒂母女都不會理財，要她簽了一份不平等合約，使她的財產被完全扣住了；這時癌症又再度侵襲她的身體，母親和妹妹竟然在一次空難中離她而去……百般猶豫中，她在「再找個長期飯票」和「自己站起來」這兩個聲音中選擇聽從後者，從證券公司的臨時業務員開始她的新生活，這時，她已經四十歲了！

沒了青春，沒了垂涎她美色的男人；沒了家產，也沒了退路，只好靠自己，茱蒂憑著一股勇氣從基層做起，混進了清一色都是男性業務員的證券業，以她獨到的眼光以及重視小客戶的熱誠，為自己開創一條生路。她的事業越做越大，不

女 人 有 錢 有 尊 嚴

217

到十年，她已經獨立門戶，成為一家著名投資銀行的董事長。

「我富有過，我窮過，有錢比較好過！」就是她的心聲。

她成功的第一步，就是告別：「好女孩不該對錢太精明。」的觀念，又在萬念俱灰中體認了一個事實：「靠男人不如靠自己！」在決定靠自己謀生之後，她發現自己的經營智商遠遠比自己想像的更聰明，對金錢的敏感度更勝過白手起家的父親！

伸手折煞尊嚴

從前的女人，老愛以「愛情當然比麵包重要」或「愛情就是我的全部」為清高。生活在現代，時代已經不同，請別再把這樣的老話掛在嘴上。現代女子都明白，錢雖然不能買來一切，但常可以買來尊嚴和自由。

有位婚姻專家私下就做過一個有趣的統計，她說，一個現代婆婆若有兩個媳婦，即使都不住在一起，她往往不知不覺的會對「職業婦女」的媳婦比「家庭主婦」的媳婦寬容些。她下意識可能覺得「家庭主婦」的媳婦是跑不掉的，凡事要仰仗自己的兒子，所以家事當然要做得好些，她對這個媳婦的標準自然提高了許多。

相反的，「職業婦女」的媳婦在她眼裡是在幫她兒子挑半邊天，手頭也比較有些閒錢可以慰勞婆婆，所以常得婆婆歡心。

這個調查蠻現實的，但在我印證起來，準確度也很高。

很多女孩在純真少女的時代，往往還希望找到一張長期飯票，家裡的女性長輩也往往希望她嫁給一個賺錢像打開水龍頭一樣容易的男人，但很少人能誠實告訴女人：仰人鼻息，跟男人伸手，有多麼折煞尊嚴。

現在的經濟環境十分詭譎，今天看他起朱樓，明天他可能就樓塌了，就算真的找到一張長期飯票，其實也可能變成壁紙。

以前我在唸法律系的時候，還有所謂的「票據犯」——我們曾經做過統計，百分之九十的女票據犯都不是自己開票把錢花掉，而是被老公拿來當人頭的。結果，公司周轉有問題，女人坐了牢。有的女人本來心甘情願替丈夫坐牢，期待男

女 人 有 錢 有 尊 嚴

人在外頭東山再起，結果等她坐牢回家，女主人已經換人。現在雖然取消了票據

刑責，但我還是看過不少女子，家產已經掏空了，她還渾然不覺，沒了男人後，

還幫他背負了鉅額的債務。她們心中的憤怒與委屈，真是有苦無處訴。

沒有經濟能力，「運氣」這兩個字在婚姻中就有百分之八十的影響力；有獨

自的經濟能力，代表在婚姻中有應變的能力。

女人有錢有尊嚴，沒有獨立的經濟能力，「做妳自己」其實都是個口號而

已。

好命女守則

現代女人或多或少還是有找長期飯票的想法。

請記得，「拿人的手短，吃人的嘴軟」這句俗諺，

問問過來人好了：妳要付的代價常比想像中高啊！

——摘自《重新看見自己》

做 個 好 命 女

220

不要允許，只要祝福

以前的女人絕對依賴認同感。

現代女人當然也需要認同感，但在追尋自己的夢想上已經比較勇敢。

這絕對是時代不同所造成的差距，兩代女性要沒有代溝幾乎是不可能的。

曉恒的母親在女兒拿到學測成績單後，心裡就七上八下，天天在想，女兒該唸哪個大學、哪個系才好呢？

她趕緊打電話問在上海經商的先生。曉恒的爸爸聽到女兒成績不錯，可以唸國立大學，很是開心，特別要太太問女兒想要什麼禮物？

「……你認為曉恒該唸什麼系呢？」

「看她喜歡吧，曉恒一向是很有主見的孩子，從小不要我們操心。」

丈夫真是不夠關心，就這樣？連孩子選系這種大事都這麼冷漠，曉恒的媽媽心裡難免犯嘀咕。

「這怎麼可以呢？」曉恒的媽媽趕緊打電話跟自己龐大的娘家求救。電話一打就是七八通，要每個曉恒的舅舅嬸嬸一起出意見，該唸師大還是台大，還是選校不選系呢？

其實，舅舅嬸嬸們大部分都沒唸過大學，有的還要考文組的曉恒填醫學系當醫生，以後大家看病就不用愁了。還有更熱心的舅舅嬸嬸又打了電話給自己認為比較有學問的親友，大家都七嘴八舌的出了意見。如果有人詳細記錄統計的話，恐怕為了曉恒的志願，大家總共撥出了上百通電話，共用掉好多個小時殷勤討論吧！

媽媽將所有的意見搜集起來，細細記在腦海裡，等著參加營隊的曉恒回來，好好分析利弊得失給她聽。沒想到曉恒一開口就說：「媽，我老早就決定好了，我打算唸社工系。」

生在不同世代的人各有優缺點。

然而，未來的趨勢將永遠是比我們年輕的人所決定的。

「可是妳大舅舅認為以後當老師比較好……二舅媽的哥哥是老師，又建議唸企管比較好，大阿姨的親戚在美國，又認為唸外文比較好……」

不等母親說完，說話一向堅定有力的曉恒馬上說：「媽，是我要唸又不是他們要唸，妳幹嘛問他們的意見？我老早就決定了，我覺得按照我的個性，唸社工比較好！」

十八歲的曉恒，因為這件事和媽媽冷戰一個星期。她覺得媽媽很無聊，媽媽覺得她很無情。

幸福只能自己決定

二十八歲的清芸在感情路上也有類似的經驗。她原本是個乖巧文靜的女孩，卻在決定婚事上，在母親眼裡由綿羊變成了猛虎。

冠霖是個攝影師，這個行業在上一代眼裡太新鮮，讓她媽媽沒有什麼安全感。在她與冠霖才在談戀愛的階段，母親忙不迭出了許多主意，一會兒拿八字去

不要允許，只要祝福

223

問算命先生，說這姻緣總會出問題，而且還拚命的調查冠霖的身家，又不斷拐來好幾個伯伯叔叔嬸嬸和鄰居的意見，雖然沒有直接阻擋，卻給清芸好大的壓力。

有一天，母親急著向剛回家的清芸陳述「某某人的意見」時，清芸忽然回答了一句：「今天我們已經到法院公證結婚了，我們也不打算請客，所以妳不必擔心那些意見很多的親戚會怎麼說！」

「這……怎麼可能？妳怎麼可以……」

「媽，我要的不是允許，那些三姑六婆的意見，跟我的幸福無關，我要的是祝福！給我祝福就好了，我會自己負責的！」

清芸婚後有好幾年的時間，母女間的氣氛相當尷尬。

祝福的雅量

我觀察到「上一代」女人跟這一代女性，在觀念上確實已經有相當大的代溝。最大的對立在於現代的女人認為決定前途是自己的權利，而她們的上一代仍不自覺的認為，這樣太冒險，沒有親友一同的支持都很危險。照她們的習慣，在做任何決定之前，她必先得到別人的允許。

她們幾乎都很害怕特立獨行，只要一結婚，就自動把人身自由權交給丈夫或婆家，所以她們習慣徵詢很多人的意見。而因為生活環境有限的關係，一個不相干的遠親或鄰居隨便說的閒話，也常常在她的生命中成了千斤重量。

以前的女人絕對依賴認同感。現代女人當然也需要認同感，但在追尋自己的夢想上已經比較勇敢。這絕對是時代不同所造成的差距，兩代女性要沒有代溝幾乎是不可能的。在年輕一代看來，某些固執的上一代會變成「自己不懂又愛給意見」，上一代又覺得下一代如此剛愎自用，會吃虧在眼前。

生在不同世代的人各有優缺點。然而，未來的趨勢將永遠是比我們年輕的人所決定的。

我總建議為下一代著急的上一代：在事關下一代前途時，別急著廣徵眾人意見，或頑固的鐵嘴直斷，先聽聽當事人心中的意見吧！他們需要的已經不是長輩的允許，而是祝福，上一代得有如此雅量。

不要允許，只要祝福

請在意妳的身體

沒有任何東西比妳自己的身體值錢。

對自己好一點，並不是浪費。

記住這一點，才有資格當好命女。

我到朋友的眼科醫院檢查視力時，一位先生帶著太太，急急的走進了候診室，對著醫生說：「醫生，我太太說她快看不見了！」

先生相當瘦小，太太卻胖得不得了，身軀大概是由兩個吹漲了的氣球組成的吧！行動很遲緩，眼神已略顯呆滯。

我雖然不是醫師，但看著太太的體態，我的判斷也八九不離十，我想，她一定是得了糖尿病，卻不自知！

糖尿病跟肥胖的關連實在太密切了。

稍稍檢查了她的眼睛，我的眼科醫師朋友也說出了類似的建議：「你可能要帶她先看新陳代謝科，這不單純是眼睛的問題呢！」

這一對夫妻，大概是五十多歲。「對不起，我可不可以請問一下她什麼時候變成這樣的身材呢？」

「好多年了，都記不得了。」太太雖然人不舒服，還挺有幽默感的：「我先生、孩子都瘦得要命，只有我胖得像豬！都怪我們一家總是不把我煮的菜吃完，我怕可惜，只好都吃菜尾，吃了這麼多年剩菜，習慣了，怎麼瘦得下來！」

說自己從沒鄭重看過醫生的中年太太，眼中閃爍著神聖的光輝。類似的說法，醫生朋友聽過無數次，好多省儉持家的女人，發胖的理由都跟她一樣！

貪小，卻失大

有些人基因裡頭就帶著「胖」字。如果能夠接受自己的胖，也是好事，但發胖到有糖尿病又不自知的地步，真是太不在乎自己的身體了。難道，健康比剩菜不值錢嗎？

浪費自己的健康、自己的身材，才是最嚴重的浪費呢！他們不愛吃，妳可以不必煮得那麼多，何苦爲難了家人又爲難了自己？

上一代的女人成長在物質不豐厚的時代，勤儉持家是一種美德，但卻常常在小小的省儉和犧牲中換取成就感，而大大的犧牲了自己的健康，或糟蹋了自己的身體。貪小，卻失大。

有時，過度省儉，也造成別人的心理壓力。太偉大的犧牲者往往很難相處，因爲她律己甚嚴，待人也難太寬，免不了要覺得吃香喝辣的家人對不起她。

即使女人不必再以犧牲自己來讓全家溫飽了，犧牲還會幻化做很多方式。有一位朋友就爲家中過多的舊物傷腦筋不已：「衣服穿到不能穿了，想要送給舊衣回收中心，被我媽媽看到了，覺得我浪費，又收了回來，擺進她自己的衣櫃塞得滿滿的，就是捨不得給人。冰箱裡的東西過期了很久，她也一樣拿來吃。我領到第一份薪水後，就急著搬出那個到處都是垃圾的家！」

做 個 好 命 女

228

別當垃圾桶

當然，這種典型的女人，不只儲存舊衣服，還儲存一切舊東西。朋友一回家就像進入舊貨商店一樣，一進家門就聞到一種「復古」的氣氛。

這樣的人並不是真正無怨悔，有時她也會感傷自己貧寒枯槁的一生，說家人從沒對自己好過，只是當大家的垃圾桶。

最可悲的是，當垃圾桶當久了，家人總以為妳當垃圾桶才會快樂——我們幾曾餵垃圾桶吃好貨？

我贊同省儉是環保，是自古有之的美德。然而卻不能食古不化，也不能不分輕重。沒有任何東西比妳自己的身體值錢。

對自己好一點，並不是浪費。記住這一點，才有資格當好命女。

減一公斤肥肉的價錢比一公斤的廚餘高，還好這一點，新一代的女人多半已經懂了。

讓他有機會對妳好

就讓妳的付出對象，也有機會對妳好吧！

讓他學會付出，妳才能真正的無怨，

感情中總得要禮尚往來，才能穩定平衡！

怡娟氣呼呼的跟我抱怨：「我的那個小姑，不知道是什麼意思，新婚時，我想要對她表示好意，送給她一床羽毛被，她第二天就回了另一床高級蠶絲被給我，好像在諷刺我送她的東西不夠高級；過了一個月，我又送了她一籃水蜜桃，她馬上又回送一籃富士蘋果，真是氣死我了，她是不是根本不屑拿我的東西啊？」

禮尚往來原本是一件很有人情味的事情，小姑送回來的東西明明也很看得起人，為什麼怡娟反而會生氣？問題就出在，這個禮物回送得太快，讓人馬上會聯想到「她只想表明她不想佔我便宜，並非真正接受我的好意」，就算小姑也真心想要對這個剛進家門的大嫂好，也難免會惹來這樣的猜測。

詩群也對她的婆婆略有微詞：「她是個很熱心的人，很幫忙我們小夫妻。婚後我們每個月都會匯生活費給她，逢年過節紅包也都沒少過，她總是把我們給她的錢，原原本本的用各種名目還給我們，讓我對她心生感激。可是這一次我到婆家去過年，卻不小心聽到她跟鄰居抱怨，說她命苦，到現在沒有真正拿過孩子一毛錢！是她自己不要的啊，卻把我們說得很不孝！」

俊杰對他的女友也很頭痛：「每次情人節、生日問她要什麼，或想買什麼給她，她都叫我不要浪費錢，結果上個禮拜我們吵架，她卻罵我小氣鬼，說我們認識這麼多年，我根本沒送過她一樣值錢的東西！」

練習讓別人對妳好

以上的問題都出在類似的地方：「想對人家好，卻沒有讓人家有機會對妳

好。」這些讓人頭痛的人物，本意其實都是善良的。只是沒有把別人的感受想得

通透，所以反而變成一個「難搞的人」。

想對人家好，是女人最可愛最善良的天性。然而也得瞻前想後，以免弄巧成

拙，徒然製造心結。讓他也有被需求感，讓他也能回饋，雙方關係才能平衡，他

才不會因為被拒絕，而漸漸不想對妳好，是所有克勤克儉、做牛做馬的女人都要

學會的課題。

就讓妳的付出對象，也有機會對妳好好吧！讓他學會付出，妳也才能真正的無

怨，感情中總得要禮尚往來，才能穩定平衡！

做個好命女

吳淡如
暢銷作品

《紅樓夢》 定價269元

吳淡如以現代白話,將《紅樓夢》原著重新編
寫成一部最精朵新穎、最精簡易讀的愛情史
詩,不僅重現繁華家族的興衰史,
更將賈寶玉、林黛玉、薛寶釵等紅塵男女的愛
慾情癡描繪得淋漓盡致。

《人間詞話》 定價220元

本書收錄王國維《人間詞話》中最菁華的六十
四則詞論,
加上吳淡如精妙易讀的文字解說、
一篇篇扣人心弦的詞作欣賞,
讓你輕鬆自在閱讀古典,提昇文學涵養。

《幸福人的座右銘》

定價230元
幸福,常常被忘記,
幸福,需要被提醒,
幸福,從沒有人能真正給予,
幸福,可以用創意和真心尋覓。

吳淡如 暢銷作品

《心靈點滴》 定價220元

想活得好的人，
會用溫柔而有條理的聲音引導自己，
給自己溫柔的鼓聲，
行進的節奏才得以安穩而有力，
不會迷失在其他的雜音裡。

《做自己最快樂》 定價220元

有人說做事容易做人難，有人說做人不難做自
己最難。
其實做自己並不難，總比從別人耳中東聽一點
西聽一些支離破碎的拼出自己的形象容易。
走自己的路不後悔，過自己想過的生活，人生
不浪費。

《早知道早幸福》 定價220元

我們活在歷史上最有權利幸福的年代，
你有理直氣壯享受幸福的權利。
這本書讓你在歡笑中明白：
什麼事早知道，早幸福，
不要走太多冤枉路。

吳淡如 暢銷作品

《學會過生活》 定價220元

真正的人生在尋常的日子發生，
學會用自己最喜歡的方式過日子，
愛上生活中的小小事，
就擁有世界上最美味最實在的幸福。

《昨日歷歷晴天悠悠》

定價220元

沿著對小弟的追憶，吳淡如一路回溯自己的成
長。今天我們所認識的，教大家「人生以快樂
為目的」「愛情以互惠為原則」的吳淡如，過去
也曾有一張陰鬱的臉，但她愛戀陽光的美好、
春日的燦爛，所以不斷的尋找、嘗試，終於重
新看見自己，面向有陽光的道路。

《在遠方等待的海》 定價150元

不久前，吳淡如透過電視節目，終於把熱愛攝
影的小弟吳育誠生前散失各處的作品一一尋回。
把這些美麗的照片集結成冊，與大家分享弟弟
眼中的美麗世界，是吳淡如最快樂的事。

《重新看見自己》 定價200元

沒有問題單純是外在的問題，自己總有一點責任。如果一個問題會困擾你，你必然也在潛意識中說了「歡迎光臨」。

只要我們好好審視自己，會發現我們所擁有的正是我們所渴望的。

《新快樂主義》 定價210元

有自信的人，才會真正尊重人，活得開心，人人願意和你在一起；別把生活的臉孔繃得太緊，愛自己，人人更愛你。請看吳淡如的新快樂主義：

◆腦袋清楚，活得舒服◆拿捏分寸，人人信任
◆先愛自己，他更愛你◆放過小事，計較大事
◆尋找定位，解放胸襟

《愛情以互惠為原則》

定價210元

一般人談戀愛，常不知不覺的以「互毀」為原則，然而，真正的愛是尊重，是成長，是如魚得水，是不愛之後，還希望他活得好。如果想要在愛中成長，我們要學習：

◆打破完美主義的假象◆別找錯愛情專家◆幸福的首要條件

《創造好心情》 定價200元

人生其實可以更簡單，只要你能： ◆觀察壓力，善待自己◆治療「人際關係花粉熱」◆懂得感情世界的溝通與談判◆承認欲望，與心靈真情相對◆無論如何，總要往好處想

樂天不是膚淺，在陷入僵局時，再想一次，就不會那麼慘。

《活得更聰明》 定價190元

混亂的世界中，想得越清楚，就能活得越開心，讓我們撥開雲霧，學會學校沒有教的事：活得更聰明！

吳淡如相信，人生若不快樂，就不值得活，

但是，快樂可不是鬼混裝傻，

真心的快樂需要一顆更清醒的、懂得思考的心。

《自戀總比自卑好》 定價190元

吳淡如透過本書為我們重新解讀：

「自戀」其實不是我喜歡有什麼不可以，

「自戀」更不是自我膨脹目中無人；

「自戀」其實是願意給自己多一點的機會和時間，

「自戀」更是有能力和自信選擇愛與被愛。

《非常誠實有點毒》 定價190元

本書提供你如何快樂生活的三帖完全開心處方：
1. 愛情不能讓你快樂，如果你自己不開心
2. 環境不能讓你快樂，如果你自己不開心
3. 朋友不能讓你快樂，如果你自己不開心
善用這三帖開心處方，保證讓你人生中的各種疑難雜症，藥到病除，心情快樂無比。

《給愛一條活路》 定價190元

本書提出三道破除愛情魔咒的錦囊妙招：
兩性幽默---每個愛情都有趣
危險關係---每個愛情都危險
愛情ICQ---每個愛情都要有創造力

《真愛非常頑強》 定價180元

提供你捍衛愛情的十九道致勝法寶：
付出---好女人製造男性生活低能症，願意---妳心「乾」情「怨」過一生？夢想---人人心中一座麥迪遜之橋，糾纏---小狗，別咬自己尾巴，EQ---你的情緒智商及格嗎？傾聽---以智慧，施恩惠，很實惠，逃避---有些男人喜歡逃避承諾，交換---女人拿身體換承諾，溝通---男女溝通不是說服。

融合印度、中國、日本……等
風水、太極、靈氣、宗教和瑜珈精髓
SPA 音樂精靈

由音樂師、心理分析師、按摩治療師…等專業人士,集結印度、中國、日本等各國之相關風水、太極、靈氣、宗教以及瑜珈之精髓,研究出此套協助人體自療的 SPA 音樂。讓緊繃的身體及心靈得到寧靜、舒坦,甫推出即受到專業 SPA 中心歡迎!聆聽音樂時,若搭配以專業的按摩指壓,將更能發揮療效,達到完美和諧的境界。

★全套共十七片★
本書隨附「微笑心靈 SPA 音樂 CD」為其精選特輯

瑋秦音樂
E-mail:welchenm@ms35.hinet.net
TEL:(02)89236434-6　FAX:(02)89236437
台北縣永和市秀朗路二段 232 號 7 樓

值得珍愛的才華洋溢好命女
瑋秦音樂感性之旅

羅瑞塔琳的妹妹，也是美國
鄉村歌后的 Crystal Gayle
克莉絲朵蓋兒，其著名代表
作" Don't it make my
brown eyes blue 別讓我的
棕眼憂鬱"，表現風情萬種之
美，以最感性之美聲，詮釋
得淋漓盡致，呈現給您唯美
的、知性的、感性的結合表
象。

法國影歌紅星 Edith Piaf
伊蒂絲皮耶夫（又稱小麻
雀）" La vie en rose 玫瑰
人生" 是其膾炙人口的代表
作歌曲。

美國鄉村歌手 Loretta Lynn
羅瑞塔琳，其著名代表作為
電影" Coalminer's daugh-
ter 礦工的女兒" 的主題曲。

瑋秦音樂

E-mail：welchenm@ms35.hinet.net
TEL：(02)89236434-6　FAX：(02)89236437
台北縣永和市秀朗路二段 232 號 7 樓

The Eurasian Publishing Group
圓神出版事業機構
用心與你對話・視野無限寬廣

方智出版社
Fine Press

http://www.booklife.com.tw　　inquiries@mail.eurasian.com.tw

自信人生 039

做個好命女

作　　者／吳淡如

發 行 人／簡志忠

出 版 者／方智出版社股份有限公司

地　　址／台北市南京東路四段50號6F之1

電　　話／（02）2579-6600・2579-8800・2570-3939

傳　　真／（02）2579-0338・2577-3220・2570-3636

郵撥帳號／13633081　方智出版社股份有限公司

資深主編／林秀禎

主　　編／呂燕琪

責任編輯／呂燕琪

美術編輯／黃昭文

印務統籌／林永潔

監　　印／高榮祥

校　　對／吳淡如・連秋香・呂燕琪

法律顧問／圓神出版事業機構法律顧問　蕭雄淋律師

印　　刷／祥峯印刷廠

2003 年 8 月　初版

定價 220元　　　　　　　　ISBN 957-679-886-8

國家圖書館出版品預行編目資料

做個好命女／吳淡如著
-- 初版.-- 臺北市：方智，2003 〔民92〕
面； 公分. --（自信人生；39）

ISBN 957-679-886-8（平裝）

855   92011205